THREE PARADIGMS OF REALITY:

FROM HOMER TO EINSTEIN

BY
RON DUDUM

2009

Published by InterOrthodox Press
of the Patriarch Athenagoras Institute
2311 Hearst Avenue
Berkeley, CA 94709
United States of America

ISBN: 1-932401-11-3
ISBN-13: 9781932401110

Visit www.amazon.com or www.threeparadigms.com to order
additional copies.

To my children, Alia, Ramzi, and Karim.
I hope these pages will help you to find meaning in life.

Contents

Foreword
by Metropolitan Nikitas

Director of the Patriarch Athenagoras Orthodox Institute
Graduate Theological Union, Berkeley, California

In *Three Paradigms of Reality: From Homer to Einstein*, Ron Dudum offers the reader three ways to view reality—ways that have shaped human thought patterns throughout the ages. Dudum not only clarifies what these patterns are, but also challenges us with case scenarios to confront the central questions that attend the search for truth. While the author is inspired by the Judeo-Christian tradition, he also draws on the rich resources of philosophy—always grounded in real life, so that the arguments do not remain abstract theories, but become principles for living.

In fact, this book can be thought of as a passionate intellectual journey that parallels the "odyssey" of the world's great thinkers, with commentary on the persons, places, and situations that have shaped intellectual history. Dudum gleans insights from the ancient philosophers, quotes from the Patristic tradition, and draws from the principles of the natural sciences. Like others who have embarked on the sacred quest to discover truth, he addresses the issues of freedom, self, and virtue, wisely defining the battle between competition and humility.

Many readers will quickly discover that Dudum's text is filled with persons and places largely unknown to them, for we have neglected to study the once-beloved disciplines of philosophy, theology, and history, as the great thinkers once did. But Dudum invites us into the world of those persons and places, making us comfortable there. Along with the writings of Plato and Aristotle, he quotes liberally from Athanasius, Cassian, Maximus, and ecclesiastical figures often overlooked in the dusty pages of history.

Dudum's argument implies an ascent of sorts that leads us to a higher plane, especially those of us who seek to be cleansed and purified through God's grace. This ascent allows us to enter into a dialogue with the divine. Dudum forwards the beautiful theological expression of restoration, commonly referred to in the Eastern Orthodox tradition as *theosis*. This theological concept, until recently unknown in Western theological circles, has been embraced by many scholars and theologians.

As a student of theology and the classics, I was both challenged and enlightened by Dudum's approach. As a Christian, I found his knowledge and understanding of the Eastern tradition most refreshing after years of reading and studying texts that have another style and focus. I hope that when others read this book they will learn from its wealth of knowledge and wisdom. Most important, though, I hope that readers will be challenged to enter into a discipline of struggle to overcome evil as they seek to attain virtue, love, humility, and truth.

+Metropolitan Nikitas

�֍ ✧ ✧

Introduction

This book is about three ways to view reality, and therefore three ways for human beings to govern their lives. Two of these ways promote cooperation among all individuals, peoples, cultures, and societies; the third promotes competition.

The earliest of the three paradigms, historically, was the ancient Greek paradigm, which saw reason as the key to comprehending the universe and envisioned two forces that bind human beings in harmony, both with the universe and with each other. The positive force, which inspires right conduct, the Greeks called "virtue" (*areté*). The negative force, which discourages wrong conduct, they called "shame" (*aidos*). Although the ancient Greek paradigm required citizens to seek harmonious cooperation, it did not dictate which authority was higher, the state or the divine. That decision was left up to the individual—a freedom that ultimately promoted self–interest and individualism and led to the unraveling of the paradigm in Greek society.

Next came the early Christian paradigm, which saw reason as insufficient for comprehending the universe unless it was accompanied by faith and humility. Early Christians understood that dedication to this paradigm would entail suffering and sacrifice, but the reward of eternal life would more than compensate for the temporal struggle. Like the ancient Greek paradigm, the early Christian paradigm called for personal commitment to harmonious cooperation among all people. However, there was no longer any question about whether the state or the divine was the higher authority. To obtain eternal life, one must unconditionally accept the absolute authority of the Father, the Son, and the Holy Spirit.

Next came the modern paradigm of self, which was born between the fifteenth and the eighteenth centuries, with the Renaissance and the Age of Enlightenment, when reason conquered faith. After Copernicus knocked the Earth out of the center of the universe, people no longer saw the need to look to religious institutions for answers to cosmic questions. Instead, they could rely on their own ability to consider evidence and draw their own conclusions. Now religion, or religious mystery, which is beyond evidence and inaccessible by reason, could be dismissed as mere fantasy—a clever invention, as the Sophists argued twenty–five hundred years ago, for politicians to control the masses. The consequence of this skeptical outlook, however, is that it promotes competition between everyone and everything, leading ultimately to narcissism, loneliness, and intellectual chaos.

Thus, today there are three ways to approach reality: through sensory perception (empiricism), through rational reflection (reason), and through faith in mystery (religion). Ironically, modern quantum mechanics and Heisenberg's uncertainty principle have shaken the modern *belief* in the infallibility of scientific empiricism and rationality. This has opened the door to the possibility that knowledge of truth and reality can be acquired through empirical evidence, intellectual reflection, *and* the realm of mystery.

Each of the three primal paradigms of reality embraces a unique understanding of absolute truth. *Three Paradigms* does not advocate a preference for any of the three, but rather identifies and accepts the underlying premise of all three. Which version of absolute truth may actually be the Absolute Truth is left up to the reader. This book will have succeeded to the degree that the reader considers the role of paradigms in interpreting history, evidence, and reality itself.

❖ ❖ ❖

Chapter 1

The Ancient Greek Paradigm

One Law, Two Ideals, Three Principles

The ancient Greek paradigm contained three principles: (1) a transcendent Law inspires cosmic harmony; (2) faith in reason will yield understanding of that Law; and (3) duty binds individuals and their communities to the cosmos in an organic relationship. Furthermore, duty itself comprises two ideals: excellence or virtue (*areté*), which inspires right conduct; and holy shame (*aidos*), which discourages wrong conduct.

Werner Jaeger (1888–1961), an eminent professor of classics, wrote, "The history of what we can truly call civilization—deliberate pursuit of an ideal—does not begin until Greece."[1] Other civilizations dealt with issues of mystery and experience, duty and authority, but the Greeks were the first to look for a single law, a transcending truth, that united mankind with the cosmos.[2] According to Jaeger, the ancient Greeks believed that education was "the ultimate justification for the existence of both the individual and the community."[3] This ancient Greek paradigm accepts the idea of a single law and interprets all human behavior and interactions through the lens of that transcendent truth. The logical consequence of this paradigm is that if everyone, individuals and communities alike, learns and accepts this transcendent truth, the result will be universal harmony and stability.

The contemporary reader must accept that our modern understanding of individualism did not exist in ancient Greece. In Jaeger's words, the Greek mind did not consider any part of the cosmos to be "separate and cut off from the rest, but always as an element in a living whole."[4] On a societal level, the Greeks saw the city–state, or *polis*, as an organic whole from which individuals could not live apart, just as a leaf or branch cannot survive apart from a tree. There was no concept in ancient Greece of a personal conscience; all considerations of self were organically one with the public conscience.[5] If a diseased leaf were self–conscious of its potential contamination of the tree, it would willingly sacrifice itself for the good of the whole. Within times of peace, the unity between citizen and state might be relaxed, but in times of war, which were frequent, the individual and the state were merged in what Jaeger calls a "universal I."[6]

The best example of this unity between a state and its citizens was the city–state of Sparta in the ninth century B.C., where men lived, ate, and studied publicly, dedicating themselves, as Jaeger says, "to the hunt, the practice of war, and their official duties."[7] As the historian Plutarch (ca. 46–ca. 119 A.D.) observed about ninth–century B.C. Sparta, "Nobody was free to live as he wished…. He did not belong to himself but to his country."[8] Plato (ca. 428–ca. 348 B.C.) greatly respected Spartan communal life and used that model as the basis for the leadership training that he proposed in the *Republic*.[9] The discipline and obedience of Spartan society, not only admired by Plato but also by Xenophanes of Colophon (ca. 560–ca. 478 B.C.) and other Greek philosophers, became the model for citizenship within the Greek city–states for centuries.

Greece's most famous poet, Homer (9th–8th? cent. B.C.), celebrated the societal role of the nobleman and hero, whose stature was measured by *areté*—that is, virtue, excellence, goodness, the best one can be. "Strength and health," explains Jaeger, "are the *areté* of the body, cleverness and insight the *areté* of the mind."[10] *Areté* was earned through words and deeds.[11] The desire to preserve *areté* became the basis for Greek *paideia*, the term used by Jaeger to represent the ancient effort to advance *areté* between generations. Homer believed that the evidence of a man's nobility was his sense of duty.[12] Noble deeds, he felt, should be celebrated by the individual and heralded by the *polis* (city–state).* Given the organic character of the ancient Greeks, the *areté* of a hero was shared with his community. Noble *areté* became the standard for "right conduct" and established an aristocracy that, over time, sought to maintain its privileged status.

Greece's second greatest poet, Hesiod (ca. 800 B.C.), wrote of the valiant struggle of his fellow peasants and the virtue developed through hard work. The word *peasant*, Jaeger notes, "had not come to mean 'uncultured.'"[13] Hesiod, deprived of his inheritance by an influential brother, passionately challenged the greed and laziness of the aristocracy in general.[14] While Homer wrote of justice, Hesiod embraced the concept with a reformer's zeal, so much so that Jaeger identifies him as the "prophet of a new age."[15] The gods, Hesiod believed, proved their divinity through their victory over injustice. "With Hesiod," writes Jaeger, "we see the beginning of that spiritual leadership which is the distinguishing mark of the Greek world."[16]

Freedom and Cooperation

Ideas of individual freedom originated in the city–state of Ionia, which was recognized as the intellectual center of Greece.[17] Ionian society could not organize its free individual citizens into a military force, but instead unleashed the political framework, as Jaeger puts it, that "helped to create a vitally new ideal of the state."[18] The poet, the lawgiver, and the statesman were the undisputed leaders of the *polis*.[19]

---

*Christian sentiment against sinful pride would not influence behavior for hundreds of years.

Each influenced the evolving idea of *areté*, but the question of which educational method best leads to *areté* had not been settled. With the age of Sophocles (ca. 496–406 B.C.), a sophistical humanist spirit sprouted from the roots of Ionian intellectualism, culminating in Protagoras's (ca. 485–410 B.C.) epigram, "Man is the measure of all things."[20]

Where words and deeds were the historic currency of *areté*, the Sophists sought to educate leaders in the techniques of rhetoric.[21] "In return for money," Jaeger writes, Sophists "would teach virtue," which Jaeger defines as political *areté*—that is, intellectual power and oratorical ability. With man as the measure of all things, human happiness became the primary goal of life. The first poems of hedonism, celebrating what Jaeger calls "the individual's right to sensual happiness and beauty,"[22] are found in this era.

According to the ancient Greek paradigm, the transcendent truth bound individuals and their community together with the cosmos in an organic relationship that defined harmonious cooperation. This unity was held together by a communal understanding of duty. Noble *areté* inspired right conduct, and *aidos* (holy shame) discouraged conduct that was unbecoming a member of the *polis*.

Over time, a third enforcement mechanism, self–preservation, came to modify personal behavior. Self–preservation represented an internal self–interested motive to conform to societal standards. While there was no modern sense of self within the ancient Greek paradigm, and no sense of duty to oneself, this paradigm accepted self–preservation as an innate characteristic of humanity.

The final element of mankind's beingness involved the nature of the soul.* Pre–Socratic philosophers did not believe in the soul's immortality.[23] To them, death was final. Thus, the only way for a man to exist beyond death was to be remembered by the *polis* for his heroic deeds. According to Jaeger, "a new ideal of *areté*…for the first time emphasized the central importance of the *psyche*, the 'soul,' in all culture."[24] With Socrates in the fifth century B.C., the immortal fullness of the soul would guide human experience through time.

The status of the aristocracy and the general sense of duty to the city–state were elevated by Homer. The *areté* of the masses and a higher sense of justice were celebrated by Hesiod. The discipline and obedience of Sparta were contrasted with the emerging sense of individual freedom in Ionia. When the *areté* of the state began to be questioned, the immortality of the soul sought a higher standard of being. People were then confronted with a personal crisis, having to choose between their duty to the state and their duty to the divine.

These political and spiritual differences came together in the Athens of the fifth and fourth centuries B.C. When the state condemned Socrates (470–399 B.C.) to death, Plato appealed to a higher authority beyond the state, believing, according to Jaeger, that "the principle of action which guides society and the state is the same as that which guides the moral conduct of the individual."[25] As Jaeger explains:

> Socrates transferred the contrast between slavery and freedom into the inner moral world. A new idea of spiritual freedom now arose, to correspond to that

---

*According to Werner Jaeger (*Paideia: The Ideals of Greek Culture*, 2nd ed., trans. Gilbert Highet, vol. 1 [New York: Oxford University Press, 1945], pp. 50 and 153), the fundamental laws of being are the essence of humanity. Being is the deepest problem of life. Plato's essential "truth about being exists in our soul" (*Paideia*, vol. 2, p. 169).

development of "self–control" as the rule of reason over the desires…. So moral autonomy would mean, for him, to be independent of the animal side of one's nature: it would not contradict the existence of a higher cosmic law, of which this moral phenomenon, self–control, would be an example.[26]

Plato, bringing together the two human characteristics of self–interest and self–control, advanced the idea of the highest Good. Jaeger describes the pivotal point:

For us, politics means policy, realistic policy; and ethics means individual morality…. It is difficult for us to accept without question the ancient Greek view…that the law of the state is the source of all standards of human life, and that the virtue of the individual is the same as the virtue of the citizen. That harmony between state and individual had for the first time been seriously challenged in the age of Socrates.[27]

Within the ancient Greek paradigm, right conduct meant harmony between a citizen and his city–state. As Jaeger explains, "The old free ideal of the heroic *areté* of the Homeric champion now becomes an obligation to the state, a duty to which all citizens alike are bound."[28] Harmony through right conduct—that is, allegiance to the state—was the responsibility of everyone. With Socrates, the state and the individual were no longer in harmony. Plato sought the divine Good that transcends the city–state and found harmony and spiritual freedom through self–control.

A citizen could now choose to find harmony with his city–state *or* with the divine. A citizen maintained harmony with the state so long as he willingly subordinated himself to the state's ultimate authority. A citizen was "free" to do whatever he wanted, within the limits prescribed by *areté* and his obligation to the state. On the other hand, a citizen who sought harmony with the divine Good struggled to control his desires. Self–interest would challenge the internal harmony with the divine, a harmony that could only be achieved through self–control. In each of these alternatives, the citizen decided whom to serve: the state or the divine. The ancient Greek paradigm required a citizen to seek harmonious cooperation, but did not dictate which authority was higher, the state or the divine. That decision was left up to the individual. Ultimately, however, the harmonious paradigm was unraveled by the seeds of self–interest sown in Ionia.

The Role of Personal Will

In the pre–Socratic period, when citizen and state shared an organic identity, freedom was contrasted with slavery.[29] Typically, slaves were defeated foes, who were expected to subordinate their personal will to that of free citizens. Whether one was a slave or free citizen, however, his (or her) status could be attributed to the external influences of fate and destiny in conformity with the transcendent law.[30]

Personal will, the freedom to choose without coercion from the transcendent paradigm, was not part of the ancient Greek paradigm, but Socrates' emphasis on an inner moral world laid the foundation for the Christian concept of free will. A free citizen's duty was to the highest authority—whether the state or the divine. A slave's duty, on the other hand, was to his master. Within the ancient Greek paradigm, there was no duty to oneself. Jaeger explains:

> The Greeks in the classical era…thought that political morality and personal morality were practically identical: since the state was the sole source of all moral standards…. In the fifth century, there were only two possibilities: either the laws of the state were the highest standard for human life and coincided with the divine government of the universe, in which case a man was a citizen, no more and no less; or else the standards of the state conflicted with those established by nature or God, so that man could not accept them, in which case he ceased to be a member of the political community, and the very foundations of his life dissolved.[31]

While Socrates respected the authority of the state, he was more concerned, as Jaeger notes, "with the problem of the individual, of human life in general, than with the problem of the state, as most of the great Athenians had been until his time."[32] Plato modified the Sophist epigram of man being the measure of all things to God being the measure of all things.* Socrates, in Plato's view, found harmony in his service to both the civil and divine authorities. He respected the authority of the state and willingly accepted its decision to end his life. Socrates did not fear death, believing that a divine authority would accept his efforts to control personal desires and grant him a place in the divine realm.

---

*In both the Republic and the Laws, Plato elevates the Good and the Divine. In the Statesman, he refers to the Good as "the most exact measure" (quoted here from Jaeger, Paideia, vol. 2, p. 286, note 46).

The three enforcement mechanisms that encouraged right conduct were the Homeric concepts of *aidos* and *areté*, plus self–preservation. Within the ancient paradigm, the sense of holy shame (*aidos*) represented an external influence on the individual to subordinate self–interest in his service to the city–state. The concept of *aidos* would eventually expand to include the ideas of esteem and respect, thus becoming, in Jaeger's words, "the basis for ethical conduct."[33]

In Sparta in the ninth century B.C., there was no need for coercion to maintain the organic unity between citizens and state because the sense of *aidos* permeated life in the *polis*. Duty, *areté*, and obedience to the state were universally accepted, and individuals who failed to live up to those standards were punished accordingly. As the Ionian sense of individual freedom grew, however, right conduct through *aidos* gave way to right conduct motivated by self–preservation. By the fifth century B.C., the authority of the state and the standards of justice had merged into a general obedience to the laws, which were enforced by punishment.[34] Religious authority represented the last remaining proponent of morality, which the Sophists challenged as a clever invention of the politicians.[35] Socrates was obedient to the authority of the state and willingly accepted the ultimate punishment of death. But his fearless approach to death and his higher duty to the divine directly challenged the worthiness of obedience through fear of temporal punishment.

According to Jaeger, Plato found in Socrates' example "the most perfect vision of the cosmos of human and daemonic powers. Knowledge is central in that picture, because knowledge of [eternal beauty] is the creative force which leads and orders everything. For Plato, knowledge is the guide to the realm of the divine."[36] The Sophists' elevation of man as the measure of all things did not achieve final victory in the West until the Enlightenment.

Individualism Versus Conformity

The defining characteristic of the ancient Greek paradigm was a core belief in a single transcendent law that brought harmony within the cosmos and truth to man's life. The right conduct of a citizen toward his community can only be understood within this transcendent harmony. There was no external struggle between the citizen's duty and his state. Without the organic relationship with the state, the foundations of a citizen's life would dissolve. Duty to the state defined right conduct, and right conduct was enforced through *aidos, areté*, and self–preservation. When the authority of the state began to be questioned, Plato did not abandon the obligation of duty required by the ancient paradigm, but sought a higher authority of justice that retained the cosmic harmony. Those citizens who chose to challenge the authority of the state were guilty of wrong conduct and were subject to shame and punishment.

Socrates exemplified a new understanding of right conduct: obedience to the state's temporal authority and self–control as the means for eternal harmony. The internal struggle pitted innate desire for momentary satisfaction against the eternal reward offered by the divine Good. Individuals who chose hedonism over self–control (of course, within the accepted boundaries of *aidos* and the *polis*) might avoid temporal punishment, but sacrificed divine harmony.

A modern Westerner will find great difficulty in accepting the ancient Greek paradigm of duty, which seems to ignore the self. Yet, there are contemporary examples of this paradigm. Many tribal societies will immediately recognize themselves in an ancient paradigm that respects elders, reprimands individualism, and expects conformity. These characteristics can be found within every community on Earth. The only difference is in the degree and type of enforcement mechanism used to maintain communal harmony.

In the last fifty years, American society has experienced its own paradigm shift. The changing role of women and the increased economic opportunities for minorities represent direct challenges to the powerfully privileged. Unquestioned respect for government and religious institutions has been replaced by a cynical questioning of all positions of authority. But we are getting ahead of ourselves. This train of thought will be addressed in Chapter 9.

❖ ❖ ❖

Chapter 2

From Hesiod to Aristotle

Rational Order and Absolute Truth:
The Pre–Socratic Philosophers

Chapter 1 presented the ancient Greek paradigm of mankind and the cosmos harmoniously united within the transcendent divine. Homer and Hesiod offered mythological explanations for creation, *areté*, and justice within the ancient paradigm. Their pre–Socratic counterparts, however, were more interested in the nature of the cosmos than in mythology. These thinkers called their activity wisdom.[1] The modern paradigm of self begins with the pursuit of wisdom weaving the thread of our human soul through the fabric of time.

Hesiod was the first writer in ancient Greece to weave the creation myths of the universe into a rational order: Heaven and Earth, the roof and foundation of the cosmos, were separated by the empty space of the primordial yawn of Chaos. Eros, the unique contribution of Hesiod, introduced the cosmic force that creates life.[2] The motherly Earth gave birth to the gods without assistance from the Heavenly father. Hesiod describes his myths as fables—stories of truth and praiseworthy behavior without necessarily being literally true.[3] Philosophy, the rational effort to integrate *areté* and education through intellectual discipline,[4] began in the Ionian city of Miletus on the coast of what is now Turkey.

Thales of Miletus (624–547 B.C.), the first known Greek philosopher, scientist, and mathematician, believed that water is the source of all things. According to Reginald Allen (1931–2007), a professor of classics and philosophy at Northwestern University, this implies two truths: "that all things have a source, and that the source of all things is one thing."[5] Water is alive, capable of spontaneous movement, and as such the primordial element of the ensouled universe. The idea of a single transcendent unifying source of cosmic harmony was congruent with the first principle of the ancient Greek paradigm.

This first effort to explain existence and being, however, did not yet have any ethical or religious implications. Nature, humanity, and magnets were all considered ensouled, since they were all capable of spontaneous movement.[6] The first philosophers were motivated by simple curiosity,[7] but their belief in the cosmic unity of life became the first essential characteristic in their philosophical pursuit of wisdom.

Allen speculates that Thales' belief in primordial water as the indefinite, unbounded stuff of life can be found in the water myths of the great river-civilizations of Egypt and Babylonia, which traded not only merchandise in Thales' hometown harbor but also ideas.

Anaximander of Miletus (ca. 610–546 B.C.), unable to understand how fire could come from water, proposed that everything is eternally in a constant state of opposition—for example, hot and cold or wet and dry—balanced by the judgment of time.[8] Anaximenes of Miletus (585–525 B.C.) proposed that the unbounded stuff was not water but a thick mist, which he called *Aer*. Thus, there were two fundamental notions of the unbounded stuff—one that saw it as composed of eternal elements in opposition, and the other that saw it as a thickening and thinning of one element.

Aristotle (384–322 B.C.) later identified the equilibrium of Anaximander as "something other than the elements,"[9] an unexplained, undefined, unbounded essence from which the elements would arise. Allen explains:

> In the *Physics* (187a 11), Aristotle divides the natural
> philosophers into two schools: those who hold that there

is an underlying body from which other things are generated by thickening and thinning, and those who "separate out" the opposites from the mixture. Anaximander belongs to the latter school, Anaximenes to the former.[10]

Egyptian civilization cultivated the original idea of an immortal soul (psyche).[*] However, the soul is immaterial, so neither water nor *Aer* can be its underlying source. The absolute truth of cosmic unity required a bridge between the unexplainable unbounded and the material world. The soul's ability to transcend both realms provided a solution that maintained the cosmic harmony and belief in the existence of an absolute truth. The soul is thus a vital element of the ancient Greek paradigm.

Hesiod's mythical system was formed and governed by reason,[11] but the religious embrace of the soul was not solidly rooted within Greek beliefs until the middle of the sixth century B.C., with the cult society of Pythagoras (ca. 580–ca. 500 B.C.). Greek ideas about the soul, such as immortality, salvation through purification, the freeing of the soul from the bodily prison, and reincarnation, all coalesce here. Pythagoras saw a harmonious order in the cosmos, which was structured through music and known by abstract mathematical concepts.[†]

Before Aristotle's clarity on the nature of the cosmos, important ideas were introduced through the pursuit of wisdom. Xenophanes of Colophon (ca. 560–ca. 478 B.C.) believed that one god controlled the

---

[*]Reginald Allen, ed., *Greek Philosophy: Thales to Aristotle*, 3rd ed. (New York: The Free Press, 1991), p. 35. Regarding the nature of Egyptian afterlife, also see C. W. Ceram, *Gods, Graves, and Scholars: The Story of Archaeology* (New York: Knopf, 1951), Book 3.

[†]Academics are uncertain of Pythagoreanism's philosophical origins. The cult society was extremely secretive and attributed all mathematical discoveries to its founder (Allen, *Greek Philosophy*, p. 6). For more information regarding Pythagorean cosmology, see Joseph Campbell, *Occidental Mythology* (New York: Penguin, 1991), pp. 185–186.

universe through thought. Heraclitus (ca. 535–475 B.C.) believed that the divine logos united the cosmos. Parmenides (b. ca. 515 B.C.), who drew a distinction between appearance and reality, found the truth of being through abstract reason alone, rejecting material evidence as false and misleading. Empedocles (490–430 B.C.) believed that everything was real—abstract reason *and* material evidence—and that the forces of Love and Strife govern the whole.

All these great minds could be distinguished by the extent to which they understood the transcending absolute truth as cooperative or competitive. Xenophanes, Heraclitus, Pythagoras, and Empedocles sought cooperative harmony within the transcendent divine. Anaximander and Parmenides saw dualistic competition within the transcendent divine, but even they believed that harmony could be achieved through the intervention of an arbiter. Anaximander saw time as that arbiter, whereas Parmenides, more in accord with the ancient Greek paradigm, saw reason in that role.

The notion of a transcendent absolute truth of harmonious cooperation is consistent with the ancient concept of the thickening and thinning of the indefinite, unbounded stuff of life (which, for example, Anaximenes called *Aer*). Dualistic philosophers understood the unbounded stuff as oppositional eternal elements that require an arbiter's intervention for harmony to emerge. Prior to Christianity, there was no concept of non-being, a time when the eternal nature of the unbounded stuff did not exist.

From Thales (624–547 B.C.) to Socrates (470–399 B.C.), the search for wisdom of the absolute truth of cosmic unity engaged the greatest thinkers of ancient Greece. But notice that *areté*, one's duty to virtuous conduct, which so influenced the ancient Greeks' paradigm had not been part of the history of the soul. As Hesiod's mythic understanding of the origin of the universe became more rationalized, the center of the cosmos rested in the human soul.[12]

The competing theories regarding the nature of the cosmos could not agree on a unifying single transcendent law or the nature of the soul. The obvious lack of harmony provided an opportunity for sophistry, which abandoned the search for absolute truth altogether. Instead, the Sophists challenged the moral and political beliefs of the *polis*. Allen calls this the two-part thesis of Cultural Relativity: "First, what is right or moral in one culture may be wrong and immoral in another; second, there is no 'absolute' standard to judge anything as right or wrong, apart from the attitude of a given society."[13] The Sophists' paradigm of Cultural Relativity rejected the transcendent principle of the ancient Greek paradigm, challenged the existence of the gods, and recognized man as the measure of all things.

The Sophists taught virtue through rhetorical technique. To them the substance of "absolute" truth was relative to the individual. Jaeger wrote of this philosophical perspective: "As man becomes increasingly conscious of his selfhood, he tends to consider his own will and reason independent of higher powers: and thereby he becomes more responsible for his own fate."[14] Socrates sought to challenge the moral relativity of the Sophists. The struggle between them—that is, between the ideas of absolute truth and relative truth—would confront every generation thereafter.

The One and the Many: Plato and Aristotle

Plato (ca. 428–ca. 348 B.C.) was a partisan. Inspired by Socrates' life, the Platonic dialogues guided the ancient paradigm of duty toward absolute truth in a divine realm, thereby uniting Heaven and Earth through the intellectual capacity of the human soul. Plato was not, however, naïve regarding the appeal of relativistic morality and its threat to the Greek city-state.

"It is hard, in the first place," wrote Plato in the *Laws*, "to perceive that a true social science must be concerned with the community, not with the individual…, and that it is to the advantage of community and individual at once that public well-being should be considered before private."[15] The problem would be to convince individuals to recognize the personal advantage of self-sacrifice for the common good.

In the *Republic*, Plato describes the ring of Gyges, which makes its bearer invisible. Freed from the judgment of others, will a person always act according to personal profit? Socrates' brothers, Glaucon and Adeimantus, want to be convinced, says Jaeger, "not that justice is socially profitable, but that it is good in itself for the soul of the man who possesses it."[16] In Plato's *Laws*, the character he calls the Athenian observes:

> Frail human nature will always tempt [a person in author-
> ity] to self-aggrandizement and self-seeking, will be bent
> beyond all reason on the avoidance of pain and pursuit
> of pleasure, and put both these ends before the claims
> of the right and the good; in this self-caused blindness it
> will end by sinking him and his community with him in
> depths of ruin.[17]

Here Plato identifies core characteristics of human nature: people, particularly leaders, are weak, and compelling self-interest leads to a community's ruin. If Plato correctly assesses human nature and the fabric of community, by what means can a community avoid the ruin of self-interested leadership? Plato answers, within the constraints of the ancient Greek paradigm, "To 'act beneath yourself' is the result of pure ignorance; to 'be your own master' is wisdom."[18] Nobody errs willingly; human nature cannot willingly pursue ignorance.[19] The transcendent unifying law, Plato's Idea of the Good, compels citizens to be their own masters and pursue wisdom. Jaeger indirectly acknowledges the authority of the ancient Greek paradigm when he observes:

> The thesis that nobody errs willingly presupposes that the will is directed to the Good as its *telos* [motivating goal of one's life], and since not only Plato but the other Socratics too have that idea, it is clearly Socrates' own.[20]

But if people are weak, and if human nature cannot willingly pursue ignorance, how will people avoid ignorance and gain wisdom? Plato's answer places the full responsibility on the proper teaching of *areté*.* He points to reason as the "only indwelling preserver of virtue throughout life in the soul that possesses it."[21] Through reason, humanity overcomes its weak, self-centered nature and enjoys communal harmony. For Jaeger, it is obvious that "the soul of man is the prototype of Plato's state," and that the ultimate aim of the *Republic* was to instill justice, or moral perfection, in the soul of each member of the *polis*.[22]

Plato's emphasis on *areté* through education had its limits. In his seventh letter, in which he asserts that educating the masses is not a good thing, he prefers to rely on the "few who are capable of discovering the truth for themselves."[23] Only a few can be relied upon to grasp the virtue of Plato's *paideia*. Jaeger notes, "Knowledge of good grows within us as Good itself becomes a reality taking shape in our souls."[24] It would seem that human weaknesses, however, represent a serious obstacle to reason's ability to compel right conduct. The grip of duty within the ancient Greek paradigm would be tested within the human soul.

---

*Plato, *Meno* 89a. Thus, Werner Jaeger (*Paideia: The Ideals of Greek Culture*, 2nd ed., trans. Gilbert Highet, vol. 1 (New York: Oxford University Press, 1945), emphasizes *paideia* as the teaching of *areté*.

In *Phaedrus*, Plato describes the soul as two winged steeds, whose winged charioteer is the *nous*, which is "reason alone, the soul's pilot."[25] One steed is "noble and good," the other "has the opposite character."[26] The winged steeds are impulsive and irrational. If they lose sight of the divine Good, they fall to Earth and cycle through various incarnations. It is difficult to distinguish Plato's poetic talent from his theology.* Jaeger writes, "We cannot apprehend [the soul's] true nature unless we contemplate its love of knowledge, and its high endeavour to soar aloft in the knowledge of its own divinity and immortality."[27]

Since Plato's concept of the soul has both rational and irrational characteristics, human reason's duty is to subordinate the soul's irrational inclination and guide the chariot toward the divine realm. Union with the divine is to be achieved through self-control. In the *Republic*, the calculations of reason and the irrational impulses of the soul are distinguished further. The irrational impulses are divided into two categories: "appetites" or "desires" and the incensive traits of "high spirit" or "anger."† Reason's knowledge of the divine and its struggle with desires and anger eventually re-emerged as the internal struggle of the western Christian soul. (The concept of the soul will change throughout the course of history.)

Other important characteristic of Plato's concept of the human soul is its immortality, for it exists both before and after the human body.[28] In fact, Plato (and other ancient Greek philosophers) considered the human body a prison for the soul, which becomes free once the body dies.[29] In other words, the soul is man's true being, whereas the body is a mere creature.[30] Furthermore, the soul reincarnates from the divine

---

*According to Jaeger (*Paideia*, vol. 2, p. 297), the revolutionary concept of theology was founded by Plato and described in the *Republic*.

†Plato, *Republic* 4:439d. Cf. 441b. *Incensive* is a term used to describe *spiritedness* or *anger*.

realm through various lives until it attains moral perfection.* For Plato, the divine realm, the Idea of the Good, was the ultimate reality. Human intelligence could guide the soul toward this absolute truth, but "divine revelation" represented the surest path.[31]

The ancient Greek paradigm reached its apex in Plato's theology.† But if reality is the invisible realm of the divine, what can be said about the pre-Socratic "unbounded stuff"?

The ancient Milesians had no religious or ethical motivations in their quest for wisdom. They identified three characteristics of the cosmos: an invisible unbounded; visible stuff; and an idea of equilibrium. Plato's understanding of wisdom united these three characteristics of the cosmos. Jaeger explains, "It is, as Plato describes it, the penetration of thought from the phenomena to the true nature of *areté*, an act of intellectual vision, which sees the One in the Many."[32]

Only the *nous* ("mind") is capable of this intellectual vision, this divine revelation. As Plato writes in the seventh letter, "Suddenly, like a blaze kindled by a leaping spark, it is generated in the soul and at once becomes self-sustaining."[33] However, the ancient Greek understanding of *nous* was far more encompassing than its modern translation of "mind" or "intellect." According to Plato, the *nous* was the highest capacity of the human soul, the purest of ideas, the ultimate idea.[34] The *nous* was, in fact, the only human capacity that could both know and experience divine perfection. In contrast, mathematical thought (*dianoia*) could only provide abstract understanding, and knowledge of the material world or empirical evidence (*pistis*) was mere opinion.[35]

The soul of the ancient Greek paradigm accepts the unity of the One in the Many. Plato's belief in the ancient paradigm was unconditional.

---

*References to the transmigration of the soul are found in Plato's *Meno* 81b; *Phaedo* 70c, 81; *Phaedrus* 248c; and *Republic* 10:617d.

†Jaeger notes, "The God who is the 'measure of all things'…is identical with the One…it is theology" (*Paideia*, vol. 3, p. 352, note 376).

Aristotle, Plato's most significant student, while sharing his teacher's faith both in the divine and in reason, sought knowledge of the One *from* the Many. According to Richard Tarnas (1950–), a professor of philosophy and psychology at the California Institute of Integral Studies, in San Francisco, "The crux of their difference involved the precise nature of the [Ideas of the Good] and their relation with the empirical world. Aristotle's intellectual temperament…took the empirical world on its own terms as fully real."[36]

Another way to understand the differences between Plato and Aristotle can be seen in the way each understood the nature of being. For Plato, the Idea of the Good was "beyond being."[37] The soul ascends from the darkness of the cave (described in the *Republic*) toward the light of the intelligible world.[38] "The essential thing for Plato," writes Jaeger, "is the realization that 'truth about being exists in our soul.'"[39] Plato's soul ascends and descends through reincarnation, until the soul perfects its knowledge of the divine.

For Aristotle, all being is within the natural world, where it is either "actual" or "potential." The only connection between the supreme Form of Good and the natural world was the *nous*, the eye of man's soul.* Tarnas explains, "Only because man shares in the divine *nous* can he apprehend infallible truth, and the *nous* constitutes the only part of man that 'comes in from outside.'"[40] The divine and earthly realms are separate and distinct. Yet, Aristotle accepts the existence of both. His worldview continues to be influenced by the ancient paradigm of the transcendent divine. Its precarious unity depends on the existence of the divine *nous*. When Aristotle wrote the *Nicomachean Ethics*, the

---

*Plato describes the *nous* as divine intelligence in *Cratylus* 407b, and as the soul's pilot in *Phaedrus* 247c. Andrew Louth notes that the *nous* as the eye of the soul is used by St. John of Damascus (645–749 A.D.) (*St. John Damascene: Tradition and Originality in Byzantine Theology* [New York: Oxford University Press, 2002, p. 44]). The significance of the *nous* to early Christianity will be covered in Chapters 4 and 5.

Politics, and the *Metaphysics,* he identified distinctions of "the Many" while accepting the unity of the divine realm.

Lost in Translation: From Greek to Latin

When the Greek understanding of *nous* lost its meaning of apprehending divine revelation and assumed the Latin meaning of reason or intellect, the unity of Aristotle's physics and metaphysics came undone. Aristotle had seen divine harmony between physics, which treated the realm of evidence, and metaphysics, which treated the realm beyond evidence. Owen Barfield (1898–1997), a British philosopher, author, poet, and critic, shed important light on the evolution of meaning in language:

> At the heart of early Greek philosophy lay two funda-
> mental assumptions. One was that an inner meaning lay
> hid behind external phenomena…. The other assumption
> concerned the attainment by man of immortality.[41]

An example of the inner meaning of external phenomena can be found in the gospel of St. John (3:8):

> The wind blows where it wishes, and you hear the sound
> of it, but cannot tell where it comes from and where it
> goes. So is every one who is born of the Spirit.[42]

The Greek word *pneuma* is translated here in the first instance as "wind" and in the second instance as "Spirit." By separating the internal ("Spirit") and external ("wind") meanings of *pneuma,* the original complexity of the word is diminished. The shared essence, synergy, and unity of the two concepts are lost.

Another example that Barfield identifies is *Logos*, which in ancient Greek meant both "word" and "reason":

> *Logos* in Greek had always meant both "word" (an ex-pressed meaning) and the creative faculty in human beings—"Reason." ...The Stoics were the first to identify this human faculty with that divine Mind (*Nous*) which earlier Greek philosophers had perceived as pervading the visible universe.[43]

Plato and Aristotle were bound by the ancient Greek paradigm, but by significantly different degrees. Barfield observes:

> While Plato had concentrated his intellectual effort on mapping out what we should now call the "inner" world of human consciousness, starting from the point of view of ancient traditions and myth, and working outward..., deducing the sense-world from the spiritual world; Ar-istotle turned to the acquisition of knowledge about the outer world of matter and energy—that is to say, that part of the world which can be apprehended by the five senses and the brain. The two philosophers were alike in their emphasis on the importance of cultivating im-mortality..., but otherwise there were few resemblances indeed.[44]

Both philosophers accept the absolute truth of the transcendent divine and emphasize the "importance of cultivating immortality."

Aristotle's effort to categorize the cosmos, however, would become the intellectual forerunner of modern science. Knowledge of the earthly realm would come through abstract reasoning or empirical evidence. Anaximander's "separating out" would eventually evolve into the invisible realm of Cartesian rationalism, and Anaximenes' materialism would become the forerunner of the visible realm of Hume's empiricism. Jaeger concludes:

> [Plato] explains that there are two sources for man's belief in the existence of the gods: knowledge of the orbits, eternally the same, in which the heavenly bodies move; and the "eternal stream of being" in us, the soul. No human philosophy has ever gone beyond this—from Aristotle, who took these two motives for the belief in God into his own theology, to Kant's *Critique of Practical Reason*, which after all his revolutionary theoretical arguments ends in practice with the same two thoughts.[45]

These twin foundations for man's belief in the existence of the gods would each be challenged over the next two thousand years. The belief that these foundations support the absolute truth of the ancient Greek paradigm would have consequences for the elevation of man's Self by the eighteenth century.

As with Plato and Aristotle's unconditional faith in reason, the Sophists' belief that man was the measure of all things was equally unconditional. The Sophists' rejection of the existence of the gods, however, was unthinkable to most of their contemporaries. As early as Parmenides (b. ca. 515 B.C.), the idea of non-being was considered meaningless. Plato saw the unity of the One in the Many. Aristotle thought it was "proper to start from the known" through investigation of the natural world, for knowledge of the "first principle."[46] Both Plato and Aristotle accepted the ancient paradigm of a transcendent truth, but sought knowledge of it in completely different ways. Their pursuit of absolute truth, however, represented important areas of agreement that united them in their opposition to the cultural relativity of the Sophists.[47]

The One *or* the Many

Upon closer examination, Plato's One was not Aristotle's unmoved mover. For Aristotle, the divine unmoved mover represented the first principle and cause of all being. The unmoved mover initiated the eternal cycle of cause and consequence in the cosmos. The unmoved mover remained unmoved and unchanging in itself.[48] Twentieth-century British philosopher and mathematician Alfred North Whitehead (1861–1947) identified Aristotle as the last great European philosopher to consider dispassionately the metaphysical character of God, not as a moral personality but as a requirement of his physics.[49]

Aristotle regarded life's goal as happiness. Life guided by enjoyment (i.e., hedonism) was fine for common people and animals, but humanity's intellectual capabilities have a higher duty.* Unfortunately for Aristotle, there is no objective external standard to guide behavior. Without a transcendent One and its single standard of right conduct, people essentially define and arbitrate their own standard of intellectual happiness.[50] This relative understanding of happiness, however, complemented the cultural relativity of the Sophists. When rhetoric eventually

---

*Aristotle, *Nicomachean Ethics*, Book I, Chapter V. See Allen, *Greek Philosophy*, pp. 387–388. Aristotle categorized the "generality of mankind," his term for the human condition, as follows: the life of enjoyment, the life of politics, and the life of contemplation.

conquered the philosophical education of Plato and Aristotle, the latter's scientific methods unwittingly contributed to the sophistic victory.[51]

Aristotle proposed that humanity guide personal behavior through the Doctrine of the Mean. As noted earlier in this chapter, the pre-Socratic philosopher Anaximander was the first to present the idea of a transcending battle of opposites guided by the judgment of time. Reginald Allen speculates that the warring opposites came from "the perpetual war between winter (the moist and cold) and summer (the hot and dry); the cycle of the seasons, and perhaps the lesser cycle of day and night."[52] Nature's examples of opposites provided the perfect subject for Aristotle's intellectual curiosity.

In the *Nicomachean Ethics*, Aristotle identifies two kinds of *areté* (virtue): Intellectual and Moral. In pursuit of *areté*, right conduct for individual happiness seeks the mean by avoiding the extremes of deficiency and excess.[53] For example, in the area of self-expression, the extreme excess of boastfulness and the extreme deficiency of understatement both represent vice. The virtuous mean would be truthfulness. For the incensive power of anger, the extremes of irascibility and lack of spirit would have a virtuous mean in patience; and in the case of fear, the virtuous mean of courage is bracketed by the vices of rashness and cowardice.

Plato's quest for divine knowledge was not the mean between opposites, but the perfect ascent of the soul. At the heart of Plato's appreciation for self-control was the belief that short-term sacrifice would produce long-term rewards.[54] Jaeger summarizes Plato's reliance on obligation in the *Republic* as follows: "The rulers, the guards, and the working class—all have their fixed and definite duties."[55] Jaeger deduces:

> Prudent self-control...[ensures] concord between the three classes, based on the voluntary subordination of

that which is by nature worse to that which is by nature or training better. It is to penetrate all three classes, but its principal demands are made on the class which is expected to be loyally obedient.[56]

In Jaeger's exploration of the health of society and the health of the soul, justice is the common denominator and arbitrator. It is "moral perfection" and "the health of the soul" and the "realm of true freedom." Thus, Jaeger writes, justice "does not lie in separate actions, but in the... permanent state of having a good will."[57] Voluntary subordination, or self-control, is necessary for justice. Having a permanent attitude of good will ensures the health and stability of both the soul and the state.

Plato's respect for self-control, however, was not consistent with the ancient Greek culture. According to Jaeger, "Homer believed that the denial of honor due was the greatest human tragedy."[58] According to the Doctrine of the Mean, understatement in self-expression is an extreme deficiency and therefore a vice against the mean of truthfulness. If one is good and does not tell others, that is bad. Humility was not a virtue in ancient Greece, although Socrates' example of intellectual humility clearly inspired Plato.

Plato and Aristotle both considered courage a virtue, but Aristotle had a much more tangible understanding of justice because it deals with interactions between people, as opposed to the personal disposition of an individual.[59] This different emphasis regarding justice is consistent with Plato's and Aristotle's particular points of view. Both rely on and have faith in reason, yet the exercise of reason has interesting consequences for the two perspectives. According to Barfield:

> [Consider] the almost lost distinction between the word "hypothesis" and the word "theory." ...The Greek word [*theoria*] meant "contemplations" and is the term used

in Aristotle's psychology to designate the moment of fully conscious participation, in which the soul's potential knowledge (its ordinary state) becomes actual, so that man can at last claim to be "awake." ...It does emphasize the difference between a proposition which it is hoped may turn out true, and a proposition, the truth or untruth of which is irrelevant.[60]

In the beginning of the *Nicomachean Ethics*, Aristotle suggests that *areté* is a virtuous habit accomplished through practice. The ancient Greek term *praxis* meant "a doing action." Remember that both Plato and Aristotle believed that knowledge of the divine realm could be achieved through reason. Through the exercise of reason, knowledge of the knowable should lead to knowledge of the divine. The exercise of reason should demonstrate the union of *theoria* (knowledge of the divine) and *praxis* (a doing action). Theory was not an abstract hypothesis whose innate truth was irrelevant, but an absolute truth that could be proved through effort. Plato and Aristotle mutually relied on reason, but their different emphasis would result over time in vastly different points of view. Albert W. Levi (1911–1988), a professor of philosophy at Washington University in St. Louis, observed:

Philosophers since Plato and Aristotle have taken for granted the centrality of the intellect, and from this belief has grown a faith that the unity of nature can be best expressed in the abstract and geometrical form imposed by the intellect.[61]

Socrates had steadfastly refused to involve himself with politics, which Jaeger speculates was "not a sign of lack of interest, but the result of a profound intellectual and spiritual conflict."[62] Jaeger compares

Plato's intent in writing the *Republic* and writing the *Laws*. The *Republic*, he argues, promotes the voluntary acceptance of self-sacrifice by each member of the *polis*. The *Laws*, on the other hand, "represents the lower plane of opinion," where government is responsible for maintaining harmony.[63] But even in the *Laws*, the whole tenth book is concerned with theology.

It seems impossible for Plato to consider divine duty and civic duty as separate and distinct responsibilities. We have seen how Plato's and Aristotle's mutual reverence for reason moved in vastly different directions. Knowledge of the divine does not provide a compelling reason for self-sacrifice. An atheist, for example, would consider knowing the divine a frivolous effort. Governmental punishment for wrong conduct provides a compelling argument to an individual's innate desire for self-preservation. Jaeger summarizes his three-volume effort on *Paideia* as follows:

> State and church, in the modern world, are separate. Plato made them one and the same in the conception of the polis. And yet what was it that did most to separate them, and to found a spiritual kingdom beside and above the kingdom of this earth? It was the enormous demands made by Plato on the educational powers of human society. The state built around Plato's central educational ideal moves, from *The Republic* to *The Laws*, nearer and nearer to the kingdom ruling over the souls of men which the church later brought into being. But Plato always maintains his principle that this kingdom is nothing but the inner spiritual nature of man himself, led to action by superior intelligence. It is the rule of the higher in us over the lower: the fundamental axiom laid down in *The Laws*.[64]

The personal struggle between our higher duty and our lower inclinations would forever frame Plato's understanding of freedom. External events may influence personal decisions, but ultimately, for Plato, freedom would be an internal struggle to control our irrational desires and incensive anger. The next chapter will identify the external influences in that period known as Middle Platonism.

❖ ❖ ❖

Chapter 3

From Middle Platonism to Neo-Platonism

Plato, Politics, and Morality

With the previous background on the Greek pursuit of wisdom as a foundation, we now approach that period of history known as Middle Platonism. It is a period of significant transition from the Greek city-states to the unity of the Roman Empire. I introduce here the role of Plato, Isocrates, Philo, Plotinus, and the teachings of the Stoics, Epicureans, Skeptics, and Gnostics. However, this chapter is not intended to be a thorough review of each personality or philosophical idea that sought to replace the ancient Greek paradigm. We begin this part of our effort with the most prominent of the ancient Greek city-states, Athens.

Plato was a descendant of Solon (638–558 B.C.), whom Jaeger praises as "the first Athenian."[1] Solon's legendary selfless reign over Athens was an example of the highest *areté* of the ancient Greek paradigm. Jaeger observes that Solon "never tires of declaring that he did not use his position to make himself a rich man or a tyrant, as most men would have in his place; and he is willing to be called a fool for missing the chance."[2] Solon credits his guiding principle to right judgment, *gnomosyne*, because, as Jaeger notes, "it always suggests the *gnome*, which is both true insight and the will to put it into action."* Furthermore, two of Plato's uncles, Critias and Charmenides, were part of a political

---

*Werner Jaeger, *Paideia: The Ideals of Greek Culture*, trans. Gilbert Highet, vol. 1 (New York: Oxford University Press, 1945), p. 149. This principle of gnomic willingness was referred to by early Christian theologian St. Maximus the Confessor (ca. 580–662 A.D.), who distinguished the two wills of Christ as human and divine, as will be covered in greater detail in Chapter 5.

uprising against Athenian democracy. It is no wonder that Plato explored the relationships among individual *areté*, societal governance, and divine authority.

The structure of Plato's ideal society, described in the *Republic,* was not a democracy but rather a benevolent tyranny, the supreme rule of one person, like Solon, devoted to the well-being of the *polis*. To ensure the selfless character of the ruling elite, Plato proposed that every aspect of society that encouraged selfishness, such as private wealth, would be condemned, and family relationships would be abolished. Breeding would be officially controlled by the state; nurseries would be set up for mothers to suckle the children without any knowledge of which was their own baby.[3] "The best state," Jaeger explains, "is the state where most citizens think 'mine' means not something individual and separate, but something common to all."[4] Leaders who are selfless govern not as masters but as helpers. They would, as Jaeger notes, respect "common people not as servants but as breadwinners and providers."[5]

Plato believed that the proper training of every citizen was the responsibility of the city-state. His strategy for teaching *areté* was through the creation of school communities where students would spend decades learning many subjects, including gymnastics and the Pythagorean disciplines of astronomy, music, and mathematics. The framework of the curriculum for these first universities was outlined in the *Republic*. At the heart of the effort was Plato's belief that the nature of man was both social and moral. The guiding authority of the ancient Greek paradigm brought together Plato's faith in a transcendent divine, his belief in the moral nature of humanity, and his reliance on reason for knowledge of the universal truths. The eighteenth-century philosopher Jean-Jacques Rousseau (1712–1778) understood that the *Republic* was not a political system "but the finest treatise on education ever written."[6]

While the Pythagorean disciplines were prominent in the curriculum of Plato's Academy, he was critical of the Pythagorean emphasis on sense-perception. His students were taught to seek *theoria*, that moment of fully conscious participation with absolute truth. This is another example of the unity of *theoria* and *praxis*, theory and practice, in Plato's philosophy and explains why the Academy's curriculum was based on gymnastics and the Pythagorean disciplines. Plato believed that "every citizen [would] recognize the divine truth of the eternal God."[7] Atheists, who did not believe in the gods proclaimed by Socrates, would be punished; although, with the proper training, they could redeem themselves. Punishment was not considered retribution but a means of education. According to Jaeger, Plato considered punishment "a cure for the sick soul."[8]

The tyrant represents the highest unity and concentration of the collective *will* of the *polis*.[9] As such, the tyrant can be just or unjust, depending on the ethos (the spirit and way of life) of the city-state. Neither the collective *will* nor the tyrant's *volition* was automatically presumed to be *gnomic*. External laws could not advance justice if the ethos of society was not good.[10] Only personal knowledge of the absolute truth of the divine would justify the authority and power of honorable governance.[11] Plato hoped for a teachable tyrant to ensure the happiness of the future city-state.[12] He was aware, however, that even the most successful tyrannies would collapse within two or three generations. The failure of the tyrant's sons or grandsons to maintain their inherited power, or their despotic misuse of power, would doom their reign.[13]

There was no consensus among the Athenians that their leadership should come from Plato's tutelage, nor was there consensus about what constituted the proper training of *areté*. Alternative schools were established. Plato's belief in educating a selfless tyrant, a philosopher-king, to lead the people was challenged by Isocrates' belief in democratic governance.

Ethnicity Versus Empire

Isocrates (436–338 B.C.), the father of "humanistic culture,"[14] believed that a tyrant could not be relied on to restrain his inclination toward self-interest through the virtues of justice and self-control alone. Isocrates also did not believe that the state had any responsibility to educate the *polis* toward moral perfection,[15] nor did he believe in a moral order within man's soul.[16] He was a nationalist, who believed that the idea of Greek cultural superiority would unite the *polis*. Jaeger credits this nationalistic spark for advancing Greek *paideia* as universally valuable. He believes it was the "basis for Macedonian Greek world-empire," without which "the universal culture which we call Hellenistic would never have existed."[17]

Isocrates accepted the cultural relativity of the Sophists and emphasized the virtues of oratory and rhetoric. He believed that the state should amass material greatness to ensure the prosperity of the *polis*.[18] Contrasted with Plato's emphasis on self-control, this was a compelling message. Jaeger summarizes:

> When philosophical educators preached that every activity must be subordinated to eternal values, that seemed to many to be too lofty an ideal; but there was a general demand that politics should be inspired by higher principles, and many of the younger generation must have felt that Isocrates' national morality was a happy and timely mean between the extremes of ethical skepticism, on the one hand, and philosophical retreat to the Absolute, on the other.[19]

Despite the appeal of Isocrates' nationalistic rhetoric, the geography and inclination of the ancient Greek *polises* resisted the formation of an empire combining the various Greek enclaves. There were constant battles between city-states and against outside forces such as the Persians and Macedonians. The Macedonian king Philip II (382–336 B.C.) was successful in conquering the various Greek city-states, which would not regain their independence for two thousand years. His son, whom history knows as Alexander the Great (356–323 B.C.), proceeded to conquer Persia, the eastern Mediterranean, and Egypt. Aristotle, who was a young product of Plato's Academy, was Alexander's tutor. The success of the Macedonian Greek empire, however, could not overcome Alexander's death, as Plato might have predicted. Without a clear successor, the Macedonian political institutions were too weak to survive.

At about the same time, Roman military victories were occurring throughout the Mediterranean. The Romans' mind-set was more structured than the Greeks' in the areas of political and legal discourse. This different intellectual emphasis accounts for the relative long-term stability within the much larger Roman Empire. Once the Macedonian Greek territories had been absorbed into the Roman Empire, however, the more sophisticated Greek culture and philosophy overwhelmed the Romans, creating what historians call the "Greco-Roman" period. Greek culture is often recognized as having conquered its conquerors, and the most prominent families of the empire were fluent in both Latin and Greek. "Without Greek cultural ideas," Jaeger states, "Greco-Roman civilization would not have been a historical unity, and the culture of the western world would never have existed."[20]

Many peoples were absorbed within the geographic sphere of the Roman Empire, and most accepted the divinity of the Greco-Roman deities. The definitive scholar on the Roman Empire, Edward Gibbons, stated that "the various modes of worship which prevailed in the Roman world were all considered by the people as equally true; by the philosopher, as equally false; and by the magistrate, as equally useful."[21]

But the people of one tribe, the Israelites, had their own understanding of the divine. The most famous Jew in history spent his whole life in the Roman province of Palestine. Jesus was born in Bethlehem, grew up in Nazareth, and was crucified in Jerusalem. His followers believe that he is the incarnate word of God and that three days after his crucifixion he rose from the dead. It is an historical fact that no single person has had a more significant impact on humanity than this Palestinian Jew. The calendar of the Western world begins with his life, and today a third of the Earth's peoples accept the truth of his resurrection from death.

Followers of Jesus were first identified as Christians in the Roman city of Antioch, in what today is Turkey (Acts 11:26). Both Jews and Christians were considered pagans by the Roman religious authorities, but Christians were particularly persecuted for their reluctance to accept the supreme authority of the Roman emperors and their gods. During the first three hundred years after Jesus, his followers could only worship in secret. Despite the persecution, however, their numbers and influence grew. In early 313 A.D., Constantine, the ruler of the western half of the Roman Empire, proclaimed the Edict of Milan, which was accepted by Licinius, the ruler of the eastern half of the empire, giving Christianity equal status with the Greco-Roman religious establishment. In 324 A.D., Constantine defeated Licinius and united the Roman Empire under his leadership.

During the six hundred years between the death of Alexander the Great and the imperial rule of Constantine, the people within the Roman Empire were bombarded with competing ideas about the nature of being and the purpose of life. Various Roman leaders built roads throughout the empire, which facilitated economic commerce, allowed for the efficient movement of troops, and inspired the exchange of ideas. During this period, the Greco-Roman academic and religious traditions gave rise to a number of social and moral influences, including Stoicism, Epicureanism, Gnosticism, and Skepticism.

To fully appreciate the important transitions that occurred between Alexander and Constantine, we need to briefly revisit Plato's motivation for writing the dialogues. For Plato, the political leadership of his day had lost its moral authority. The ancient Greek paradigm had begun with the acceptance of a transcending divine, of which each person's soul was a part. The divine was absolute good, and each person had a soul that shared the essence of that absolute good. The Sophists' rhetoric of cultural relativity was interpreted by Plato as a direct assault on the authority of the divine. The dialogues, therefore, were an attempt to refocus the *polis* on the benefits of knowing the divine through an inner struggle between reason and irrational impulses. But the sense of duty embodied in the ancient Greek paradigm did not distinguish between the authority of the state and that of the divine. Each member of the *polis* had to choose the authority to which he would pledge his allegiance. The Sophists rejected humanity's subordinate role to either the state or the divine, seeing man as the measure of all things. Therefore, they saw no reason to endure sacrifice of any kind.

In Chapter 2, we saw how Plato and Aristotle approached divine knowledge in very different ways. Although both philosophers relied on reason to discover knowledge of the divine, Plato sought it through internal contemplation, whereas Aristotle sought it through exploration of external natural phenomena. We also noted in that chapter Barfield's comments on the difference between the Latin tendency to separate the internal and external meanings of words and the Greek language's fuller appreciation of meaning. Finally, we contrasted Plato's strategy of governing society through a selfless tyrant patterned after his ancestor, Solon, with Isocartes' call for a democracy that would unite the people on the basis of nationalism. The convergence of all of these influences represents the point when the ancient Greek paradigm began to break down.

Up until this point, there was a broad-based acceptance of an undefined transcendent law that united the cosmos. In Chapter 1, we spoke of personal will, and at the beginning of this chapter we identified Solon's reliance on *gnomosyne*, which is volition with, in Jaeger's words, "true insight and the will to put it into action."[22] Members of the *polis* who exercised their will did not necessarily act in the best interests of the community. People have choices, and the Sophists challenged individuals to determine their own standards of morality.

Right conduct would no longer be universally recognized by the guiding principle of a single transcendent law, which distinguished the ancient Greek paradigm. Isocrates lamented the loss of holy shame, *aidos*, to enforce mutual respect.[23] In the absence of *aidos*, the government would define and enforce right conduct through punishment. Solon's reliance on *gnome* no longer had a universal standard that everyone could accept. True insight would be relative, and all members of the community would act according to their own measures of morality.

In this environment, philosophical alternatives began to distinguish themselves. The Epicurean school, founded in Athens in 306 B.C., emphasized an empirical approach to logic and stressed pleasure as the highest good.[24] Stoicism aligned an individual's personal exercise of reason with the divine reason that determines the order of each person's life. Only complete detachment from passions would unite the individual with the universal reason.[25] Skepticism questioned the capacity of reason to know anything with certainty. The *probability* that a particular outcome would manifest itself would be all that one could expect from reason.[26]

These alternative belief systems, which defined right conduct in the service of a guiding principle, would entice each person's allegiance. Jaeger writes:

> Philosophy becomes a set of dogmas aimed at guiding
> human life by its teachings and giving it an inner security
> no longer found in the outside world..., thereby fulfilling
> a religious function.... Stoics and Epicureanism satisfy a

nonrational religious need to fill the vacuum left by ancient Greek cult religion…. But cool research…of human mind was still strong enough for Greek philosophical thought to end in heroic scepticism denying all dogmatic ideas.[27]

The alternative philosophical dogmas essentially represented alternative systems of arbitration for each person to accept or reject. Barfield's linguistic distinction between the external and internal evolution of meaning began to manifest itself once ethnicity became a subset of empire.

Middle Platonism and Neo-Platonism: Philo and Plotinus

As the various ethnic communities within the emerging Roman Empire traded goods and ideas, a clearer conception of God evolved beyond Plato's vague realm of the divine Good. Self-interest, selflessness, the divine, and the state offered competing understandings of happiness and the meaning of life. The ancient Jews, however, who had been brought into the empire by the military successes of Alexander, had their own unique belief in God. Their personal relationship with the one God was completely foreign to both Greek and Roman culture. While many historians refer to this period as the Middle Platonist transition toward the Neo-Platonism of Plotinus (ca. 205–270 A.D.), Andrew Louth (1944–), a professor of theology and religion at Durham University, draws a clearer distinction, recognizing the fuller definition of God as a unique characteristic of Middle Platonism.[28] In Louth's view, Philo (ca. 13 B.C.–ca. 50 A.D.) was the most prominent Middle Platonist when he merged his Jewish theology with Platonic principles.

Philo, who lived in Alexandria, was a contemporary of Jesus, although there is no evidence that they ever met. He was a devout Jew from a wealthy family and was well versed in Greek philosophy. In fact, Philo referred to the divine *logos* proclaimed by the pre-Socratic philosopher Heraclitus (ca. 535–475 B.C.) as the "only-begotten son."[29] In other words, he personified the originally abstract concept. Philo wrote extensively about the first five books of the Bible, the Pentateuch, revered by Jews as the scriptural foundation of their faith, and he brought together the common themes of Greek philosophy and Jewish theology.

Philo believed that the highest virtue was humility, whose roots could be found in the Pentateuch. For example, Moses is recognized there as humble, Isaiah speaks of a contrite and humble spirit, and the Psalms of David are full of references to humility.[30] Philo's concept of humility is compatible with Plato's respect for self-control, but incompatible within Aristotle's Doctrine of the Mean.

Philo claimed that God is both unknowable in essence and knowable in energy. According to Louth, Philo believed that "the soul is not an essentially divine being that belongs to the divine realm.... [Rather, it] is a creature, created by God, and nothing in itself."[31]

If Philo sought to merge Jewish and Greek traditions, the third-century Neo-Platonist Plotinus sought to distinguish Plato's theology from Gnostic influences, which saw reality in dualistic terms, such as good and evil or light and darkness.[32] Gnostic mysticism competed with the mystery of early Christianity. Gnostics merged Hesiod's (ca. 800 B. C.) mythology of Mother Earth into the Goddess of Heaven, which they referred to as Sophia, the Greek word for wisdom.[33] Plotinus had broad influence throughout the Roman Empire and was particularly important for detailing the orthodoxy of Platonic theology. As the Irish classical scholar E. R. Dodds (1893–1973) observed:

> [In Plotinus] converge almost all the main currents of
> thought that come down from eight hundred years of

Greek speculation; out of it there issues a new current destined to fertilize minds as different as those of Augustine and Boethius, Dante and Meister Eckhart, Coleridge, Bergson, and T. S. Eliot.[34]

Any difference between Plato's One and Aristotle's first principle of the unmoved mover were resolved by Plotinus. Historians' confusion with regard to Plato's dialogues as mere poetry was resolved in the dogma of Plotinus. Recognized as the premier Neo-Platonist, Plotinus spoke of "the flight of the alone to the Alone."[35] Andrew Louth sees Plotinus' mystical quest of the soul toward the divine as:

> a solitary way that leads to the One, sovereign in solitary transcendence. The One has no concern for the soul that seeks him; nor has the soul more than a passing concern for others engaged on the same quest: it has no companions.[36]

Plotinus recognized a hierarchy of three principles: the One as Plato's Idea of the Good; the *nous*, or mind (discussed in the previous chapter), humanity's intellectual capacity to apprehend divine revelation of the Good; and *psyche*, or soul, the center of man's being, our individual experience with the sensory world. According to Henry Chadwick (1920–2008), a distinguished historian at Oxford University, Plotinus spoke of the One, the *nous*, and the soul "as if all souls participate in one common soulness, and separateness or individuality is entirely a matter of body."* Louth summarizes the distinction between *nous* and the One:

---

*Henry Chadwick, "Philosophical Tradition and the Self," in *Interpreting Late Antiquity: Essays on the Postclassical World*, ed. G. W. Bowersock, Peter Brown, and Oleg Grabar (Cambridge: Harvard University Press, 2001), available at http://www.myriobiblos.gr/texts/english/chadwick_tradition.html. Notice the similar difficulty that Descartes had in distinguishing intellect from extension.

> [The *nous*] is Plato's realm of the Forms. Here knower and known are one, here knowledge is intuitive…. For Plato this was ultimate reality. For Plotinus, not so…. Beyond the realm of [the *nous*]…is the One, which is absolutely simple, beyond any duality whatsoever, and of which, therefore, nothing can be said. It is the One, because beyond duality; it is the Good, because it has no need of anything else. It is the source of all, it is beyond being.[37]

The distinction that Louth makes regarding the essential nature of the soul may seem like a distinction without a difference, but the attempt to reconcile the unity of the One and the multiplicity found in the world's natural diversity still plagues Western philosophers to this day. In Chapter 2, we identified the ancient Greek paradigm's acceptance of unity between one and the many and their implied cooperation through the transcendent divine. In the Middle Platonist era, the underlying obligation to cooperate was challenged by the struggle between various philosophical alternatives, whose competition produced new allegiances.

For Plotinus, the flight of man's eternal soul to the Absolute One could only be achieved through contemplation. But unlike the ancient Greek cooperation between *theoria* and *praxis*, whereby contemplation is always fulfilled through action, Plotinus sought *theoria* without an obligation to *praxis*. In this respect, that flight shared the Stoics' disinterest in the sensory world and their mutual dependence on contemplation without action. Note, however, the significant difference from Plato's understanding of *theoria* and *praxis*, whereby contemplation is always fulfilled through action.

In Chapter 2, we identified the simultaneous internal and external meanings of the Greek language. After Rome conquered and then embraced Hellenic culture, the different emphases of Plato and Aristotle became more profound as Greek ideas were translated into Latin. Barfield notes:

> Words which are genuinely of Latin origin...are very often concerned with the material outer world, [whereas] words of Greek origin are more likely to be landmarks in the world of thoughts and feelings.[38]

Over time, this linguistic distinction separated internal from external in reference to matter and spirit, particular and universal, noumena and phenomena, and visible and invisible.* The different emphases in language would contribute to Plotinus' ultimate conclusion that the One is separate and distinct from any multiplicity. Barfield concludes:

> As time went on, Roman religious feeling quickly changed in two almost opposite ways. On the one hand, it attached itself more and more to concrete and material objects, and, on the other, its gods and goddesses were felt less and less as living beings, and more and more as mere abstract intellectual conceptions.... Thus, the mythical world was much less real to the Romans than it had been to the Greeks.[39]

Philosophical Alternatives in the Roman Empire

The differences between Plato's inward and Aristotle's outward perspective were further exaggerated by the Latin- and Greek-speaking

---

*Immanuel Kant first made the distinction between noumena and phenomena in his *Critique of Pure Reason*, trans. Norman Kemp Smith (London: Palgrave Macmillan, 1985).

peoples of the Roman Empire. The Stoic disinterest in life could be interpreted as a lack of concern for others. The Epicurean interest in momentary happiness could justify hedonism. Philo's attempt to reconcile Plato and the Pentateuch provided the rationale for the early Christian church. Plotinus' definition of orthodox Platonic theology lingered throughout the centuries of Western philosophical inquiry. The Gnostic claim to know the religious mystery of personal salvation blurred the distinctions between myth, philosophy, and theology. The people of the Roman Empire had plenty of philosophical alternatives to choose from, each one representing a belief system with its own standard of right conduct and its own enforcement mechanism.

A cursory summary of the guiding principles of these belief systems will immediately demonstrate the spectrum of choices that a Roman citizen had. Epicureanism, founded by Epicurus (341–270 B.C.), accepted the belief in the divine, where atoms exist in an infinite void. The goal of life would be material happiness, and prudence would be the foundation of virtue.[40] Stoicism valued physics and recognized a universal reason that determined the boundaries of natural law. Adherents of this belief system, such as the Roman statesman Seneca (ca. 4 B.C.–65 A.D.), were known to commit suicide if they felt they had failed in their public duties.[41] Gnostics believed in varying combinations of a dualism of good and bad, light and dark; a Great Mother Goddess who descends into the material world; and a Savior who battles evil, bringing salvation of the elect believers.[42]

While each belief system represented a different interpretation of right conduct, there was no overseer to discipline the casual initiate, nor was there any requirement for perfect discipline within a belief system. People were free to pick and choose which belief system they adhered to and change their mind at any moment. Each belief system attempted to enforce right conduct through some version of *aidos*, peer pressure, or punishment. But the effectiveness of these enforcement measures depended directly on the degree to which an initiate freely submitted to the authority of the belief system's guiding principles.

While these belief systems were very different from one another, they were all compatible with Hesiod's mythological description of the creation of the universe. In all of them, the mysterious heavenly father and earthly mother were infinite and eternal, and the material world was equally eternal. The possibility of regeneration was more explicit in Plotinus and Hesiod, but generally speaking there was a compatible acceptance of visible and invisible realms with no particular initial creation event. Even Aristotle's unmoved mover was at best vague about the initial event. Philo, however, had a different explanation for creation. One God, he argued, created everything, including heaven, earth, time, and the cosmic void. Therefore, all beings exist through the intention of the One Creator. Jaeger distinguishes these two cosmic origins as follows:

> The Logos [of the Hebrews] is a substantialization of an intellectual property or power of God the creator, who is stationed *outside* the world and brings that world into existence by his own personal fiat. The Greek gods [described by Hesiod] are stationed *inside* the world; they are descended from Heaven and Earth, the two greatest and most exalted parts of the universe; and they are generated by the mighty power of Eros…. Thus they are already subject to what we shall call natural law.[43]

Skeptics suspended final judgment about every aspect of every belief system. Twentieth-century philosopher and historian Richard Popkin (1923–2005) asserted that virtually all contemporary philosophy is either skeptical or concerned with answering the claims of skepticism.[44]

Whatever belief system a Roman citizen chose would define his standard of right conduct and his perspective on freedom. In this period, however, Plato's internal struggle for freedom through self-control was transformed into the individual's freedom to consider alternative belief systems. The Sophists' notion of man as the measure of all things began to make inroads over the ancient Greek paradigm as Romans wrestled with their moral choices. The cultural relativism and absence of a universal Greco-Roman belief system empowered each citizen with the choice of whom to serve. The personal acceptance of each belief system's administration of justice would advance the Sophist mantra. Chadwick said of the popularity of the belief systems of the time: "In the early Roman Empire of the first and second centuries, Stoic teachers ranked high in the popularity stakes, [and] from the third century onward, Platonism became more and more dominant."[45]

With Constantine, the Roman Empire united under the banner of Christianity for the next four centuries, but the philosophical alternatives were never silenced. Competing believers proclaimed their versions of absolute truth, while the less committed citizens modified their behavior as the moment dictated. The transcending authority of a single Christian belief system was under constant assault from the internal Platonic struggle of self-control and the competing advocates for alternative belief systems.

❖ ❖ ❖

Chapter 4

The Christian/Neo-Platonist Era

From Communal to Personal Standards of Morality

From the Middle Platonist period, we enter an era in which there were two dominant belief systems: Neo-Platonism and early Christianity. On the surface, both shared a common understanding of freedom as an internal struggle between reason and the irrational passions of desire and incensive rage. The shift away from communal standards toward personally defined standards of morality had begun, but the general sense of duty of the ancient Greek paradigm continued to frame the majority attitudes of morality and ethics. The competing messages between multiple belief systems blurred their distinctions, but Neo-Platonism and Christianity shared a number of attributes.

Although the ancient Greek paradigm continued to influence the communal sense of duty of Roman society, individuals decided to whom they owed their allegiance. The overlapping and complementary doctrines of many of the alternative belief systems led to much confusion among the Roman population. For example, Stoic detachment from passions could easily be confused with the Platonic indifference of the Absolute One; Epicurean hedonism could complement the Skeptical view of deferred reward; and Gnostic mystery bore superficial resemblances to both Neo-Platonism and what would become mainstream Christian mystery.

As a consequence of the evolving standards of morality and ethics, many people straddled the different belief systems with their own rationales for behavior. As today, citizens were free to pick and choose their favorite morality with each momentary decision. Freedom from external obligations was only beginning to demonstrate itself. In other words, self-interest independent of the obligations of duty began to exercise more influence, but the modern idea of Self did not establish itself for another millennium. The appeal of the Sophists' emphasis on cultural relativity began to empower individuals to accept the behavioral expectations that seemed appropriate at any particular moment.

The Knowable and the Unknowable

While both Neo-Platonism and early Christianity accepted the ancient Greek paradigm of duty to the divine, they approached this responsibility with conflicting strategies. Both grew in prominence during the three hundred years after Jesus. We shall consider their similarities before we explore their differences. Both Neo-Platonism and Christianity claimed knowledge of the absolute truth, the single transcending authority that unites the cosmos. Both sought wisdom, but a distinction between theology and philosophy had not yet emerged. Both respected the power of reason, but we begin to see a difference in how they employed reason.

Recall in the previous chapter the writings of Philo of Alexandria (ca. 13 B.C.–ca. 50 A.D.). Through his Jewish theology, he distinguished two aspects of the one God: the unknowable essence and the knowable energy. For Philo, both aspects existed simultaneously within God. Philo unconditionally accepted both the inability to know the divine essence and the ability to know the divine energy. Here is what he imagined God said to Moses on Mount Sinai:

> I only bestow such gifts to him who is deserving of my
> favour all the gifts which he is able to receive. But not

only is the nature of mankind, but even the whole heaven and the whole world is unable to attain to an adequate comprehension of me. So know yourself, and be not carried away with impulses and desires beyond your power; and let not a desire of unattainable objects carry you away and keep you in suspense. For you shall not lack anything which may be possessed by you.[1]

Philo saw no inconsistency in accepting the supreme authority of revealed divine knowledge that is beyond the capacity of human reason. This position is significantly different from the Platonic tradition, which believed that knowledge of the divine *could* be achieved through reason. Plato and Aristotle's common faith in reason was the basis for them to seek the divine through contemplation (Plato) or through evidence (Aristotle). There was no limit, they thought, to what reason could know, no boundary between what was knowable and unknowable.

One of the most highly regarded students of both Christian and Platonic theology was the Christian philosopher Clement of Alexandria (ca. 150–215 A.D.). According to early church historian Hans von Campenhausen (1903–1989) of the University of Heidelberg, Clement "deliberately avoided established formulas and slogans, and never came to an end with his questioning, research, and thinking…. Despite his extensive knowledge, [he was] not really a scholar."[2] Clement respected the relative truth of philosophers, but accepted the absolute truth of the prophets and the divine Logos of Christianity. Clement referred to Plato as "the friend of Truth."[3] His search for truth moved from the reasoned approach of philosophy to the supreme authority of unconditional love for God and the divine command to willingly provide for one's neighbor.[4]

Christian-sounding themes in Plato's dialogues provided shelter for Clement's ambiguity. These themes included the following from Plato's

Timaeus: "But the father and maker of all this universe is past finding out, and even if we found him, to tell of him to all men would be impossible."[5] With regard to the authority of divine revelation, Plato wrote in *Phaedrus*: "When one who is fresh from the mystery…beholds a godlike face…, first there come upon him a shuddering and a measure of that awe which the vision inspired, and then reverence as at the sight of a god."[6] A similar experience of Saul of Tarsus on the way to persecute Christians in Damascus resulted in his conversion into the Apostle Paul.[7] According to Louth, Clement's philosophical spirituality was not considered anti-Christian so much as independent of Christianity.[8] Specific Christian dogma regarding the nature of the Divine Essence was not established until the second Ecumenical Council of 381 A.D.

The distinction between philosophy and theology became more apparent through the writings of Clement's younger contemporaries, Plotinus (ca. 205–270 A.D.) and Origen (ca. 185–232 A.D.). Both were students of the philosopher Ammonius Saccas (ca. 175–242 A.D.), who is credited with founding the Neo-Platonic school in Alexandria. Little else is known about his principal teachings. We have already met the influential Plotinus, whose scripture was Plato's dialogues.

The orthodoxy of Plotinus was both clear and straightforward. The body, in his view, was bad; the soul was good. Contemplation allows the soul to ascend to the Absolute (but indifferent) One. If the soul fails to achieve its final union with the One, it will try again. A closer exploration of Plato's concept of the human soul reveals the roots of Platonic orthodoxy. The soul is immortal[9] and pre-exists the human body, which Plato considered a prison that frees the soul only through death.[10] The soul is man's true being; the body is mere creature.[11] Furthermore, the soul reincarnates from the divine realm through various lives until it attains moral perfection.[12]

For Plato, the divine realm, the Idea of the Good, was the ultimate reality. Human intelligence could guide the soul toward this absolute truth, but "divine revelation" represented the surest path. The material world is one of shadows. Plotinus fine-tuned the Idea of the Good into the Absolute One of indifference, but his intellectual union of the One, the *nous*, and the soul left the attributes of their distinction ambiguous. Henry Chadwick summarized the resulting confusion:

> Was it correct to say that the soul becomes "identical in being" with *nous*, and if so, does that imply that in *nous* itself there are higher and lower levels? It seemed easier to hold that soul is in principle distinct from *nous* and on an inferior level of being.[13]

Plotinus might have benefited from Philo's acceptance of both the unknowable divine essence and the knowable divine energy, but he was not inclined in the same way as the Christian theologians of the fourth century.

Origen began his studies with Ammonius Saccas as a Christian, and not, like Clement of Alexandria, as a convert from philosophy.[14] When considering the ascent of the soul, Origen accepted the divinity of Jesus and concluded that Christ's union with the human soul was activated through baptism. Andrew Louth observed about this:

> Origen [wrote] about the life of the baptized Christian within the Church; Plato and Plotinus about the search for ultimate truth by an intellectual elite, either in the company of other like-minded souls, or as "the alone to the Alone."[15]

Despite his Christian inclinations, however, Origen remained significantly influenced by Platonism. He did not recognize Philo's unknowable nature of divine essence, and early-Christian scholar Vladimir Lossky (1903–1958) thinks Origen was "insensitive to the unknowability of God."[16] Origen accepted Plotinus' common understanding of man's soul—that is, that it shares a common essence with the immortal One and pre-exists the body.* Through contemplation, he believed, the soul frees itself from the bodily prison and ascends to Christ's divine kingdom.[17] Origen saw God as "a simple, intellectual nature admitting of no complexity whatever in itself.... He is Monad and Unity and Spirit; the source and origin of all intellectual and spiritual nature."[18]

In Platonic fashion, Origen accepted humanity's innate capacity to distinguish good from bad, the real good of the divine from the temporal illusion of good.[19] He did not "acknowledge the existence of 'absolute evil' or the possibility of eternal separation and damnation," according to von Campenhausen,[20] who summarizes Origen's position as follows:

> He combined the unphilosophical tradition of the Church
> with the Gnostic–Neo-Platonic tendencies of the century
> on a higher intellectual plane.... But he had no feeling
> for the deeper, objective problems of a truly Christian
> theology.... They were the solutions of a theorist of ge-

---

*Henry Chadwick ("Philosophical Tradition and the Self," in *Interpreting Late Antiquity: Essays on the Postclassical World*, ed. G. W. Bowersock, Peter Brown, and Oleg Grabar [Cambridge: Harvard University Press, 2001], available at http://www.myriobiblos.gr/texts/english/chadwick_tradition.html/) notes: "In the second book of his commentary on the Song of Songs, Origen gives a list of questions concerning the soul: Is it corporeal or incorporeal? composite or simple? created or uncreated? transmitted to the embryo with the physical sperm or independently from some external power?... (Parallels to this list in...Seneca...suggest that there was a standard list of questions in philosophical schools.)"

nius who constructed reality from the idea, without being moved at a deeper level by doubt and suffering.[21]

With so much similarity to Plotinus, what distinguished Origen's
Christianity was his belief in the absolute truth of "the person and pattern of Christ."[22] According to von Campenhausen, "the Bible remains
the all-important document, guarantee, and support of his faith."[23] Despite Origen's devotion to Christianity, "he remains a prisoner of the
assumption of his Platonizing and Gnosticizing philosophy," von Campenhausen concludes, "incapable even of seeing what separates him
from the Old and New Testaments."[24] Origen's interpretation of Platonic
theology through the lens of Jewish-Christian traditions garnered him
the epithet of "barbarian" from the Platonic establishment.[25] The persecution of Christians would intensify over the next hundred years.

Defining Christianity

In 324 A.D., Constantine the Great (ca. 274–337 A.D.) united the
western and eastern provinces of the Roman Empire with his defeat
of Licinius (ca. 250–325 A.D.). Constantine's mother, Helena, was a be-
liever in the Christian story and clearly had a powerful influence on
her son. In any case, through a vision, Constantine foresaw his military
victory under the banner of the cross of Christ. Consequently, when he
consolidated the Roman Empire, he relieved the persecution of Christians. Since the Platonic religious establishment was well entrenched in
Rome, he established Christianity in the city of Byzantium (Istanbul in
modern Turkey) on the coast of Asia Minor, declaring it "New Rome."
However, the name did not take, for the masses referred to the city as
Constantinople, the city of Constantine.

The emperor did not dismantle or persecute the Platonic establishment, but he did assist the development of Christianity by seeking, in true Roman fashion, to *organize* the newly freed Christian faith. For the first time, Christian religious elders, who traced their lineage back to the Apostles, assembled to discuss their beliefs. This assemblage, in 325 A.D. in Nicaea (modern-day Iznik, in Turkey), was the first of seven Ecumenical Councils, whose authority was universally recognized by all Christians. This is not to say that everyone in the Roman Empire was Christian, nor was every Christian free from the influences of Platonism, Gnosticism, Stoicism, Epicureanism, or Skepticism. However, after these Councils, there was a single understanding of dogma, which mainstream Christians accepted as revealed divine knowledge.

The first two Councils, in 325 and 381 A.D., established the nature of the Divine Essence of the Trinity. Father, Son, and Holy Spirit would be One Essence, Light of Light, Very God of Very God. Utilizing Philo's formula, the Trinitarian mode of being would recognize Divine Essence beyond humanity's capacity to know as the Un-Begotten Father. The mode of the Divine Essence that *can* be known would be referred to as the Only-Begotten Son, the incarnate person Jesus Christ. Finally, there is the mode of being of the Divine Essence known as the Proceeding Holy Spirit. (If the reader's knowledge of Christianity evolved through the Latin tradition, this Trinity formula may raise questions, but Christianity would not experience its Great Schism for another seven centuries—a topic to be covered in Chapter 6.)

The understanding of Trinity in Unity and of Unity in Trinity is difficult to accept through rational explanation. In fact, the early Church emphasized that understanding the Trinity was impossible because it was beyond human comprehension. There is, however, a modern explanation of the physics of an electron that similarly reveals this Trinitarian relationship—namely, its having mass, charge, and spin. In 1925, Dutch physicists George Uhlenbeck and Samuel Goudsmit, exploring the properties of light, concluded that electrons both revolve and rotate. The work of Uhlenbeck and Goudsmit was summarized by physicist and author Brian Greene (1963–): "The spin of an electron is an *intrinsic* property, much like its mass or its electric charge. If an electron were not spinning, it would not be an electron."[26]

The modes of being are not parts of the whole. Each *is* the whole. The Trinity is One in Essence, One in Divine Will, and not additive. The Begotten Son and Proceeding Holy Spirit are one hundred percent of the Un-Begotten Father. The Un-Begotten Father and Proceeding Holy Spirit are one hundred percent of the Begotten Son. The Un-Begotten Father and Begotten Son are one hundred percent of the Proceeding Holy Spirit. Similarly, today's understanding of an electron is not mass plus electrical charge plus spin. The absence of any one characteristic would simply "not be an electron."[27] The modes of being help humanity approach knowledge of what is fundamentally unknowable. This is not the only example in which the physics of quantum mechanics and the early Christian understanding of Trinity complement each other. We shall have more to say about this in Chapter 8.

Note that Constantine the Great had reunited the Roman Empire and in so doing had brought back together both Latin- and Greek-speaking Romans. After the Edict of Milan in 313 A.D., both Latin- and Greek-speaking Romans were free to practice their particular belief systems. Christianity was centered in "New Rome," the ancient city of Byzantium, where Greek was the primary language. The proceedings of each Ecumenical Council were in the Greek tongue, and then translated into Latin. To this day, both Latin- and Greek-speaking Christians recognize the authority of the first two Ecumenical Councils.

Ex Nihilo or Eternal: Athanasius Versus Arius

The decisions of these Ecumenical Councils would be summarized by twelve articles of faith known as the Nicene Creed. To be a Christian meant complete acceptance of those twelve articles of faith. The Councils were not unanimous love feasts, for there had been no formal communication between the scattered underground Christian communities for almost three hundred years. First and foremost, there was disagreement and dissension over the divine nature of Jesus. Athanasius of Alexandria (ca. 298–373 A.D.) was the one figure in particular who most dominated the proceedings.

Athanasius was the first Church Father* to use theology as a weapon against the academic philosophizing of earlier Church leaders.[28] Von Campenhausen describes Athanasius' struggle to defend the dogma of the first two Ecumenical Councils as follows:

> For forty-five years he continued to wage it with unvarying tenacity, agility, and energy, showing versatility in his methods and formulations, relentless on the essential issues, reassured by no partial success, and discouraged by no failures…. The whole subsequent development of the Greek-Byzantine Church was based on the struggle and success of this one man.[29]

Athanasius did not view the Church as a sacramental institution, but as the sacred dogma of absolute truth. He and his friends advocated the Christian Church's transcendence over the civil authority of the Empire.[30] Von Campenhausen observes:

---

*Early Christian theologians are referred to as "Fathers of the Church." More will be said about this designation in Chapter 5.

Even to his own contemporaries Athanasius seemed an
almost mythical figure; even pagans credited him with
supernatural knowledge.... He maintained the essential
character and spiritual independence of Christianity in
his struggles with the emperors and all the authoritative
representatives of the theological world. As a result of his
labors, belief in Christ remained, in the strictest sense,
belief in God and was kept distinct from all pagan philosophical and idealistic theories.... Athanasius saved the
Church from becoming entangled in the idea of progress
and from the snares of political power.[31]

Athanasius was a master at impressing the masses and enjoyed strong
support throughout the Empire, particularly among Latin-speaking
Romans.[32] However, he got into trouble with the civil authorities after
Constantine the Great died in May 337, which led to the division of the
Empire among his three sons. The oldest, Flavius Claudius Constantinus, known as Constantine II (316–340 A.D.), ruled Britannia, Gaul, and
Hispania. The youngest, Flavius Julius Constans, known as Constans
I (ca. 320–350–A.D.), ruled Italia, Africa, and Illyricum. The middle brother, Flavius Julius Constantius, known as Constantius II (317–361 A.D.),
ruled the East, where Athanasius lived. Constantius, who liked to maintain political harmony among the population, considered Athanasius a
troublemaker, and so the latter was exiled five times in seventeen years
for approaching high treason. But Constantius was ultimately forced by
Constans to readmit Athanasius, who was the first to advocate the separation of Church from State with his idea of "Church freedom" from the
civil authority of the Emperor.[33]

The most profound distinction between Christianity and Neo-
Platonism was their mutually exclusive understanding of creation.

Athanasius was a forceful proponent of the idea that the Triune God created everything from nothing: *ex nihilo*. Christianity accepted a complete distinction between Creator and created. The Middle Platonist and Gnostic attempt to find an intermediate zone was rejected by the Council of Nicaea in 325 A.D. The ambiguity of Clement was clarified, and the Platonic influence of Origen was rejected. After the Council of Nicaea, the perfect union of the cosmos, the union of unknowable Creator and knowable creation, was found in the unique dual nature of the Only-Begotten Son. Louth summarizes the new understanding as follows:

> Contemplation is no longer a means of divinization: it is simply one of the activities of the divinized soul. No longer is the soul made divine by that which it contemplates, as in Origen. Rather, to quote Athanasius: "The Word became man that we might become divine; he revealed himself through a body that we might receive an idea of the invisible Father."[34]

Recall that Hesiod's mythology of an eternal cosmos inhabited by an earthly mother and heavenly father included material worlds. We saw in Chapter 2 the ancient Greek attempt to identify the single source of the unbounded. Whether the unbounded was a thickening and thinning, or an opposition of eternal elements, the eternal elements were just that, eternal. The idea of "non-being" was completely rejected by Greek philosophy. Christianity stood alone in accepting a pre-eternal Creator. From an ancient Greek perspective, such a Creator would by definition require acceptance of an initial state of non-being.

Recall Jaeger's summary of Plato's evidence for man's belief in the gods: "knowledge of the orbits, eternally the same, in which the heavenly bodies move; and the 'eternal stream of being' in us, the soul."[35]

Both proofs of God were rejected by the first two Ecumenical Councils, which maintained that the orbits are not eternally the same, and the soul is not part of the eternal stream of being. Rather, both are products of the unconditional love of the Triune God.

The acceptance of creation *ex nihilo* set up the most significant controversy of fourth-century Christianity—that which surrounded Arianism. Named after Arius of Alexandria (ca. 250–336 A.D.), it is noteworthy that both Arius and Athanasius rejected the creation myth of Hesiod. Arius argued that if God created everything out of nothing, then Jesus was a creature. Even if Jesus existed "before all worlds," as was stated in the second article of the Nicene Creed, Arius speculated that there could have been a moment when the Only-Begotten Son did not exist. The victory of Athanasius at the first two Ecumenical Councils established the eternal unity of divine Trinity as the only acceptable Christian understanding of God. Arianism was denounced as heresy, but the dual nature of the Only-Begotten Son was not fully resolved until the Sixth Ecumenical Council, in 681 A.D.

Humility As the Path to Salvation

To appreciate the full significance of the dual nature of the Only-Begotten Son, the modern reader must accept the role of humility within the early Church. According to the Nicene Creed, all creation is subordinate to the Triune God of Un-Begotten Father, Only-Begotten Son, and Proceeding Holy Spirit. As Lossky summarized the belief, "all energy originates in the Father, being communicated by the Son in the Holy Spirit.... The Father creates all things by the Son in the Holy Spirit."[36] To be a Christian meant literal and unconditional acceptance of the incarnation of the Logos by the Proceeding Holy Spirit and the Virgin

Mary in the person of Jesus. The unconditional love of the Triune God is demonstrated by the Word's willful example of humility. God's unconditional love for humanity underlies humanity's ability to willingly reciprocate unconditional love.

The early Church saw humanity's willful exercise of humility as the only reliable path to salvation. Humanity could ascend to participation with the divine energy through the willing exercise of unconditional humility. People today who are engulfed in Western culture may find it difficult to accept the degree of humility pursued by the early Christians, but there are thousands of examples from Church Fathers regarding the virtue of humility. The Abbot of St. Catherine's monastery on Mount Sinai, St. John Climacus (ca. 525–606 A.D.), provides an example that demonstrates the depth of virtue found in humility:

> I once saw three monks receive the same injury at the same time. One felt the sting of this and was troubled, but kept silent; the second rejoiced at his injury for the reward it would bring him, but was sorry for the wrongdoer; and the third, thinking of the harm his erring neighbour was suffering, wept fervently. And fear, reward, and love were to be seen at work.[37]

The first monk's silent acceptance expresses his humility. The second monk is aware of the consequence of humble acceptance; he knows that the assault will garner rewards in eternal life, and he feels sorrow for the perpetrator. The suffering that the perpetrator will experience as a consequence of his actions overwhelms the third monk, who fervently prays for the eternal welfare of the perpetrator.

The Councils of Nicaea had profound implications for those Romans who sought common ground among the alternative belief systems. With

Christianity, the body and soul were both regarded as created. Therefore, the body was no longer regarded as inherently bad, and the soul was no longer regarded as inherently good. Moreover, the soul did not pre-exist the body, nor did it share an essence with the spiritual realm. Contemplation would no longer be thought of as elevating the soul to the divine, because there was no kinship with the Creator. The divine was not indifferent to the soul's ascent, but was the living example of unconditional love.

Only through the operation of God and the cooperation of man could humanity experience synergy with the divine energy. Participation required both divine grace and the willingness to cooperate. Humanity was not by nature one with divine essence, but could call the Un-Begotten Father through the divine grace of adoption.[38] Finally, the concept of regeneration or reincarnation was rejected outright. Accepting the dogma of the Ecumenical Councils as divine revelation required the personal embrace of humility as the only reliable path to salvation.

Gnosticism

The intermediate zone between Christianity and Platonism was best represented by Gnosticism. There is no consensus among historians regarding the origin of the various Gnostic sects, which sought personal salvation for initiates through knowledge (*gnosis*). Whether Gnostic mysteries came via Babylon or were a merger of Judaism and Greek mythology, Gnosticism blurred the growing divide between Neo-Platonism and Christianity. Compatible with Hesiod's mythology, Gnostic mystical rites and magic words guided initiates through the dual realms of good and bad, light and dark, and protected them from demons. Gnostics also believed in a Christian sounding Primal Man or Savior who would vanquish the dark realm.[39]

Gnostic influence was greatest in the second century A.D., but waned in the third century as the influence of Manichaeism grew. Mani (ca. 215–ca. 274 A.D.) was born in Babylonia and proclaimed himself the latest incarnation of God's messengers, which included Buddha in India, Zoroaster in Persia, and Jesus in Palestine. The realms of Light and Darkness were more clearly defined by Mani than by the preceding Gnostic sects. However, Zoroastrian priests had Mani executed.

In the twentieth century, a number of Gnostic texts were discovered in the Egyptian desert, especially the Nag Hammadi monastery collection, which includes the Gospel of Thomas and the Gospel of Mary Magdalene. Along with the Dead Sea Scrolls and the recently discovered Gospel of Judas, these texts demonstrate the competing myths regarding absolute truth. The reemergence of these Gnostic texts provides fodder to modern historians, unrestrained by early Christian humility, to deduce multiple variations of the Christian myth. But Jesus was not a myth. His actual life, and the faith and actions of his followers, would inspire converts.

Knowledge and Mystery: Augustine and Cassian

The belief systems of Christianity, Neo-Platonism, and Gnosticism sought converts among Greek-speaking Romans. In Chapter 3, we noted Owen Barfield's comments regarding the different emphasis in meaning in the Latin and Greek languages. Latin-speaking Roman Christians relied on the translations and Christian insights of their Latin brothers who were fluent in Greek. In the fourth century, there were many of these, of whom the most significant included St. Ambrose (ca. 340–397 A.D.), St. Jerome (ca. 340–420 A.D.), and St. John Cassian (ca. 360–ca. 435 A.D.).*

The most significant Latin-speaking Christian of the fourth century was St. Augustine (354–430 A.D.), who was born in a small North African town in what is today Algeria. Although his mother was Christian, the young Augustine fully investigated the pleasures of the world. After reading Cicero, he was inspired by the quest for truth. He was also attracted to the teachings of Mani and remained with the sect for ten years. Platonic discipline and the Gnostic mystery of Mani, seamlessly merged with Latin linguistic characteristics, deeply influenced Augustine.

At the age of thirty-two, Augustine heard a homily by St. Ambrose of Milan that caused him to embrace Christianity, and he eventually became the Bishop of Hippo. St. Ambrose remained in close contact with Greek-speaking theologians, and *The New Advent Catholic Encyclopedia* speculates that the Great Schism would never have happened had "East and West continued to converse as intimately as St. Ambrose and St. Basil."[40] The dogma of the Trinity, which had been established in the first two Ecumenical Councils, had been extensively developed by three Greek-speaking Roman theologians known as the Cappadocian Fathers—St. Basil the Great (329–379 A.D.), St. Gregory of Nyssa (d. ca. 386 A.D.), and St. Gregory of Nazianzus (ca. 325–389 A.D.).

Augustine was well-regarded as a defender of orthodoxy against the heresies of Pelagianism and Donatism. Pelagianism was named after Pelagius (ca. 354–ca. 420 A.D.), an ascetic monk who denied the doctrine of Original Sin from Adam, rejected the sacrament of Baptism, and taught that people can earn salvation through their own efforts without relying on the grace of God. Donatism was named after Donatus Magnus (ca. 311–ca. 355 A.D.),

---

*St. John Cassian was never formally canonized within the Latin Church. However, Pope Gregory the Great (ca. 540–604 A.D.), who was later sainted himself, regarded Cassian as a saint, as did the Greek-speaking Church.

a bishop of Carthage, who held an unyielding standard of perfection for clergy. Donatists challenged the validity of sacraments preformed by clergy who failed their standards, and therefore required these sacraments, such as baptism, to be performed again by a Donatist-approved cleric.

Augustine's writings were unparalleled in their introspective and psychological self-probing.[41] However, despite Augustine's extensive writing and his recognition as a Father of the Church, he had little knowledge of the Greek language and no influence on Christian dogma among Greek-speaking Romans. Throughout his life, he revised and updated his earlier writings to reflect his better understanding of theology, and he humbly implored his readers, "Let all those who will read this work imitate me not in my errors."*

We have already noted the early Christian formula for salvation through the cooperation of man and the grace of God. The Latin linguistic tendency to separate meanings manifested itself in Augustine's treatise about the cooperative effort between the gift of divine grace and the act of free will.[42] Augustine's logical inclinations emphasized the gift of divine grace at the expense of humanity's free will. The nineteenth-century Russian philosopher Ivan Kireyevsky (1806–1856) observed:

> No single ancient or modern Father of the Church showed such love for the logical chain of truths as Blessed Augustine.... Perhaps because of this he was sometimes carried too far, not noticing the inward one-sidedness of his thinking because of its outward order.[43]

---

*Quoted here from Fr. Seraphim Rose, *The Place of Blessed Augustine in the Orthodox Church* (Platina, CA: St. Herman of Alaska Brotherhood, 1996), p. 22. In *On Trinity*, Augustine cautions the reader: "Wherever...he is certain, there to go on with me; wherever...he hesitates..., join with me in inquiring; wherever he recognizes himself to be in error..., return to me; wherever he recognizes me to be so..., call me back; so that we may enter together upon the path of charity, and advance towards Him, of whom it is said, 'Seek His face evermore'" (Chapter 3:5, translated by A. W. Hadden, available at http://www.ccel.org/fathers).

St. John Cassian criticized Augustine's teaching on grace.[44] Cassian, who was equally versed in Latin and Greek, emphasized the harmony of cooperation between grace and free will. Prosper of Aquitaine (390–465 A.D.), a Latin-speaking layman with great ardor for religious controversies, immediately came to Augustine's defense and criticized Cassian:

> At this point, by a sort of inscrutable contradiction, there is introduced a proposition in which it is taught that many come to grace without grace, and that some also, from the endowments of the free will, have this desire to seek, to ask, and to knock.... On your [i.e., Cassian's] part there is complete agreement with neither the heretics nor the Catholics. The former regard the beginnings in every just work of man as belonging to the free will; while we (Catholics) constantly believe that the beginnings of good thoughts spring from God. You have found some indescribable third alternative, unacceptable to both sides, by which you neither find agreement with the enemies nor retain an understanding with us.[45]

Augustine never abandoned a belief in free will's responsibility to cooperate, but succeeding generations drove a wedge between divine grace and free will. Greek-speaking Christians recognized the synergy that resulted from unconditional cooperation between humanity's free will and the operation of divine grace.

St. John Cassian wrote:

> Both grace and free will seem indeed to be contrary to each other; but both are in harmony. And we conclude that, because of piety, we should accept both, lest taking one of these away from man, we appear to violate the Church's rule of faith.[46]

For Augustine, the cooperative relationship was a difficult intellectual question, as he stated in his letter to Abbot Valentinus of Hadrumetum: "[It is] a question which is very difficult and intelligible to few."[47] This revealing statement underlies the influence of intellection.

Augustine's attempt to explain dogma led to misunderstandings and misinterpretations among later generations of Latin theologians. Augustine was not wrong in his understanding of theology so much as he was constrained by the limits of intellect to understand what could only be accepted by faith. St. Cassian, who was intimately familiar with the Greek linguistic understanding of theology, accepted the operation of grace and cooperation of free will without the obligation to explain it.

The Latin mind sought an intellectual explanation that would not be satisfied by Cassian's orthodox theology. Prosper of Aquitaine was representative of Latin-speaking Christians who found the "indescribable third alternative" unacceptable. Philip Sherrard (1922–1995), poet, translator, literary scholar, theologian, and interpreter of the Orthodox tradition, distinguished Augustinian intelligence, which was a superior mental faculty of the soul itself, from the spiritual intellect of the Greek *nous*, which was "heart-centered."[48] The competition between head and heart would grow in the Latin west. The cooperation between head and heart maintains Christian unity and defies intellectual judgment.

The disagreements between Cassian and Augustine must be viewed as differences in the presentation of Christian dogma. Neither accused the other of heresy. Although both were recognized as Church Fathers, over time Cassian would be given greater respect among Greek-speaking Romans, and Augustine would be given greater respect among Latin-speaking Romans. However, their differing emphases would have no impact on Christian dogma for another four hundred years.

From the time of the pre-Socratic philosophers, Western societies relied on reason for knowledge of the divine. Intellection has certain innate characteristics, such as discerning differences, categorizing, analyzing, prioritizing, and judging evidence. Owen Barfield wrote, "The essential function of the human being…is to think."[49] Similarly, French philosopher and historian Étienne Gilson (1884–1978) wrote, "Man is best described as a rational animal; deprive man of reason, and what is left is not man, but animal."[50] Augustine relied on faith, not reason, to bridge skepticism,[51] but succeeding generations of the Latin mindset separated these two paths toward knowledge. Reason and faith will be more thoroughly discussed in Chapter 6.

❖ ❖ ❖

Chapter 5

The Early Christian Paradigm

The Authority of the Ecumenical Councils

In Chapter 4, we were introduced to the influence of emphasis in the theological understanding of dogma. It must be reiterated that from the fourth to the eighth centuries A.D., all mainstream Christians accepted the authority of the Ecumenical Councils. After the fourth century, Aristotelian logic reemerged. Combined with the Neo-Platonic traditions, logical reasoning tainted individual consideration of all belief systems. Von Campenhausen describes this trend as "Byzantine scholasticism, a scientific theology of such rigidity and complication that only the most learned specialists, monks, and clerics could find their way about."[1] Jaeger recognized fifth-century B.C. Sophists as the forerunners of philosophers of the modern Enlightenment.[2] Byzantine scholasticism embraced the fifth-century Sophist regard for reasoned logic and solidified the dogma of the early Christian paradigm.

The city of Rome fell to the Goths in the fifth century A.D., but the empire continued to be governed from its second capital, Constantinople. Over time the Roman Empire, embodied in its historic Greco-Roman ethos, partitioned along the linguistic preferences of particular provinces. The authority of the seven Ecumenical Councils, however, continued to unite all Latin- and Greek-speaking Christians under one umbrella. The average Roman accepted the authority of the Ecumenical Councils without concern for the rigid scholasticism that sought reasoned explanations for principles of faith. The early Church recognized five seats of Church authority—in Rome, Constantinople, Antioch,

Jerusalem, and Alexandria. A bishop, referred to as Patriarch, administered each seat. The Patriarch of Rome, recognized as the "first among equals," was given the title of Pope.

Although the first two Ecumenical Councils established the Trinitarian relationship of Un-Begotten Father, Only-Begotten Son, and Proceeding Holy Spirit, there was considerable controversy regarding the dual nature of the divine and the human in the person of Jesus. Gnostic efforts to link Jesus with the concept of Primal Man and Savior further confused the masses. How could Jesus exist "before all worlds" *and* be born like any other man? How could the human creature ever be equal to the divine essence? How could the divine essence experience death? And how could Jesus' body experience suffering? These were not simply academic questions, but fundamental principles whose answers would validate the Christian claim of absolute truth against all other belief systems.

The Two Natures of Jesus: St. Leo and Maximus the Confessor

It would take four Ecumenical Councils to resolve the confusion over the dual nature of the Only-Begotten Son. The most significant contributions to this resolution came from St. Leo the Great (died 461 A.D.), who was Pope of Rome from 440 to 461 A.D., and Maximus the Confessor (580–662 A.D.). By the time of Pope Leo's reign, the city of Rome had long since lost its military superiority, but the eastern capital, Constantinople, continued to exercise civil rule. On November 8, 449 A.D., a council of bishops met to settle a dispute with Eutyches (ca. 380–ca. 456 A.D.), a member of the clergy. At issue was Eutyches' unorthodox beliefs regarding the dual nature of the Only-Begotten Son. Flavian (d. 449 A.D.), the Patriarch of Constantinople, was compelled to excommunicate Eutyches, after which he notified Pope Leo of his decision. Pope Leo gave his approval in a letter that became known as the *Tome of Leo*, in which he articulated the degree of cooperation between the divine essence and the humanity of Jesus:

> There is nothing unreal about this oneness, since both the lowliness of the man and the grandeur of the divinity are in mutual relation. As God is not changed by showing mercy, neither is humanity devoured by the dignity received. The activity of each form is what is proper to it in communion with the other: that is, the Word performs what belongs to the Word, and the flesh accomplishes what belongs to the flesh. One of these performs brilliant miracles; the other sustains acts of violence. As the Word does not lose its glory which is equal to that of the Father, so neither does the flesh leave the nature of its kind behind. We must say this again and again: one and the same is truly Son of God and truly son of man. God, by the fact that "in the beginning was the Word, and the Word was with God, and the Word was God"; man, by the fact that "the Word was made flesh and dwelt among us." God, by the fact that "all things were made through him, and nothing was made without him"; man, by the fact that "he was made of a woman, made under the law." The birth of flesh reveals human nature; birth from a virgin is a proof of divine power.[3]

St. Leo's Christological definition was adopted at the Fourth General Council of Chalcedon, in 451 A.D., and accepted throughout the Latin-speaking provinces. A number of eastern Christian communities, however, challenged the doctrine of Chalcedon, accepting the two natures of Jesus but recognizing one volition. The idea of one divine will guiding the two natures of Jesus provided an ambiguity that became known as Monothelitism.

By the end of the fifth century A.D., Gothic tribes had overrun the western provinces, but some of these tribes claimed allegiance to Constantinople.[4] The longest period of imperial stability after that of Augustus Caesar, who ruled from 27 B.C. to 14 A.D., was from 527 to 565 A.D., when Justinian I ruled the empire from Constantinople. Justinian worked hard to regain the empire's former glory and succeeded for the most part in uniting the lands around the Mediterranean. His successors, however, could not maintain his accomplishments. Various tribes, including the Slavs and Persians, attacked eastern provinces, and, in 661 A.D., Arab armies defeated the Persians and occupied the Byzantine provincial capital of Damascus. Emperor Constans II was so distraught that he abandoned the eastern Mediterranean in 662 A.D. and moved his court to Sicily, where he was murdered in 668 A.D.*

In addition to the political instability of this period, various religious leaders supported conflicting interpretations of the doctrine of Chalcedon. The political leadership in Constantinople sought acceptable compromises that would hold the empire together. Invading tribes and competing non-Christian belief systems contributed to the confusion. In 648 A.D., Emperor Constans II had hoped to resolve the Chalcedonian debate with an imperial decree, known as the *Typos*, which forbade "any discussion of one will or one energy, two wills or two energies."[5] Pope Martin I of Rome rejected the *Typos* and formally condemned a number of religious leaders who were not in conformance with the doctrine

---

*For a comprehensive review of the political and religious environment, see the Introduction in Andrew Louth, *Maximus the Confessor* (New York: Routledge, 1996).

of Chalcedon. The Emperor responded by arresting Pope Martin and bringing him to Constantinople. There, according to Louth, "he was deposed, defrocked, and ill-treated, and exiled to Cherson in the Crimea, where he died on September 16, 655 A.D., a confessor to Orthodoxy."[6]

Maximus's Cosmology: Philosophy Versus Theology

The sole remaining proponent of the dual nature and two wills of the Only-Begotten Son was Maximus the Confessor, who, consistent with Athanasius in the fourth century, challenged the Emperor's right to define Church dogma and also rejected outright the Monothelitist compromise. For this stand, Maximus was tried in Constantinople, convicted of heresy, tortured, and had his tongue ripped out and his right hand cut off. Shortly thereafter, he died in exile on August 13, 662. Louth notes:

> Within twenty years, the teaching for which he had given his life—the doctrine that Christ had two wills, a divine will and a human will—was vindicated at the sixth Ecumenical Council, convened at Constantinople in 680, though no mention was made there of the great confessor of Orthodoxy, St. Maximus.[7]

At this point, the caution of the previous chapter must be reiterated and emphasized. Our modern knowledge of Christianity, through the Latin lens that developed after the Great Schism, does not emphasize the unity found in the first millennium. For this reason, this chapter will explain the cosmology of Maximus in greater detail than that of other figures presented so far. The final pieces of the early Christian paradigm come together with this cosmology and distinguish this paradigm from that of ancient Greece.

We will first contrast Maximus's summary of orthodox dogma regarding the soul with Platonism, and then we will address the issue of the two wills of Christ. This version of Christianity is very different from modern perceptions.

Maximus's life demonstrates the challenges and persecutions that believers were willing to endure. The grip of the ancient Greek paradigm of duty continued to weaken, but the Christian paradigm was not based on a transcending collective sense of *aidos* ("holy shame") or on *areté* ("virtue"). The acceptance of Christianity grew from personal experience with real events. The life of Jesus, the blood of martyrs, and the witnessing of miracles all contributed to the personal experiences that spread the hope of life after death. Only through *praxis*, the act of doing, could *theoria*, fully conscious participation with absolute truth of the Divine Trinity, be achieved. Theologian Hierotheos Vlachos (1945–) explains:

> It is emphasized by the Fathers that the saints do not theologize in the Aristotelian way, that is, through intelligence and philosophy, but in the manner of a fisherman, that is, through experience (like the Apostles, through the Holy Spirit), after inner purification and disclosure of the *nous*.[8]

Here the difference between philosopher and theologian becomes evident. The philosopher speculates about God through a lens of reasoned logic. The theologian beholds God with a purified *nous* ("mind").* The philosopher uses intellect alone to interpret everything experienced. The theologian experiences God through his purified *nous* and uses intellection to describe the moment.[9] Barfield's distinction between Greek and

---

*Recall Philip Sherrard's heart-centered *nous* in Chapter 4.

Latin linguistic tendencies manifested itself in the evolving distinction between philosopher and theologian.

The early Church recognized unconditional humility as the only reliable behavior for salvation. The example of humility offered by the Only-Begotten Son, and emulated by true believers, was a personal lifestyle of choice. Only one's complete embrace of the orthodox Christian paradigm would justify selfless humility. This commitment required complete cooperation between *faith* in the Triune God and *reason* in the service of faith. Reason without faith is incapable of understanding divine revelation. Faith without humility lacks the experience of *praxis*. Humility without reason and faith is blind and aimless. As Vlachos explains, "we acquire knowledge of our inner world not through intelligence, but through watchfulness, purification of the *nous*, ascetic living, and repentance."[10]

Maximus did not invent a cosmology for Christianity to fill the void left by the rejection of Hesiod's mythology. Louth describes Maximus as

> a speculative theologian of genius, [who] sees himself as interpreting a tradition that has come down to him.... Theological controversy was forced on him because theological error threatened the authenticity of a Christian life of love in response to God's love for us in the Incarnation: for that reason it mattered, and mattered to the point of death.[11]

With the spreading influence of Aristotelian logic, the ambiguity of earlier Christian theologians would be held to a different, more logical standard of accountability.

Maximus's cosmology is indebted to the writings of preceding Christian theologians, including Clement of Alexandria (ca. 150–215 A.D.); St. Gregory of Nyssa (d. ca. 386 A.D.), the youngest Cappadocian Father; Evagrius Ponticus (ca. 345–399 A.D.); the Macarian Homilies (written at the end of the fourth century A.D.); Diadochus, the Bishop of Photike in Epiros in the middle of the fifth century A.D.; and Pseudo-Dionysius the Areopagite (believed to have lived in the fifth century A.D.).* Maximus, however, took these writings much farther than their authors and exercised a precision that clarified ambiguity and abandoned the shadows of Platonism. The times demanded clearer understandings of divine revelation, and Maximus delivered.

The Heart-Centered *Nous* and Free Will

Maximus saw the human creature as more than rational capacity. Humanity, Louth summarizes, "loves with a love that integrates the several layers of our being, layers some of which we share with the non-rational, and even non-animal creation."[12] In earlier chapters, we noted that the Greek term *nous* evolved in its Latin translation to mean "mind" or "intellect." Maximus distinguished *nous* from intellect, recognizing it as the heart and center of our being with the capacity to see things clearly. Intelligence formulates and expresses what is seen and heard.[13] The heart-centered *nous* in its natural state sees clearly, and the intellect analyzes and judges what is seen and heard. The implications are significant.

Distinctions between *nous*, soul, heart, and mind are beyond the scope of this book.† However, a few brief examples will demonstrate the depth of Maximus's insight. For example, Maximus identified the

---

*For a detailed description of these influences, see Louth, Introduction, *Maximus the Confessor*.
†Hierotheos Vlachos's *Orthodox Psychotherapy* (Levadia, Greece, Birth of the Theotokos Monastery, 2000), is an excellent book, but may be too complicated for someone outside the Orthodox Christian tradition. Baby steps are the best steps.

power of the Divine Energy that emanates from the Divine Essence and reveals its authority in all living creation:

> The soul's powers are for nourishment and growth, for imagination and appetite, for reason and understanding. Plants share only in the first powers, irrational animals share in the second as well, and men in the third in addition to the first two. Moreover, the first two powers prove to be perishable, but the third is imperishable and immortal.[14]

Using an antinomy, Maximus described the relationship between the *nous* and God as "still-flowing."[15] Antinomies, whose theological use began with Philo of Alexandria (ca. 13 B.C.–ca. 50 A.D.), attempt to describe God both by what He is (cataphatic theology) and by what He is not (apophatic theology). Pseudo-Dionysius used many antinomies to describe the Trinity, including "ever-moving standing," "stationary movement," and "brilliant darkness."[16] Only characteristics that are completely contrary, yet remain accurate in both extremes, can begin to describe the unknowable Trinity. Negative theology is used to communicate the unknowability of the Divine Essence and Energy.

The Un-Begotten Father, Only-Begotten Son, and Proceeding Holy Spirit created time and the universe out of nothing. "Faith," wrote Maximus, "is the foundation of everything that comes after it, I mean hope and love."[17] Hope is the strength that unites faith and love. Love fulfills faith and hope. Maximus continues:

> For love gives faith the reality of what it believes and hope the presence of what it hopes for, and the enjoyment of what is present. Love alone, properly speaking,

proves that the human person is in the image of the Creator, by making his self-determination submit to reason, not bending reason under it, and persuading the inclination to follow nature and not in any way to be at variance with the *logos* of nature.[18]

Maximus understood self-determination as "the unhindered willing of a rational soul towards whatever it wishes."[19] But free will is not directionless. Louth, who traces Diadochus and Clement of Alexandria as the root of Maximus's understanding of free will, concludes: "Human beings are creatures whose nature finds its fulfillment in their freely turning towards the God to whom they owe their being. What is meant by freedom, in this sense, is lack of coercion."[20] In other words, without coercion, our heart *naturally* desires union with its Creator.

The ancient Greek paradigm's sense of duty was understood by the early Christian Fathers as deterministic coercion, which they rejected. Free will is a natural characteristic of being that imposes neither an external duty to others nor an internal struggle between self-interest and self-control. Thus, the creation of humanity in the image and likeness of God (Genesis 1:26) is the gift of natural free will, which Maximus recognized as true freedom. In the early Christian paradigm, humanity is wholly responsible for directing its natural will.

All humanity shares this natural desire for its Creator. Whether or not the modern reader accepts this natural yearning as an innate characteristic of humanity, Maximus's understanding provides a rational explanation for Aristotle's recognition of man as a "social being." Alternative modern explanations for our social character did not develop for another thousand years.

Adam and Eve were made in the image of God, but lacked the maturity to exercise their natural will and achieve the likeness of God. When they pursued their own interests, they freely moved away from their natural disposition toward God and experienced the fall. The moving away from God represented sin. From their natural state, they were wrapped in "garments of skin" (Genesis 3:21) and experienced the consequence of sin—namely, death. Maximus explained:

> Thus humankind has brought into being from itself the three greatest, primordial evils..., ignorance..., self-love, and tyranny, which are interdependent and established one through another. For out of ignorance concerning God there arises self-love. And out of this comes tyranny towards one's kin.... For by the misuse of our powers—reason, desire, and the incensive power—these evils are established. For reason, instead of being ignorant, ought to be moved through knowledge to seek solely after God; and desire, pure of the passion of self-love, ought to be driven by yearning for God alone; and the incensive power, separated from tyranny, ought to struggle to attain God alone.[21]

Reason, desire, and the incensive power of anger also made up the Platonic soul, with reason governing the irrational aspects of desire and incensivity. Maximus reiterated the Christian position that the fall from grace corrupts the whole *nous*, which is now subject to passions, overwhelmed, and disoriented. But Maximus distinguished between humanity's natural goodness and the misuse of natural powers in the fallen condition:

> It is not food which is evil but gluttony, not the begetting of children but fornication, not possessions but greed, not reputation but vainglory. And if this is so, there is nothing evil in creatures except misuse, which stems from the mind's negligence in its natural cultivation.[22]

Reason, no longer the Platonic path to knowledge, is subject to misuse and corruption in the fallen state, where the sick *nous* substitutes self-interest, including material wealth and praise from others, for participation with the divine. Maximus frequently identified self-love as the cause of all sin.[23]

For the sick *nous* to return to its former natural healthy state requires purification. Maximus taught three stages of the ascension of the *nous* to perfect union with the Triune God: purification, illumination, and deification. Purification through prayer and fasting reduces the distractions of sensual stimulation and incensive anger. As the *nous* becomes purer, a person begins to experience the Uncreated Light of Divine Energy. This witness is not merely one of perspective. The Uncreated Light, while always present, remains unseen by the sick *nous*.

Illumination represents the stage of purification of the recovering *nous*. People continue their efforts to purify their *nous* in the hope of achieving deification, becoming "partakers of the divine nature" (2 Peter 1:4). Those who achieve deification are commonly referred to as saints. Through the operation of divine energy and the cooperation of human synergy, any person can reach deification.[24]

Purification through prayer and fasting is very different from Platonic contemplation or Stoic detachment. "The soul," wrote Maximus, "is pure when it is removed from ignorance and illuminated by divine light."[25] Where contemplation acts to deaden the body (recognized as bad within the Platonic tradition), the focus of prayer and fasting is God's unconditional love. Maximus rejected contemplation. "As the memory of fire does not warm the body," he wrote, "so faith without love does not bring about the illumination of knowledge in the soul."[26] Louth explains "mere thoughts" as thoughts uncorrupted by passion. For Maximus, he writes, they "are a sign of that detachment that enables us to engage in the world and with others in a non-possessive way—with respect."[27]

The Stoic understanding of detachment from passions sought "tranquility of [the] soul," according to Wilken.[28] Passions were criticized for driving behavior against reason. Maximus, however, saw detachment as spiritual freedom, explaining:

> As a little sparrow whose foot is tied tries to fly but is pulled to earth by the cord to which it is bound, so does the mind which does not yet possess detachment get pulled down and dragged to earth when it flies to the knowledge of heavenly things.[29]

Early Church Fathers refer to detachment and spiritual freedom as *dispassion*. This should never be confused with absence of passion, but is the free exercise of unconditional love. Maximus explains:

> The one who is perfect in love and has reached the summit of detachment knows no distinction between one's own and another's, between faithful and unfaithful, between slave and freeman, or indeed between male and female.... For in him there is neither Greek nor Jew, neither male nor female..., but Christ is everything and in everything.[30]

Only in the state of detachment and dispassion can one truly and unconditionally love an enemy (Matthew 5:44). Love is not merely an emotion, but the experience of divine grace that seeks unity with the Creator and the image and likeness of the human creation (Genesis 1:26). If readers are disturbed by the continual references to Church "Fathers," that is because they have not achieved the perfect love of dispassion that sees "Christ is everything and in everything."*

---

*This quote, when taken out of the context of the early Christian paradigm, can seemingly support the heresy of polytheism.

Adam and Eve were created in the natural state of illumination before the fall. Humanity's natural condition is illumination in the image of God. Through unconditional humility, we can ascend to the state of deification and share in the likeness of God. The human creature created in the image and likeness of God can never be the Creator, but through the operation of divine grace and the willing cooperation of one's body and soul, humanity can achieve deification.

The purpose of the Church, the Body of Christ, is to heal one's *nous*. Just as eyes that are sick cannot see well, the Church acts as both hospital and doctor, curing the infirmity and allowing the *nous* to ascend to its natural state before the fall.[31] Louth explains that "knowledge of God is, for Maximus, a transforming experience, which is why he lays such stress on deification as the goal of human life."[32] Faith in the hope of eternal salvation inspires reason to distinguish good stimulation from bad and helps Christians to maintain a humble attitude, the only reliable strategy to purify the *nous*.

Maximus used the biblical story of transfiguration to demonstrate the cure of the *nous*:

> This is shown on the mount of the Transfiguration of the Lord when both the brightness of his garments and the light of His face made Him known, and drew to God the knowledge of those who were after Him and around Him. For as the eye cannot, without light, grasp sensible things, neither can the mind, apart from the knowledge of God, receive spiritual contemplation. For there light gives to sight the perception of visible things, and here the vision of God grants to the mind the knowledge of things intelligible.[33]

The Trinity of Uncreated Light never changes. Only through purification of the *nous* can humanity change and become capable of perceiving and knowing the Uncreated Light of the Trinity. The beatitude
"Blessed are the pure in heart, for they shall see God" is a literal truth.

Maximus clearly distinguished Christian dogma from Neo-
Platonism. The soul, he argued, is neither good nor bad, but willful and
disoriented. The spiritual body before the fall becomes wrapped in the
garments of skin after the fall. But Maximus went further when raising
the stature of the body. The body cannot be bad or a prison, he said,
"for he did not come to debase the nature which he himself, as God
and Word, had made, but he came that that nature might be thoroughly
deified."[34] Raising the ante even further, Maximus categorically stated a
dogma that is clearly neither Platonic nor Origenist:

> Unless the Incarnate Word guards without loss the prop-
> erties of both natures [divine essence and human being]
> out of which and in which he properly is, even after the
> union, then he exists as a defective God. His Godhead is
> then altogether imperfect.[35]

The final quality of the Platonic soul was regeneration. Origen hereti-
cally taught the circular reality, or reincarnation, of preexisting souls. In
union with the divine essence, he contended, the soul becomes satiated and
bored and moves into the body, only to seek a return to unity with the divine essence. Augustine had written against the theory of cycles as a never-
ending process, but Maximus's cosmology went further. Louth explains:

> Adam in paradise should have moved towards and around
> God, and in that way found rest. Instead he moved away
> from God and towards beings lower than himself, and

condemned himself to continual movement, leading to further movement, and not to an ultimate rest at all.[36]

Humanity comes into being through God's creation of soul and body. Adam's fall represents movement away from God. Returning to God requires both the operation of divine energy and the cooperation of human synergy. Humanity can never be satiated, because the effort to unite with the divine essence can never be satisfied. Recall Maximus's and Pseudo-Dionysius's antinomies of still-flowing, ever-moving standing, and stationary movement.

To illustrate the antinomic process, imagine an ever-spinning pinwheel. The center point holds the pinwheel together, the outside of the pinwheel moves much faster, but the speed is reduced as one advances toward the center of the pinwheel. Thus, the closer one gets to the center, the slower one moves. The mover can approach the center, but never *be* the center.

Early Christian Freedom

The need to cooperate with divine grace has been mentioned a number of times. Now we will address Maximus's understanding of volition. The human condition after Adam's fall from paradise would "experience coercion in trying to love what cannot give fulfillment."[37] Louth summarizes Maximus:

> In their fallen state, rational creatures are no longer aware of their true good, which is God. Various apparent goods attract them: they are confused, they need to deliberate and consider, and their way of willing...[is] in accordance with an opinion, or intention, or inclination.[38]

Maximus is clear that our natural will did not change with the fall, but became disoriented and ill as a consequence of the fall.

Maximus used the same Greek term to designate human will that Solon (638–558 B.C.) had used, *gnomic will*. But Solon's understanding of what Jaeger calls the "true insight and the will to put it into action"[39] implies more than Maximus's precision allows. If our natural will was free before the fall, the mere intention toward volition is evidence of corruption after the fall. Maximus explained the distinction between natural will and gnomic will as follows:

> The Fathers...openly confessed the difference between two natural, but not *gnomic*, wills in Christ. They did not, however, say that there was any difference of *gnomic* wills in Christ, lest they proclaim him double-minded and double-willed, and fighting against himself, so to speak, in the discord of his thoughts, and therefore double-personed. For they know that it was only this difference of *gnomic* wills that introduced into our lives sin and our separation from God. For evil consists in nothing else than this difference of our *gnomic* will from the divine will.[40]

An example will help to clarify the distinction between natural will and gnomic will. Imagine that you are leaving a friend and want to go across town to your home. For purposes of this example, assume that there are only five paths home, of which one is the fastest and safest route. The natural will would never consider alternative routes. There is no need for choice. It knows *naturally* what is good, and is eager to get there. With humility as the guide, obstacles that might be encountered are opportunities to arrive home safer. Along the way, passers-by suggest alternative paths that the natural will knows to be false. You do not get sidetracked but remain on course. The gnomic will, however, does consider alternative routes. It evaluates weather conditions, traffic patterns, crime statistics, and so on, and reconsiders. The gnomic will encounters obstacles, evaluates the available information, and makes another decision. The other routes are less certain, and the gnomic will doubts.

In this example, the human will of the Incarnate Word is in its *natural* state, before the fall, without sin. There is no doubt or hesitation. Maximus pointed to evidence that the Incarnate Word has by nature both a human and a divine will:

> He [Jesus] humanly begged to be spared from death, saying, *Father, if it be possible, let the cup pass from me* (Matt. 26:29), in order to manifest the weakness of his own flesh. So his flesh was acknowledged by those who saw him not to be a phantom deceiving the senses, but he was in truth and properly a human being…. And again, that the human will is wholly deified…is clear when he shows that all that matters is a perfect verification of the will of the Father, in his saying as a human, *Not mine, but your will be done*, by this giving himself as a type and example of setting aside our own will by the perfect fulfillment of the divine, even if because of this we find ourselves face to face with death.[41]

Maximus quotes Athanasius (ca. 298–373 A.D.), the most dominant theologian at the First Ecumenical Council, to demonstrate that God is not afraid of death when the human will begs to avoid death:

> Two wills are manifest here: the human, which belongs to the flesh, and the divine. For the human will, because

of the weakness of the flesh, seeks to avoid the passion; the divine will is *eager*.[42]

Only perfect cooperation can unite the two wills of the Only-Begotten Son and the Incarnate Word. Any misinterpretation results in heresy, either of atheism or polytheism. If the human will were merely gnomic, then the possibility of competition would divide the Un-Begotten Father from the Only-Begotten Son. On the other hand, if there were only one divine will that permeated all creation, the result would be polytheism. As Maximus stated:

> The one, afraid of confusion, flees from the hypostatic union and makes the essential difference a personal division. The other, afraid of division, denies the essential difference and turns the hypostatic union into a natural confusion. It is necessary to confess neither confusion in Christ, nor division, but the union of those that are essentially different, and the difference of those that are hypostatically united, in order that the principle of the essences and the mode of the union might be reverently proclaimed.[43]

Cooperation resolves the Platonic dilemma between Unity and Multiplicity. The three Persons are One in Essence and Light of Light. But the Person of the Only-Begotten Son has two natures and two wills—the latter in perfect cooperation within the Incarnate Word. Unity in multiplicity and multiplicity in unity are found in the Triune God. Only the perfect divine will and the perfect human will of Jesus cooperate perfectly. The rest of us struggle with our imperfect gnomic will to cooperate with the operation of divine grace.

Maximus and Absolute Truth

The early Christian paradigm was fully articulated by Maximus and recognized as authentic divine revelation by the authority of the seven Ecumenical Councils. The ancient Greek paradigm existed among a homogeneous community that accepted duty. *Areté* and *aidos* were sufficient to enforce the common standard of moral behavior. The early Christian paradigm required the conscious personal decision of cooperation between faith, reason, and humility. A life dedicated to the early Christian paradigm would necessarily entail suffering and sacrifice. The lives of Maximus and the many martyrs provided numerous examples of temporal persecution. But the reward of eternal life would more than compensate for the temporal struggle.

A member of the ancient Greek *polis* had an organic relationship to the whole. The early Christian paradigm spoke of the "Body of Christ." For example, one's body cannot exist without a properly functioning heart, lungs, and kidneys, each of which has a specific duty. None of the organs aspires beyond its duty. Clearly, each organ is distinguished from the others and approaches its duty in completely different ways. Imagine that each organ could *freely* choose to perform its duty. How long would the body survive? Clearly, only as long as each of the different organs subordinated its personal free will to the common survival.

The obligation of duty within the ancient Greek paradigm was replaced by the new sense of personal responsibility and humility toward the Triune God in emulation of the example of the Only-Begotten Son. Complete cooperation would now mean unconditional self-sacrifice for the common good. Such a standard was exemplified when Jesus, the Only-Begotten Son and Incarnate Word, washed the feet of the disciples at the last Passover Seder. Jesus said to Peter, "If I do not wash you, you have no part with Me" (John 13:8). And then to all of the Apostles, he said, "If I then, your Lord and Teacher, have washed your feet, you also ought to wash one another's feet" (John 13:14).

There is only one sin in the early Christian paradigm: whenever you think, say, or do something that does not give glory to the Triune God, you have turned away from God. It is an impossible standard for any human creature to fulfill. The Orthodox Christian funeral service clearly states, "No man lives and does not sin." With such an impossible standard, who can be saved? Jesus answered, "With men this is impossible, but with God all things are possible" (Matthew 19:26). Is there a limit to God's mercy? A person can be forgiven up to "seventy times seven" (Matthew 18:22).

With such a generous standard for forgiveness, why should someone worry about sinning? Similar to the three stages of purification, Maximus describes three stages of being:

> The sixth day reveals the principle of being of things, the seventh indicates the manner of the well-being of things, the eighth communicates the ineffable mystery of the eternal well-being of things.[44]

The eighth day refers to Judgment Day, when all human creatures will be held accountable for their thoughts, words, and deeds. Those deemed worthy will experience eternal well-being. Those found wanting will experience eternal ill-being. Hell is not a place but the condition of eternal ill-being. Those who subscribe to the early Christian paradigm believe completely in the reality of the eighth day and fervently appeal to God's mercy to find their unworthy effort worthy of eternal well-being.

In our current fallen unnatural condition, the *nous* is disoriented and the intellect exercises more influence on our gnomic will. Recall that

Maximus identifies self-love as the mother of all sins. Intellect discerns differences, categorizes, and analyzes the evidence used to justify self-love. The only reliable restraint on self-love is humility. "The way of knowledge," he writes, "is detachment and humility, without which no one will see the Lord."[45] Reason without faith and humility is an unreliable ally in the early Christian paradigm.

Maximus humbly offered a *Commentary on the Our Father*, the Lord's Prayer, which Eastern Orthodox Christians interpret literally. "Thy will be done on earth as it is in heaven" is an admonition to subordinate our human will in unconditional cooperation with divine grace. Maximus, reinterpreting the Platonic soul in Christian terms, wrote:

> Our reason...should therefore be moved to seek God, the force of desire should struggle to possess him and that of anger to hold on to him.... The whole mind should tend to God.[46]

Or simply stated by Jesus as the first commandment: "Love the Lord your God with all your heart, with all your soul, with all your mind" (Mark 12:30).

Jesus identified the second greatest commandment as "You shall love your neighbor as yourself." In the Lord's Prayer, Maximus interpreted "Forgive us our trespasses as we forgive those who trespass against us" as an admonition against judging others: "He summons God to be to him as he is to his neighbors."[47] In fact, Orthodox Christians believe that the degree to which we judge others (judgment being an intrinsic quality of intellect) will be the degree to which we are held accountable by the Only-Begotten Son on Judgment Day. This represents the heart of the enforcement mechanism, about which Maximus wrote:

The fear of the Lord is twofold. The first type is produced in us from threats of punishment, and from it arise in proper order self-control, patience, hope in God, and detachment, from which comes love. The second is coupled with love itself and constantly produces reverence in the soul, lest through the familiarity of love it become presumptuous of God.[48]

Maximus stepped up to meet the challenge of Byzantine scholasticism, but in the end salvation depends on two simple ideas: love God and love your neighbor. Unconditional love alone, dispassion, will overcome the gnomic will and lead to deification, allowing our natural will to act without coercion. Maximus wrote:

The reward of self-mastery is detachment and that of faith is knowledge. And detachment gives rise to discernment while knowledge gives rise to love for God.[49]

Since detachment gives rise to discernment, it frees the heart-centered *nous* to seek God naturally. Discernment allows intellect to distinguish humility from self-interest. St. John Climacus wrote:

Many have been speedily forgiven their sins. But no one has rapidly acquired dispassion, for this requires much time and longing, and God.[50]

Now *freedom* becomes fully defined within the early Christian paradigm. To free the *nous* from its fallen gnomic condition requires an internal struggle with self-love. The enforcement mechanism is the fear of eternal ill-being and the hope of eternal well-being. The surest behavioral strategy is humility. No external obligation represents a greater duty than the personal commitment to salvation. The internal struggle of Neo-Platonism and the early Christian paradigm may seem to involve the same effort, but for very different reasons.

Emperor Constans II's desire for political compromise between the various constituencies of the Byzantine provinces would be completely understandable to modern-day pragmatists. Self-preservation, understood by the ancient Greek paradigm as an innate characteristic of humanity, was understood by the early Christian paradigm as the misdirected natural desire for everlasting union with the Creator. For individuals who do not accept the early Christian paradigm, self-preservation once again motivates their personal commitment to the relative standards of their community. The personal struggle between self-interest and self-control that distinguished Plato's understanding of *areté* is now satisfied by numerous alternatives. But the history of Christianity in the first millennium was one of unity, with a single understanding of theology. Humility represented a higher standard of personal sacrifice. The trinity of faith, reason, and humility would underlie one's personal commitment to, and acceptance of, the authority of the seven Ecumenical Councils.

According to the ancient Greek paradigm, there was an organic cooperative obligation between the citizen and the state that guided behavior. Those ancient Greeks who recognized a competition between opposites found harmony through arbitration. According to the early Christian paradigm, on the other hand, there was a freely chosen personal responsibility, guided by humility, from the individual to God, without coercion from either the state or the divine. The arbiter would be the pre-eternal Creator on Judgment Day.

There is no question that the populations within the Roman Empire had to sift through an abundance of claims regarding absolute truth.

If average Romans could not understand the complexity of Maximus's cosmology, they could surely understand the commands to love God and love their neighbors, and they could easily accept the authority of the Ecumenical Councils. The Sophists' philosophy that man is the measure of all things had not defeated the obligation of duty, but the cultural relativity of belief systems and the evidence of reasoned logic would be compelling allies for individuals inclined toward self-love. Over time, the moral compasses for various provinces of the empire evolved independently of each other. Today's historians and philosophers find themselves in the same position as the people of the first millennium, deciding for themselves whether or not they accept the authority of the initial seven Ecumenical Councils.

Modern historians and philosophers point out the Platonic language used by early Christian theologians and note the overlapping mythic traditions. Through the exercise of reasoned logic, they conclude that there was a commingled evolution between various belief myths in the development of the early Christian paradigm. Evidence for this speculative conclusion is readily available. However, such conclusions ignore the authority of the seven Ecumenical Councils, which distinguished divine revelation from the plethora of speculative theological and philosophical opinions. Unless one shares the personal responsibility of the early Christian paradigm, the enforcement mechanism of Judgment Day can be dismissed as fiction.

❧ ❧ ❧

Chapter 6

The Holy Roman Empire

Empire and Personal Identity

After the death of Constantine the Great in 337 A.D., the eastern provinces of the Roman Empire maintained their cohesion and continued to act as an empire, while the western provinces were overrun by invaders. Both provinces, however, were under assault from barbarian tribes for hundreds of years to come, adding chaos to the already confusing lives of the Roman populations. By the eleventh century, the empire and Christianity irreparably divided. This chapter will review the historical events and crucial ideas that gave birth to our modern sense of Self.

Many Roman citizens viewed the fall of Rome to the Visigoths in 410 A.D. as punishment by the Greco-Roman gods, who had been abandoned for Christianity. St. Augustine (354–430 A.D.) responded to the fall of Rome with *City of God*,[1] in which he identified salvation and the Kingdom of God as beyond the temporal concerns of empire and governments.[2] But the gnomic will of fallen man was uncertain, and the remnants of the Roman Empire lacked the homogeneous identity of ancient Greece. Neither *areté* ("virtue") nor *aidos* ("holy shame") could enforce unity within the heterogeneous empire. There was no common standard of duty, obligation, or responsibility. Roman citizens would have to sort through the confusing messages of Christians, Neo-Platonists, Gnostics, and Stoics.

Byzantine scholasticism of the fifth century A.D. had infected the eastern provinces and demanded clear unambiguous explanations regarding the two wills of Christ. Answering the challenge despite torture and exile, Maximus the Confessor (580–662 A.D.) was the only one who stood up to the civil authority. The empire's efforts to silence him failed with the ultimate vindication of his teachings at the Sixth Ecumenical Council. Reasoned logic did not go away, but the average Roman, who could not be expected to understand the complex Christian cosmology, was strengthened by faith against the challenge of Byzantine scholasticism.

When Constantine the Great freed Christianity from persecution, he did not attack the establishment belief systems. He was tolerant and fair, but clear in his support of Christianity. Succeeding emperors and Christian militants were less tolerant. One example of militancy was the murder of Hypatia of Alexandria (370–415 A.D.), who was a popular Neo-Platonist, astronomer, and mathematician. Some historians believe that she was the victim of a political rivalry between Cyril (ca. 376–444 A.D.), the bishop of Alexandria, and Orestes, the civil governor.[3] In any case, Hypatia was ultimately murdered by a mob of Christian monks. Such persecutions of alternative belief systems by Christians was at the very least inconsistent with the canons of the Ecumenical Councils. Persecuting opponents was neither "turning the other cheek" nor an example of humility. When politics and religion mix, self-righteous people kill.

Maximus the Confessor's clarity on the two wills of the Only-Begotten Son left no room for ambiguity and compromise. His vigorous mind answered the challenge of reasoned logic, but could not convince those who did not share his faith. Reason, faith, and humility formed a solid trinitarian foundation, but if any one of these principles were weakened, the authority of the Ecumenical Councils would be questioned. Those who were more comfortable with ambiguity, whose faith was less certain, and whose commitment to humility was marginal were free to choose different allegiances.

The example of Hypatia represents a tragic reminder of human intolerance and self-love gone amuck. Ignorance and religious fervor are a dangerous combination. The early Christian paradigm was questioned and considered from an intellectual perspective. Many accepted the explanations of mystery provided by alternative Christian-sounding Gnostic belief systems. Others left Christian stories altogether and found comfort in Islam, which recognized God as one without the complexity of Triune explanations.

Earlier, we identified the fourth-century differences in emphasis between St. Augustine and St. John Cassian (ca. 360–ca. 435 A.D.) regarding the cooperation between divine grace and free will. Prosper of Aquitaine (390–465 A.D.), a Latin-speaking religious zealot, was not the only one who rejected Cassian's middle road of cooperation. But it is too simplistic to lay the empire's eventual division merely to differences in language. During Maximus's trial, the Inquisitors asked, "Why do you love the Romans and hate the Greeks?" To which he replied, "We have a precept which says not to hate anyone. I love the Romans as those who share the same faith, and the Greeks as sharing the same language."[4] The Roman Empire, where both Greek and Latin were spoken, had accepted the absolute truth of the early Christian paradigm. Thus, Maximus rightly identified himself with the faith of the Romans. The culture and language of the ancient Greeks were recognized as embracing the pagan gods of the early Greco-Roman empire, which Maximus rejected.[5]

Faith, Reason, and Humility in the Latin Tradition

Cassian was a Latin-speaking Roman who had personal experience with ascetic discipline and monastic life among Greek-speaking Christians. The term *ascetic* refers to the discipline of an athlete preparing for competition. The early Christian paradigm recognized ascetics as spiritual athletes who were struggling through the marathon of life toward deification. Despite his Latin origins, Cassian's differences with Augustine reduced his influence among the Latin-speaking population. But Cassian's writings influenced the founder of Latin monastic life, St. Benedict of Nursia (ca. 480–543 A.D.). Reflecting his linguistic tradition, St. Benedict developed the Rule as a legislative code of conduct. "In adapting a system essentially Eastern to Western conditions," states the *New Advent Catholic Encyclopedia*, "St. Benedict gave it coherence, stability, and organization, and the verdict of history is unanimous in applauding the results of such adaptation."[6]

In the previous chapter, we discussed the Christian reliance on humility. Appropriately, humility played a significant role in St. Benedict's Rule, where it is described as a twelve-step ladder to salvation in the seventh chapter and is referred to an additional fifteen times throughout the remainder of the text. But the trinity of faith, reason, and humility did not hold the same authority within the Latin tradition as it did among the eastern centers of Christianity.

This fact is best evidenced in modern times by the Encyclical on Faith and Reason, issued by Pope John Paul II on September 15, 1998. In over 32,000 words, the term *humility* appears only twice. The first reference, which concerns the subjective aspects of Christian philosophy, states that "faith liberates reason from presumption" and acknowledges that "the philosopher who learns humility will also find courage to tackle questions which are difficult to resolve if the data of Revelation are ignored."[7] We will explore the "data of Revelation" in greater detail in Chapter 8, but notice here that philosophy and theology have been reunited.

The second reference to humility appears in St. Bonaventure's *Itinerarium Mentis in Deum*, which, combined with three other works

(*Commentary on the Sentences*, *Breviloquium*, and *De reductione Artium ad Theologiam*), illustrates "the mutual interpenetration of philosophy and theology" that characterized the Scholastic Middle Ages.[8] Here St. Bonaventure (1221–1274 A.D.) cautions the reader to recognize the inadequacy of "reading without repentance, knowledge without devotion…, action divorced from religion…, intelligence without humility, study unsustained by divine grace, thought without the wisdom inspired by God."[9] In St. Benedict's era, Rome was politically powerless, but the leadership of the Latin Popes shined the light of truth on their Greek-speaking counterparts. By the Scholastic Middle Ages of the thirteenth century, Greek-speaking Romans were prevented from returning the favor.

The Holy Roman Empire: Culture, Nationalism, and Religion

For the first time, eighth-century conflicts within the remnants of the Roman Empire began to be framed by ethnic names instead of the names of those accused of Christian heresy—that is, the Greek East versus the Latin West, or the Franks versus the Romans.[10] Maximus's Roman faith and his respect for the Greek language would need to choose sides. The history of Europe's Germanic tribes will not be covered in this study beyond acknowledging the capture of Rome by the Visigoths in 410 A.D. and the initial alliance with the Franks during the short-lived reign of Julian the Apostate (361–363 A.D.), the half-brother of Constantine the Great. The blended allegiances between religion, nationality, and culture, which had historically formed one's personal identity, would now be challenged by the new ethnic identities. Although Greek-speaking Maximus identified himself as a Roman, future generations of Latin-speaking Romans were not obligated to see him that way.

Religious affiliation is a personal choice and a major contributor to one's understanding of who one is. In homogeneous societies, the differences between religion, culture, and nationality are difficult to discern. As societies become more diverse, however, the distinction between these three contributors to identity become more apparent. Culture, which is the most difficult aspect to discern, includes differences of class and status. For example, two families with the same nationality but from different classes may be united through the marriage of their children (assuming such a union is culturally acceptable). Only the marriage ceremony is actually religious. The events before and after the ceremony represent culture. If the families are from different social strata, the social difficulties that may present themselves represent the cultural friction that exists within many societies. If the respective families "know their roles" and respect their cultural differences, the wedding may be most enjoyable. The linking of religion and nationalism ultimately ended the unity of the ancient Roman Empire and divided Christianity. The political ambitions of Charlemagne (742–814 A.D.) manipulated the fourth-century intellectual tendencies of Augustine while creating the Holy Roman Empire.

Charlemagne's commitment to Christianity certainly seems devout. He is known to have been a great admirer of Benedictine monasticism, and legend suggests that he slept with a copy of St. Augustine's *City of God* under his pillow. But his ambition to unite Western Europe under his leadership was not constrained by Christian humility nor by respect for the authority of the seven Ecumenical Councils. As the eastern provinces were confronting the rapidly spreading influence of Islam, Charlemagne realized that Christianity could be the vehicle that would transcend and unite the various tribes of Western Europe. But first Charlemagne's vision of the Roman Empire would need to lose its Greek-speaking constituents so as to limit its exposure to the advancing Arab armies.

Within the newly relevant ethnicity of the eighth century, Charlemagne relegated Greek-speaking theologians to the Greek East, which included not only the authority of the Ecumenical Councils but also the influence of Maximus and Cassian. Like Prosper of Aquitaine, Charlemagne drove a wedge between Augustine's and Cassian's understanding of divine grace and free will, blaming Greek *hubris* for Cassian's challenge to Augustinian dogma. Fr. John Romanides (1927–2001) a prominent Orthodox Christian priest, theologian, and writer observes that the Roman Empire Latinized the Celtic band and embraced the Greek band. "One is obliged," he writes, "to speak of…a Latin North and a Greek South, but certainly not of a Latin West and a Greek East, which is a Frankish myth."[11] The significant contribution of Latin-speaking theologians and Popes in the development of the early Christian paradigm did not interrupt Charlemagne's quest for power.

The Seventh Ecumenical Council, in 787 A.D., affirmed the use of icons within the Church, but there is some evidence that Charlemagne did not agree with the Council's decision.[12] One possible reason may have been the confusion resulting from use of the Latin word *veneratio* to translate the Greek words both for reverence and for worship. The cultural differences between Greek-speaking and Latin-speaking Romans had grown so wide that by the time of Charlemagne neither side was conciliatory. The cooperation that distinguished early Christian unity had broken down along ethnic lines. Bishop Kallistos Ware notes the strong anti-Greek prejudice within Charlemagne's court:

> Men of letters in Charlemagne's entourage were not prepared to copy Byzantium, but sought to create a new Christian civilization of their own. In fourth-century Europe there had been one Christian civilization, in thirteenth-century Europe there were two; perhaps it is

in the reign of Charlemagne that the schism of civilizations first becomes clearly apparent.[13]

Empress Irene of Constantinople (ca. 752–803 A.D.) played a significant role regarding the veneration of icons affirmed at the Seventh Ecumenical Council. Her husband, Emperor Constantine V, had died prematurely in 780, and left her as the guardian of their ten-year-old son, Constantine VI, and the ruler of the Greek-speaking Eastern Roman Empire, later known as the Byzantine Empire.[14] Irene's authority to govern was challenged by many, and for a time she considered a marriage between her son and Charlemagne's daughter to strengthen her position.[15] Within the Byzantine Empire, Irene successfully consolidated her rule in 800 A.D. On December 25 of that year, Pope Leo III crowned Charlemagne as Roman Emperor after he and Charlemagne had criticized Greek-speaking Romans for accepting the leadership of a woman. Charlemagne adopted the ancient Roman title of "Augustus," and the Holy Roman Empire was born. Still, it would be another two hundred years before the Great Schism would permanently divide Christianity between the Greek East and the Latin West.

Today, the Greek East is known as Eastern Orthodox Christianity, and the patriarchates of Constantinople and Jerusalem continue to recognize themselves as "Romans," as distinct from the Vatican and the Roman Catholic Church, which they regard as "Latins."

Western Christianity recognizes the Vatican as the holy seat of the Roman Catholic Church and has been more impacted by the Protestant Reformations of Martin Luther (1483–1546), John Calvin (1509–1564), and Henry VIII (1491–1547) than by the initial Schism of 1054.

The Great Schism of 1054

Through Charlemagne's ethnic lens, Christianity's common theological roots splintered. Both the Greek East and the Latin West can legitimately consider themselves "Romans." Thus, the division was based on more than national claims or cultural differences. There needed to be a theological distinction. The particular religious issue that irreversibly divided the ancient empire was Augustine's explanation of the Proceeding Holy Spirit as the third Person of the Holy Trinity, which seemed to contradict the Nicene Creed.

Four hundred years before Charlemagne, Augustine, Bishop of Hippo, had written that the Holy Spirit proceeds from the Father *and the Son* (*Filioque*), thereby changing the essential relationship of the Triune God. Written in Latin, Augustine's explanation regarding the Proceeding Holy Spirit received much closer scrutiny in the ninth century than it had in the fifth. The need for Latin theologians who were independent of Greek influence was a priority within the Holy Roman Empire, and the numerous Latin theologians who were in harmony with the Greek East were ignored.

According to Étienne Gilson (1884–1978), a French philosopher and historian, Augustine conceived of the rational soul not only as superior to the body but as entirely independent of it.[16] Philip Sherrard distinguishes Augustine's understanding of intellect from that of early Christian orthodoxy:

> It is important to remark here that the Augustinian intelligence or intellect cannot be said to correspond to that spiritual intellect, the deiform *nous*, mentioned earlier, for this latter is, as we saw, heart-centred and of an order essentially different from and superior to the

psychophysical whole of man, while the Augustinian intelligence or intellect is but a superior mental faculty of the soul itself.[17]

Through a misinterpretation of Augustine's regard for intellect, and contrary to Maximus the Confessor and the seven Ecumenical Councils, Platonism crept back into Christian dogma. The intellectual head no longer needed to cooperate with the heart-centered *nous*.

Augustine wrote about the "spirit of man" being "freed from the body at the end of this life."[18] The similarities here to Platonism are obvious if considered independently of the Ecumenical Councils and Maximus the Confessor. Augustine confessed that *how* the Holy Spirit proceeds from the Father and the Son can only be known in eternal bliss. He considered his endeavor a failure for not accomplishing a more intelligible knowledge of the relation of the Three Persons. Augustine's limited knowledge of the Greek language would account for his difficulty in accepting a boundary between knowable and unknowable. The early Christian paradigm of humanity's ability to achieve deification and participate in the Divine Energy, but never in the Divine Essence, is not discernible in Augustine's writings.[19]

It is clear from reading Augustine's *On Trinity* that he recognized the three uncreated Persons as One God. If we sidestep the debate about what is the absolute truth of divine revelation, one observation is universally acknowledged: the *Filioque*, was not in the original version of the Nicene Creed, nor was it ever affirmed by any of the seven Ecumenical Councils. Augustine accepted that faith is superior to reason, but the cooperation between the heart-centered *nous* and the intellectual mind, which had united Christianity for centuries, would no longer influence the Holy Roman Empire.

Freed from the circumscription of humility, the duality of faith and reason remained the only acceptable means to establish Christian dogma within the Latin West (as we have seen with Pope John Paul's encyclical). The lack of a clearly defined unique role for the Holy Spirit would eventually result in perceiving the Holy Spirit as less than equal to the Persons of the Father and the Son. Maximus's concern about misunderstanding the two wills of Christ would have prophetic implications. Robert Louis Wilken (1936–), a professor of early Christian history at the University of Virginia, quotes Augustine's description of the Holy Spirit as "the 'bond of love' and the 'communion' between Father and Son"[20] Augustine's language could easily suggest that the Holy Spirit was a product of the Father and the Son. Remember that the Trinity was not additive: Three as One, and One as Three, but never two. When the Spirit becomes a consequence of the love between Father and Son, the Trinity becomes a duality between Father and Son. The cooperation found in Trinity becomes the competition of duality. In the early Christian paradigm, the only perfect duality is in the God-man Jesus.

It would be another two hundred years after the creation of the Holy Roman Empire that the Patriarch of Constantinople and the Pope of Rome would excommunicate each other. Efforts to unite Eastern and Western branches of Christianity have failed to this day. Charlemagne's ambition to unite Europe through a transcendent Latin Christian tradition would eventually succeed...somewhat. The Western understanding of freedom in Charlemagne's time would develop independently of the early Christian duty to seek cooperation between the head and the heart.

It is interesting to note that the Eastern Orthodox Church is known today by its various ethnicities: Greek, Russian, Serbian, and so on. The services of all these churches, as well as the theology and the acceptance of the authority of the original seven Ecumenical Councils, are in complete communion. Nevertheless, the ethnic distinctions represent areas of competition. Greeks and Russians regularly spar over who is more orthodox, although in truth their differences are only national and cultural. In this light, the Great Schism of 1054 could properly be recognized as the first instance of ethnic competition. Today, Greek and Russian Orthodox Christians are united in their opposition to the Latin evolution of the Roman Catholic Church!

Before we follow the development of freedom through the Holy Roman Empire, one more note about Eastern Orthodox Christianity is particularly interesting. After the split with Rome, the eastern Roman provinces fell before the military campaigns of the Arabs, and later of the Turks, until the end of the First World War. The dominant belief system in those former Roman provinces was Islam, and the Muslim majority never perceived the remaining pockets of Christians as a threat. Maintaining civil harmony had always been the responsibility of the civil authority, so for the Christians, "giving to Caesar what is Caesar's" simply meant keeping a low profile in the hope of avoiding persecution.

Over the centuries, some rulers have been more tolerant than others. For the Christian minorities, separation between Church and State was never in doubt. Freed from the duties of civil authority and the responsibilities of adjudicating crime, the Christian minorities emphasized the importance of eternal salvation. Their difficult temporal experience, they believed, would be rewarded with eternal well-being. The personal commitment to faith, reason, and humility would be elevated. Religious authorities would emphasize the Triune God's forgiveness and limitless mercy.

No Patriarch was allowed to accumulate power that might represent a challenge to the Muslim majority. In fact, whenever a new Patriarch was elected, the civil authority had to give final approval to his elevation. Even today, the Patriarchate of Jerusalem, for example, cannot install a new Patriarch without the approval of Israel, Jordan, and the

Palestinian Authority, a situation that has caused considerable confusion in recent years. This is obviously very different from the modern authority of the Pope and the Vatican.

The successful consolidation of European tribes required the Holy Roman Empire to exercise both civil and religious authority. Western Europeans were expected to blur the distinctions of nationality and culture to unite under the Latin tradition of the Roman Catholic Pope. This unity would not hold, for reasons that become clear when we evaluate the circumstances of Maximus the Confessor.

Maximus was an orthodox Christian monastic, who recognized his faith as part of his Roman national identity. But he also respected his Greek cultural identity without embracing its ancient religious implications. Charlemagne and his court, however, were under no obligation to accept Maximus's personal understanding of identity. Greek-speaking Romans were no longer relevant to the Holy Roman Empire, which would define who was in and who was out.

Exercising both civil and religious authority, the newly proclaimed Holy Roman Empire linked national and religious allegiances and subordinated tribal cultural differences. Latin was the language of religion, and the local tongues were expected to accept their subordinate status. The temporal success of this vision must be acknowledged, since the Roman Catholic Church is the largest Christian denomination in the twenty-first century. But civil authority and religious authority have different agendas. Cultural and national distinctions did not go away, and, over time, the Holy Roman Empire's grip on both civil and religious authority weakened. In fact, culture and nationalism united to undermine the authority of Rome.

The theological necessity of the *Filioque* was less about divine revelation of absolute truth and more about separating the Latin West from the Greek East. Werner Jaeger said about the evolution of Greek *paideia* (the effort to advance excellence and virtue from one generation to the next):

> At the moment of intellectual development, when the liberal meaning of the sacred books had become questionable…, giving up of those forms was out of the question, because that would have been a kind of suicide. The reason for their continuation, but with a different meaning, was not an intellectual but a sociological necessity having to do with the fact that the continuity of life depends on form.[21]

I believe that the same thing could be said about the evolution of Christian dogma in the Holy Roman Empire, which shed the traditional Christian trinitarian commitment to faith, reason, and humility in favor of a dualistic commitment to faith and reason alone. This placed Christian dogma on a weaker foundation. Charlemagnian ambition and social pragmatism were compelled by sociological necessity to balance both civil and religious authority. The separation from the Greek East was successful, and the newly defined Latin identity (religion, nationalism, and culture) had consequences for European society for centuries to come.

Absolute Truth: Take Three

The ancient Greek and the early Christian paradigms had different versions of absolute truth. For the average Roman citizen, however, the Christian belief in *ex nihilo* did not automatically invalidate the cosmology of Hesiod. Aristotle (384–322 B.C.) had formulated a cosmology in his treatise *On the Heavens*,[22] which Claudius Ptolemy (ca. 90–ca. 168 A.D.)

perfected and popularized in *The Great System*.[23] According to this theory, the Earth was the center of the universe, around which were circles that directed the motions of the moon, sun, and planets. Stars made up the background.

Hellenistic tradition rejected the concept of non-being, and, as we have seen, the alternative belief systems to early Christianity were more compatible with Hesiod's cosmology. Aristotle's and Ptolemy's understanding of the cosmos was plausible to those Romans who lacked the religious experience and faith that inspired Orthodox Christian believers to accept the dogma of *ex nihilo*.

Interest in Aristotle began to spread throughout the Muslim world from the ninth century on. Beginning with Al-Kindi's (ca. 813–873 A.D.) treatise on metaphysics, Arab philosophers explored the nuances of Aristotle with their own Islamic beliefs.* The writings of Avicenna, the Latin name for the Arabic philosopher Ibn Sina (980–1037 A.D.), translated into Latin from their original Arabic, initiated a revival of Aristotle in the twelfth and thirteenth centuries. There was also Jewish interest in Aristotle from Avicebron (1020–1070 A.D.) and Maimonides (1135–1204 A.D.).

Two hundred years after the Great Schism, faith and reason were fully united in Latin Christian dogma by St. Thomas Aquinas's (ca. 1225–1274 A.D.) brilliant *Summa Theologica*. Aquinas's work was patterned after the Commentaries of the Arabic philosopher Ibn Rushd, (1126–1198 A.D.), known throughout the Latin world as Averroes. Aquinas is credited with "baptizing Aristotle" or, more accurately, fitting Aristotle within Christian beliefs.[24] Ultimately, however, by adopting Aristotle, Aquinas was setting the stage for Protestantism, for Aristotle's belief in reason undermined the authority of faith in Western Europe.

---

*Al-Kindi was the first great Arabian follower of Aristotle. Al-Farabi combined Aristotelian and Neo-Platonic themes in the tenth century.

Aquinas is recognized as Aristotelian, in contrast to Augustine, whose emphasis was more Neo-Platonic.[25] Of course, the early Christian paradigm, which rejected Platonism, would reject both characterizations as unorthodox. Augustine had been confused about the nature of the Proceeding Holy Spirit and had not appreciated the theological distinction between Divine Essence and Divine Energy. Aquinas, on the other hand, was clear about the nature of the Divine Essence without any allowance for the concept of Divine Energy. This doctrine would further expand the theological differences of the Great Schism.

The monastic movement attributed to St. Benedict inspired other Christian communities. Significant contributions to the spread of Christianity were made by St. Bernard of Clairvaux (1090–1153 A.D.), who founded the Cistercian movement; St. Dominic (1170–1221 A.D.), who founded the Dominican Order of Preachers; and St. Francis (1182–1226 A.D.), who founded the Friars and whose Franciscan Order bears his name. Each order emphasized different aspects of Christian dogma, and, together with the followers of Augustine and Aquinas, represented the dogmatic quilt of Roman Catholicism.

Nationalism Splinters the Holy Roman Empire

Charlemagne succeeded in creating political unity in Western Europe, and the sociological necessity to praise that effort continues to this day. That sociological necessity challenges Greek theology and ignores the cooperation between Rome and Constantinople in the development of the early Christian paradigm.

In Charlemagne's day, Western Europe was populated with tribes that spoke a variety of languages, including English, German, French, and Latin. Local communities might pray in Latin, but they did not necessarily understand the language of the Church. The provocative book *Who Murdered Chaucer?* by Terry Jones presents an alternative history of fourteenth-century England and the change in leadership from Richard II to Henry IV.[26] The power struggle between the Church and the State, and particularly the role of Oxford intellectuals in challenging the tyranny of the Archbishop of Canterbury, come to life in this book. The conflicting agendas of the civil and religious authorities collapsed European religious unity.

The communal character of the Middle Ages was similar to the organic relationships of the ancient Greek paradigm and the early Christian paradigm. "Solitary activity," writes Jones, was "something to be pitied."[27] Richard II was the first king of England regarded as the protector of the English language.[28] Furthermore, as Jones notes:

> The use of the vernacular was not simply an expression of nationalism—on the contrary, it was also characteristic of the new internationalism of late fourteenth-century European courts, in which each country sought to assert its own individuality through its vernacular language.[29]

Use of the local language added to the prestige of European nobility and eventually challenged the authority of all things Latin. While communal relationships were valued in European society, the strains on an individual's moral obligations were more intense. The distinctions between civil and religious authority were becoming sharper.

Monarchs and tyrants can be distinguished by their intent. Monarchs govern in the tradition of Solon, for the well-being of their people. Tyrants seek their own interests at the expense of their subjects. Obedience to authorities represented the Middle Age equivalent of *areté*, but, as in ancient Greece, the duty to either Church or State was up to the individual. If subjects were not inclined to obey their leaders, both Church and State could enforce obedience through punishment. Both institutions could also tax the population. But the Church exercised a much more significant penalty for those who failed to pay: excommunication. Cutting people off from the religious community not only isolated them from their friends but separated them from the love of God.

Repentance and forgiveness had been part of Christian dogma from its inception. Over time these principles of faith became known as pardons and indulgences. After the establishment of the Holy Roman Empire, the use of pardons and indulgences acquired a more legal structure, particularly at the Fourth Council of the Lateran, in 1215.[30] Over the next four hundred years, the Roman Catholic Church grew into one of the most powerful and wealthy institutions in Europe.[31] There were obvious abuses in the issuance of pardons and indulgences by members of the religious establishment. Challenging the Church's accumulation of wealth, John Wyclif (1324–1384 A.D.) argued that the Church should return to its simple roots and emulate the poverty of Jesus. The German monk Martin Luther (1483–1546 A.D.) challenged the abuse of indulgences in the sixteenth century.

Wyclif claimed that the highest authority was the Bible, not the Church. Many European countries had translated the Latin Bible into the local language, and the population was very interested in discussing articles of faith in the common tongue. Thus, the Church no longer exercised exclusive authority to interpret the word of God. Terry Jones observes about this:

> The idea of the king directly ruling his people, without the hostility of a self-seeking magnate class, was not a crazy anarchist proposal; it was an ideal of monarchy recognized by political thinkers all over Europe and traceable back to Aristotle.[32]

At the end of the fourteenth century, a poll tax instituted by the magnate class in England provoked a peasant revolt that was savagely repressed. The Archbishop of Canterbury, William Courtenay, placed full responsibility for the violence on John Wyclif. Thus, the struggle between Church and State could also be understood as a class struggle between the privileged wealthy and the common folk.

Humility and the Sense of Self in the West

Jones uses an illuminating turn of phrase when discussing the Archbishop's dressing down of Oxford Chancellor Riggs. "It was," he writes, "a humiliating climb-down."[33] And again, when he says, "The barons knew how to humiliate Richard."[34] Humility in the early Christian paradigm was a personal choice in the struggle for eternal salvation. By the fourteenth century, humility was a weapon used to undermine opponents. In other words, humiliation was something you did to others, not to yourself.

The *Oxford English Dictionary* defines *humble* as "having a low estimate of one's importance, worthiness, or merits; marked by the absence of self-assertion or self-exaltation; lowly; the opposite of proud." This represents a significant change in meaning from that used in the early Christian paradigm. Plato's appreciation for humility was an anomaly in the ancient Greek paradigm, and Aristotle's more consistent Doctrine of the Mean clearly classified humility as a deficiency. Low and high self-esteem may represent the spectrum within the Doctrine of the Mean, but neither attitude would recognize the willing subordination of self that defined humility within the early Christian paradigm. If man were truly the measure of all things, finding a middle position would be a reasonable strategy.

The early Christian paradigm accepted a loving Creator who lowered Himself to the level of His creation, thereby allowing the human creature to ascend to the level of the Creator. Similarly, Plato's formula of God as the measure of all things does not recognize the Doctrine of the Mean, but rather the ascent of the soul. The early Christian paradigm accepts the Creator's unconditional love, expressed through forgiveness and mercy, as the reward for humble behavior. Attitudes of esteem and exaltation are both self-centered. Without humility as the standard for right conduct, faith and reason would be left to define duty as either an obligation or a responsibility. Humility, the only reliable path to salvation, would not be available.

There does, however, seem to be some common ground between the Orthodox Christian appreciation for humility and Wyclif's concern about the Church's accumulation of wealth. Others can speculate about whether Wyclif would have accepted Maximus the Confessor's cosmology. There is no evidence that Wyclif was aware of Maximus, although Maximus's *Ambigua* was translated into Latin by the ninth-century philosopher Duns Scotus (1270–1308).[*] Certainly, Wyclif's rejection of the authority of the Church and his espousal of personal interpretation of the Bible would have been unacceptable propositions within the early Christian paradigm, which did not rely on individual interpretation but the reinforced authority of the seven Ecumenical Councils, the Bible, Church art such as icons, the Church liturgy (which in Greek means "common work"), and the examples of saints and martyrs.[†]

----

[*]George C. Berthold, trans., *Maximus Confessor: Selected Writings* (New York: Paulist Press, 1985), p. 5, also references the seventeenth-century critical review of Maximus by Dominican patristic scholar François Combéfis (1605–1679).

[†]These five pillars of authority cooperate in maintaining the Orthodox Christian paradigm. They are identified by Fr. David Anderson in "*What We Believe* (Ben Lomond, CA: Conciliar Press, 1997), reprinted with permission in the *Orthodox Study Bible* (1993), pp. iv–xii.

Personal responsibility inspired Athanasius of Alexandria (ca. 298–373 A.D.), St. John Chrysostom (347–407 A.D.), and Maximus the Confessor (580–662 A.D.). All of these men were Christians first, Romans second, and Greeks culturally. All three could be referred to as having "steadfast humility," in the sense that their adherence to Orthodox doctrine was *never* a question of political expediency. Quite the opposite. All three endured persecution, embraced humility, and never doubted the absolute truth of the early Christian paradigm. Hans von Campenhausen explains:

> Greek Christianity knew no conflict between Church and State in the medieval sense. There were struggles for power, but they were always concerned with power inside the Church itself. Even the greatest bishops never demanded to be heard on political questions or to make political decisions.[35]

In Western Europe, Wyclif and Luther challenged the arbiters of Roman Catholic religious authority. These challenges empowered intellectuals and civic leaders, but did not offer any guidance in the quest for absolute truth. The obligation of duty or the pursuit of wisdom, which guided the ancient Greek paradigm, was not an intrinsic motive behind Wyclif or Luther. They were opposed to the oppressive hypocrisy of self-righteous arbiters. There was no tradition of humility that would frame personal duty toward obedience. The intellectual challenge to blind faith could only be suppressed by force.

To sum up, then, the contributing factors to the emergence of Self include: the change in the role and meaning of humility; the inherent competition of duality, which fractures the cooperation between faith and reason; scholastic inquisitiveness, which values rational logic and questions blind faith; an expectation of intellectual accountability; abuse on the part of Church authorities; cultural and national differences from the Latin establishment; conflicting agendas between civil and religious authorities; conflicting interests between the privileged class and the poor; and empowerment of individual moral accountability through Biblical study in various native tongues. The Holy Roman Empire advanced the Sophists' victory over duty. Man would be the measure of all things, and intellect would interpret the evidence.

❖ ❖ ❖

Chapter 7

The Enlightened Self

Faith and Reason: An Unstable Union

Linking religion, nationalism, and culture first defined and then undermined the Holy Roman Empire. Many people believe that faith and reason can cooperate—that we can make intellectually responsible decisions and at the same time have faith in a supreme deity. This chapter will finalize the development of the paradigm of self and explore the implications of our dual reliance on the heart of faith and the head of reason.

Is it possible for one's heart and head to cooperate? Can we really serve two masters? Our understanding of freedom depends on how we navigate that polarity. Until the Middle Ages, the sense of duty toward a deity, the state, or some understanding of common good was sufficient to balance the innate appeal of self-interest. Certainly, some individuals felt no qualms about self-promotion, but, generally speaking, this attitude was held in low regard by the people of Western Europe. However, self-interest was free to explore its potential once the societal commitment to humility had been abandoned.

This evolution can be demonstrated by comparing eighth-century art with the art of the Italian Renaissance. The early Christian paradigm's emphasis on humility is exemplified in Church art known as icons. These images of the holy family and of saints are not idols that are worshipped. Rather, they are revered in the same way that people cherish photographs of loved ones. Icons remind people of what they worship, but are never worshiped themselves—that is, they never replace the real persons represented by the images. The process of creating an Eastern Orthodox icon literally begins, proceeds, and ends in prayer with every single stroke of the brush. Furthermore, a proper icon should never distinguish the artist who created it; the glory belongs to God alone.

The seventh Ecumenical Council, in 787 A.D., which specifically addressed the role of icons within the Church, defeated the Iconoclast movement, which had sought to prevent Christians from venerating religious art.* A mere thirteen years later, the Holy Roman Empire was declared. Over the next four hundred years, the merged identities of religion, nationalism, and culture refocused the emphasis of religious art away from the Triune Creator and toward the human individual.

The consequences of the Great Schism can be seen centuries later in the artistic genius of Leonardo da Vinci, Michelangelo, and Raphael. And that is precisely the point. Those great artists are known through their creative talents. They are held in esteem in a way that is very different from the subjects of their art. There has never been a comparable renaissance within the Eastern Orthodox Church, for that would be contrary to the virtuous path of humility.

One might argue that the Italian Renaissance represents the perfect cooperation between Creator and Created, or between one's head and heart. But such a conclusion would impose a duty for the head and heart to cooperate that is not essential within the paradigm of self. The ancient ideas of *areté* ("virtue"), *aidos* ("holy shame"), and early Christian humility no longer encumbered Europeans. Neither religion nor philosophy imposed a duty to pursue knowledge of absolute truth. The Sophists' epigram of man as the measure of all things was unrestrained

---

*A leading defender of religious art was St. John Damascene, who stated, "I do not venerate matter, I venerate the fashioner of matter, who became matter for my sake and accepted to dwell in matter and through matter worked my salvation, and I will not cease from reverencing matter, through which my salvation was worked." Quoted here from Andrew Louth, *St. John Damascene: Tradition and Originality in Byzantine Theology* (New York: Oxford University Press, 2002), p. 202.

by any essential sense of duty, responsibility, or absolute truth. For the full development of the paradigm of self, reason needed to conquer faith, and nationalism provided the road map.

Reason Conquers Faith

Modern historians have moved away from the exclusively Italian characterization of the Renaissance. The period after the Middle Ages is today referred to as "early modern."[1] Multiple renaissances or "rebirths" are now identified by alternative nationalistic and cultural characterizations. For example, the English, French, Scandinavian, and Dutch renaissances can all be considered rebirths, as can the humanist movement.[2] It must be acknowledged, however, that the Latin lens was the first European revival of the "classical values" of ancient Greece. What is clear in all of these examples of renaissance was the early modern lens that reconsidered history through the evolving sense of self.

In the Middle Ages, as the various Roman Catholic orders (Benedictine, Franciscan, Dominican, Jesuit, etc.) reconsidered the theological history of Augustine and Aquinas, the long shadow of Platonism influenced the duality of faith and reason. This process was accelerated through the efforts of Petrarch (1304–1374), who reacquainted Western Europe with classical Greek and Latin culture and is now regarded as one of the earliest representatives of Renaissance humanism. As interest in Plato and Aristotle increased, so did knowledge of Claudius Ptolemy's "science," which placed the Earth in the center of the universe. Petrarch's successful promotion of Neo-Platonist ideas culminated in the challenge by Nicolas Copernicus (1473–1543) to the authority of the Church with an appeal to reasoned logic.

The "scientific revolution" emerged from the European realization that Copernicus's novel idea, in the words of Owen Barfield, "might not be a hypothesis at all but the ultimate truth."[3] The Roman Catholic claim of absolute truth was now held to the standard of nature as measured by the empirical methods of Copernican scientific investigation. The implications of this represented a true revolution in Western thought. Reason no longer needed dogmatic faith. Evidence of religious abuse of authority supported the challenge by Wyclif. Evidence of the Church's flawed science undermined its dogmatic legitimacy. Both challenges supported the Reformation led by Martin Luther (1483–1546).

Copernicus and Luther complemented each other's rejection of Roman authority. Copernicus's use of intellection and empirical evidence explained phenomena in terms that the average citizen could understand. Individuals no longer looked to religious institutions for answers to cosmic questions. Relying on their own ability to consider evidence, individuals could draw their own conclusions. While the Roman Catholic Church continued to assert the cooperative link between faith and reason, faith's fragile place for non–Roman Catholics collapsed with the Enlightenment. The period between the fifteenth and eighteenth centuries became the womb from which the modern sense of self was born.

A closer look at this 300-year transition reveals another duality that replaced the competition between faith and reason: the rationalism of Descartes, Spinoza, and Leibniz versus the empiricism of Bacon, Locke, and Hume. In other words, the competition became one between two forms of reasoning. Intellectual reflection and empirical evidence competed in their interpretation of temporal reality. But like the proverbial glass of water that can be seen as half-empty or half-full, the same evidence in the hands of different people does not necessarily yield the same understanding. Thus, two people considering the same glass will interpret the evidence in mutually exclusive ways. If one person insists that the other interpret the facts only in his or her way, the resulting disagreement will become impossible to bridge. Wars have started because of adherence to different paradigms. Every paradigm weighs evidence in completely different ways. One's conclusions flow from the paradigm that governs one's perspective.

What is particularly interesting about the duality of rationalism and empiricism is their mutual reliance on the individual. When René Descartes (1596–1650) discovered his cognitive ability ("I think, therefore I am"), the material evidence of reality had to be ignored. There is no place for an "extension" that exists beyond thought.* On the other hand, when David Hume (1711–1776) condemned all propositions beyond provable empirical evidence, he left no place for intuition and consciousness. Only those things that could be measured and quantified by empirical evidence would be recognized in this universal model. Yet, all people are familiar with intuition, consciousness, and material evidence. The competition of dualities does not support harmonious cooperation. The ancient Greek quest for cosmic harmony did not find fulfillment in the struggle between rationalism and empiricism. Transcendent harmony could no longer become a guiding principle for the emerging paradigm of self.

Once man was firmly placed at the center of the universe, philosophers were obligated to explain the universe without the historical crutch of divine authority. "Practically all philosophy since [Descartes'] day," Barfield observes, "has worked outwards from the thinking self rather than inwards from the cosmos to the soul."[4] Gilson's observation that Descartes' famous deduction was first articulated by Augustine in

---

*René Descartes, "Meditation Two: Concerning the Nature of the Human Mind: That It Is Better Known than the Body," in Roger Ariew and Eric Watkins, eds., *Modern Philosophy: An Anthology of Primary Sources* (Indianapolis, IN: Hackett Publishing, 1998), pp. 30–34. Here Descartes measures the "existence" of wax before and after melting, and concludes that "I now know that even bodies are not, properly speaking, perceived by the senses or by the faculty of imagination, but by the intellect alone, and that they are not perceived through their being touched or seen, but only through their being understood" (p. 34).

Book II, Chapter I of his *Soliloquies* is a footnote skipped over by many modern philosophers, who are bent on shedding any ties to faith-inspired understandings of reality.[5] It is valuable to note that Descartes, Spinoza (1632–1677), and Leibniz (1646–1716) all believed in God. Their collective failure lay in attempting to prove the existence of God through reason alone.

Like Plato, Descartes embraced intellection as the highest capacity of humanity, employing mathematics to prove the existence of the divine. Gilson refers to Descartes' "Pentecost of mathematical reasoning,"* summarizing Descartes' hubris as follows:

> The universal restoration of human knowledge was bound, out of its own nature, to be the work of a single man. He himself was that man, for he was the only one to know the true method, the only one therefore who owned the key to a rational explanation of reality.[6]

Although Descartes, Spinoza, and Leibniz all believed in God, there was no harmony between their deities. Each thought the others wrong in their rational proof. Ernst Cassirer contrasts their respective ideas as follows:

> Leibniz's metaphysics differs from that of Descartes and Spinoza in that it substitutes for Descartes' dualism and Spinoza's monism a "pluralistic universe."[7]

---

*Étienne Gilson, *The Unity of Philosophical Experience* (San Francisco: Ignatius Press, 1964), p. 109. Cf. Ernst Cassirer, *The Philosophy of the Enlightenment*, trans. Fritz Koelln and James P. Pettegrove (Princeton, NJ: Princeton University Press, 1951), p. 15, where he refers to mathematics as the "pride of human reason."

Each philosopher employed a different rational strategy, but ultimately their faith in God crashed against the intellectual limits of empirical evidence.

Science and Skepticism

Francis Bacon (1561–1626) distinguished "God's works" from "natural philosophy," separating science from theology in a way that would later be repeated by nineteenth-century intellectuals such as Charles Darwin and Ralph Waldo Emerson.[8] Bacon popularized scientific inquiry, which had previously been relegated to the secret mysteries of the occult, alchemy, and Hermeticism.

If Bacon attempted to find cooperation between religion and science, John Locke (1632–1704) challenged the authority of all institutions, religious and civil. Locke believed that reason could discern truth and determine the legitimate exercise of authority. In his "Essay Concerning Human Understanding," he attempted to identify the "horizon" and "boundary…between what is and what is not comprehensible by us."[9] That effort, however, begins and ends with man as the measure of all things. The idea of an immaterial soul does not influence human comprehension of the divine. According to Locke, the natural rights of life, liberty, health, and property provide sufficient evidence of God.[*]

The progression from Bacon through Locke provided the foundation for the skepticism of David Hume, who believed only in the empirical evidence of personal experience. In his "Enquiry Concerning Human Understanding," he wrote:

---

[*]Note, in particular, Locke's indifference to an *immaterial* soul (*immaterial* implying empirical evidence), which contrasts with his silence regarding an *immortal* soul (*immortal* implying divine).

If we take in hand any volume of divinity or school metaphysics, for instance; let us ask, Does it contain any abstract reasoning concerning quantity? No. Does it contain any experimental reasoning concerning matter of fact and existence? No. Commit it then to the flames: for it can contain nothing but sophistry and illusion.[10]

Hume's skepticism was unflinching. Ernst Cassirer summarizes Hume's rejection of religion as follows:

Appetites and passions are not only the source of the first religious ideas and dogmas; they are still the root of all religion. Religious conceptions are not shaped and fostered by thinking and by the moral will. It is the emotions of hope and fear which have led men to adopt beliefs and which support their continuance in faith. Here we have the real foundation of religion.[11]

Bacon, Locke, and Hume each represented a different tangent in understanding reality. They were united only through their common Platonic faith in reason. Even when they personally subscribed to a belief in God, their efforts to prove the unprovable only resulted in justifiable skepticism. Philosophy failed to provide any harmonious strategy to transcend temporal reality. The duality of faith and reason also failed to produce harmony within the religious domain of the Roman Catholic Church. As Gilson explains:

A Franciscan could either stick to the old doctrine of St. Bonaventura, or he could decide in favour of Duns Scotus, unless he found it more advisable to enlist

among the followers of Ockham. Were our man a Dominican he could find at the very least three theologies at
his disposal. There were Albertus Magnus and Thomas
Aquinas; and people were beginning to talk about a German preacher by the name of Meister Eckhart. There is
never too much of a good thing, but there were too many
varieties of the same thing, and the difficulty was that
since Ockham was refuting Duns Scotus, the while Duns
Scotus himself was correcting Bonaventura, or Thomas
Aquinas straightening out Albertus Magnus, they could
not all be right at the same time. But who was right? By
far the easiest way to solve the problem was to decide
that every one was wrong.[12]

Modern Western academics endlessly regurgitate the philosophical
ideas of dead white male Europeans, with no intention of seeking the
wisdom of absolute truth. Philosophers who offer competing claims of
divine truth collectively undermine all claims of divine revelation. But
the proposition that all ideas are relative abandons the quest for absolute truth. Faith and reason cannot harmonize the dissonant chords of
philosophy and theology, and clearly there is no harmony in skepticism.
Who could the average European trust for answers to the unknowable?
Science.

Descartes' mathematical epiphany led to his invention of Analytic
Geometry, the rational explanation of "geometric extension" beyond
the mind.[13] Descartes' "science," however, was short-lived. Gilson
observes:

As soon as Newton published his *Mathematical Principles of Natural Philosophy*, in 1687, it immediately

became apparent that Descartes' physics was a thing of the past. Aristotle's physics had lasted twenty centuries, Descartes' lasted about thirty years in England.[14]

Aristotle's understanding of cosmic movement, as popularized by Claudius Ptolemy, collapsed under the scrutiny of Copernicus in the fifteenth century. Euclidean geometry, named after Euclid of Alexandria (ca. 325–265 B.C.) during the reign of Ptolemy I (323–283 B.C.), provided the mathematical foundation for Newton's great scientific achievement.

The Cosmic Harmony of Isaac Newton

Sir Isaac Newton (1642–1727) was an English physicist and natural philosopher, a friend of John Locke, and a rival of Leibniz.[15] His three laws of motion sought to explain the mechanics of the cosmos, and there were three essential assumptions that supported his physics: (1) that absolute space was always at rest and unchangeable; (2) that all movement existed within a separate and distinct dimension of absolute time; and (3) that the force of gravity could be precisely calculated when the distance between the mass of two objects of material particles was known.

God was the necessary "first cause" from which the perfect creation was self-sustaining. The image of a mechanical clock provided any non-scientist with a sense of both the harmony and complexity of the universe. The Newtonian formula was relatively simple for the average European to understand, and Euclidean geometry was, in Albert Levi's words, "universally assumed to be the science of existent space."* Newton explained motion with a level of accuracy that satisfied all but

---

*Albert William Levi, *Philosophy and the Modern World* (Bloomington: Indiana University Press, 1959), p. 334. This was true until the advent of non-Euclidean geometry in the nineteenth century.

the most inquiring physicists. Today's high school students learn Euclidean theorems that are two thousand years old! In fact, Einstein's famous theories, which are based on non-Euclidean geometry, acknowledge that, as Paul Schilpp put it, "Euclidean geometry is in fact the only one which corresponds to our powers of perception."[16] For example, we naturally agree that a train moves toward a station. According to non-Euclidean geometry, the station also moves toward the train!*

Newton's substitution of Euclidean geometry for Claudius Ptolemy's discredited cosmology is not considered by historian and philosopher Ernst Cassirer to be as revolutionary as the discoveries of Copernicus. As Cassirer explains, "Newton's method is not that of pure deduction, but that of analysis…. His phenomena are the data of experience; his principles are the goal of his investigation."[17] When the seventeenth-century theories of knowledge, especially those of Descartes and Leibniz, are compared to Newton's eighteenth-century approach, there is no radical transformation. Instead, there is a shifting of emphasis, in Cassirer's words, "from the general to the particular, from principles to phenomena."[18] The use of "mathematical empiricism…stands on the threshold of skeptical empiricism," according to Cassirer, "and the step from Newton to Hume is henceforth inevitable."[19]

Newtonian physics provided the element that was missing in the paradigm of the self. Humanity naturally perceives temporal reality through the Euclidean lens. Newton's "science" accounted for a divine cosmic initiator, but did not require any providential involvement thereafter. According to physicist and author Brian Greene (1963–), "If you know where every particle is and how fast and in what direction each is moving—then, Newton and Einstein agree, you can, in principle, use the laws of physics to predict everything about the universe."[20] On the one

---

*The *relative* character of non-Euclidean geometry actually supports the perception that the train is stationary and the station moves toward *it!* Einstein's theories will be discussed in detail in Chapter 8.

hand, Newtonian physics could credit God as the source of all creation. On the other hand, religion could be dismissed as Hume's emotions of hope and fear—or as the Sophists argued two thousand years before, as merely a clever invention of politicians. Either way, man would finally be the measure of all things.

The ancient Greek paradigm was enforced through *areté* and *aidos*, and the early Christian paradigm was enforced through the cooperative efforts of faith, reason, and humility. In each case, individuals willingly subordinated self-interest to their duty to a communally accepted higher authority. With man as the measure of all things, and science providing predictable evidence, individuals had only one duty, their exercise of reason to its fullest potential. The ancient Greek stature of reason no longer required the weak sister of faith.

The mechanical universe of Newtonian physics provided rational certainty in predicting future events. Human observers actually believed they could objectively describe the mechanics of nature, and this became the goal of science. One excellent example of this triumph of reason is found in the French mathematician Pierre Simon Laplace (1749–1827), whose five-volume *Mécanique Céleste* explained, according to philosopher physicist Fritjof Capra (1939–), "the motions of the planets, moons, and comets down to the smallest details, as well as the flow of the tides and other phenomena related to gravity."[21] Capra's description of the conversation between Laplace and Napoleon clearly illustrates the diminished regard of faith:

> When Laplace presented the first edition of his work
> to Napoleon—so the story goes—Napoleon remarked,
> "Monsieur Laplace, they tell me you have written this
> large book on the system of the universe, and have

never even mentioned its Creator." To this Laplace replied bluntly, "I had no need for that hypothesis."[22]

The Cosmic Harmony of Ralph Waldo Emerson

The arrogance of Laplace was balanced by the humility of Ralph Waldo Emerson (1803–1882), who absorbed the writings of the great thinkers who preceded him. Although he became a Calvinist minister, like his father, Emerson grew restless with the authority of organized religion. Shortly after his first wife, Ellen, died of tuberculosis in 1831, he asked to be relieved of the responsibility of celebrating the Eucharist, which he considered an example of "worship in the dead forms of our forefathers."[23] By June 1835, Emerson was ready to move ahead with the new spiritual religion of the age, "First Philosophy."

"I will be a naturalist," said Emerson, which his biographer, Joel Myerson, describes as follows:

> A person who…believed that spiritual truth derived from nature, not from miraculous or supernatural revelations, and that everything from the order of the universe to the evolution of personal and cultural ethics could be discovered through the close study of nature…. Intuition enabled the observer to see through the remoteness or ambiguity of words and things to the unifying source of all in the universe: thought.[24]

Emerson introduced the world to his First Philosophy in September 1836 in his essay "Nature," which begins with two powerful questions:

> Why should not we…enjoy an original relation to the
> universe? Why should not we have a poetry and philoso-
> phy of insight and not of tradition, and a religion by rev-
> elation to us, and not the history of [our forefathers]?[25]

Not satisfied with traditional religious institutions, Emerson called
for a personal, existential relationship with the divine, which he found
in nature:

> Man is conscious of a universal soul within or behind his
> individual life, wherein, as in a firmament, the natures
> of Justice, Truth, Love, Freedom, arise and shine. This
> universal soul, he calls Reason.[26]

Man's intellectual will mediates nature, Emerson argued, and cooperates with nature's spirit for freedom. In this process, man becomes
creator. As Emerson wrote:

> Spirit creates, that behind nature, throughout nature,
> spirit is present; one and not compound, it does not act
> on us from without, that is, in space and time, but spiri-
> tually, or through ourselves: therefore, that spirit…, the
> Supreme Being, does not build up nature around us, but
> puts it forth through us…. Man has access to the entire
> mind of the Creator, is himself the creator of the finite.[27]

Emerson recognized the supremacy of man's spirit, which unites
with nature through reason. In a speech at Harvard University, commonly referred to as "The American Scholar," he spoke of the transcendent unity as follows:

> The human mind cannot be enshrined in a person, who shall set a barrier on any one side to this unbounded, unboundable empire…. It is one light which beams out of a thousand stars. It is one soul which animates all men.[28]

Emerson looked into his soul and saw the divine unity, which humbled him. In his "Divinity School Address," he spoke of humility:

> A man in the view of absolute goodness adores, with total humility. Every step so downward, is a step upward. The man who renounces himself, comes to himself…. This [religious] sentiment is divine and deifying. It is the beatitude of man…. Through it, the soul first knows itself. It corrects the capital mistake of the infant man, who seeks to be great by following the great, and hopes to derive advantages from another—by showing the fountain of all good to be in himself, and that he, equally with every man, is an inlet into the deeps of Reason.[29]

Emerson's philosophy blends all three paradigms. Both the ancient Greek paradigm and Emerson's philosophy seek to "know thyself." Plato looked inside his soul and located the transcendent divine outside himself in heaven. Aristotle looked inside his soul to find the Doctrine of the Mean. Emerson looked inside his soul to find knowledge of the transcendent divine, which he located in an unbounded sense of self.

While Plato had an appreciation for humility, Aristotle was more consistent with the Greek tradition that considered humility a flaw. Either way, the ancient Greek paradigm was enforced by the sense of duty imposed by *areté* and *aidos*, which the *polis* willingly accepted. The early Christian paradigm was enforced through the willing cooperation of faith, reason, and humility. Emerson placed duty to self as the primary responsibility of citizenship. Once individuals accept their duty, humility becomes the standard for right conduct.

With the triumph of reason over philosophy and religion, Emerson would be remembered for his appeal to self-reliance, not humility. Emerson believed that immortality could be found in union with nature, but followers of Hume's skepticism were under no obligation to share that vision. Friedrich Nietzsche (1844–1900) had great respect for Emerson, but became disillusioned with life, and in despair concluded that God was dead. He lost all sanity and died alone. Evidence of Emerson's transcendent divine was not compelling to skeptics.

Freedom and the Enlightened Self

Plato had called God the geometer.[30] Euclid and Newton provided the mathematical evidence. Immanuel Kant (1724–1804) sought to unite science and philosophy. His embrace of mathematics, however, moved him closer to physics than to philosophy.[31] Recall the Jaeger quote from Chapter 2:

> [Plato] explains that there are two sources for man's belief in the existence of the gods: knowledge of the orbits, eternally the same, in which the heavenly bodies move; and the "eternal stream of being" in us, the soul. No human philosophy has ever gone beyond this—from Aristotle, who took these two motives for the belief in God into his own theology, to Kant's *Critique of Practical Reason*, which after all his revolutionary theoretical arguments ends in practice with the same two thoughts.[32]

In other words, Kant's belief in the divine was no different from the "evidence" used by Aristotle—namely, astronomy and the eternal stream of being of the human soul. Kant referred to two realms of Spirit: Phenomena (Things of Experience) and Noumena (Things in Themselves), between which there was no bridge. The dilemma between unity and multiplicity, described earlier in Chapter 3, was rationally proved by Kant's metaphysical conclusions: that is, that metaphysics are impossible to prove. For this reason, Kant is sometimes referred to as the "last philosopher."

Emerson's world-view developed after Kant and before Nietzsche. His poetry inspired the Romantic movement, but offered no further contribution to the paradigm of self. Cassirer's correct observation about the change in emphasis from the seventeenth to the eighteenth centuries can be applied throughout the previous three thousand years. As reason influenced the development of each paradigm, the emphasis moved from the general to the particular. The ancient Greek belief in a transcendent cosmic unity gave way to a particular early Christian paradigm of personal responsibility. With the introduction of nationalism and culture, an intellectual environment of skepticism elevated human reason. One could believe in the transcendent reason of Emerson or the purely skeptical reason of Hume. By the Enlightenment, all three paradigms were fully developed. Emerson's attempt to blend the paradigms has been repeated by philosophers and spiritualists right up to the present day. One example can be found in Robert Hartman's introduction to his translation of Hegel's *Reason in History*:

> For Kant it is not God but Nature that has designs for men in history. Her cunning uses small passions within us. By them she goads us on to find a mode of living together peacefully in society. Society is the gradual result

of the antagonism between our individual and our social inclinations. Thus freedom in society is for Kant a product of Nature and history, "progress in the consciousness of freedom." This is precisely Hegel's formulation.... In Kant's definition, "progress" and "consciousness" have a more pedestrian meaning. When Hegel took over, the spirit of history began to blow through philosophy.[33]

Which brings us back to the question of freedom. Through each chapter, governing paradigms were introduced that defined guiding principles and right conduct and employed enforcement mechanisms. As time moved forward, the respective enforcement mechanisms were weakened by the internal struggle between self-interest and self-sacrifice. The ancient Greek paradigm's understanding of a transcendent law included concepts of fate and destiny that influenced a person's status in life. With Socrates and Plato, the internal struggle elevated reason above appetites and incisive impulses and strove for self-control. The early Christian paradigm sought to emulate divine love and thereby subordinate appetites, incisive impulses, *and* reason through humility.

In the paradigm of self, freedom is transformed into an external struggle from the obligations of others without a transcending sense of duty. Although the words *reason* and *freedom* are employed by all three paradigms, each interprets the words completely differently. Plato and Aristotle understood reason to share a common essence with the divine realm. Plato's ascent of the soul might sound similar to the early Christian paradigm, but we have shown the clear distinctions between Platonism and early Christianity. Aristotle's Doctrine of the Mean supported the cooperation of faith and reason in the Holy Roman Empire and in the paradigm of self's attempt to find a reasonable middle position between Nietzsche and Emerson.

Freedom within the ancient Greek paradigm is impossible to understand without the willing subordination of self-interest to the transcendent law and its implied determinism, enforced by the disciplines of *areté* and *aidos*. Freedom within the early Christian paradigm retains the notion of transcendence, but discards determinism, replacing it with free will. Furthermore, freedom within the early Christian paradigm is also completely contrary to the understanding of freedom within the paradigm of self, according to which free individuals do whatever they want in the moment. In the early Christian paradigm, on the other hand, such individuals enjoy the moment at the expense of eternal salvation. In other words, the exercise of volition separates the two paradigms. Individuals who exercise personal will without regard to divine will are either winners or losers purely on the basis of which paradigm defines their decisions.

But if reality is truly relative to individual paradigmatic beliefs, is there such a concept as absolute truth? The next chapter will investigate this question.

❖ ❖ ❖

Chapter 8

Quantum Mechanics and Absolute Truth

How We Know What We Know

In Chapter 2, we reviewed the three characteristics of the ancient Greek cosmos (an invisible unbounded; visible stuff; and an idea of equilibrium), and we explored the challenge of ancient Greek thinkers to identify the bridge between the unexplainable unbounded and the material world. The *nous* ("mind") would play an important role in this effort for the ancient Greek and early Christian paradigms. Modern science employs empirical evidence and intellectual reflection, neither of which recognizes the *nous* as relevant to scientific inquiry.

The quest for absolute truth requires a common understanding of *how* we know *what* we know. An example will take us through the three modes of knowledge. A plank of wood can be cut in half, and in half again, and again, and again. The material particles that are easily recognized by most of humanity can be empirically measured. After a particular division, the empirical evidence leaves the realm visible to the naked eye and continues its "existence" in an invisible realm. With scientific equipment, we can continue to verify the empirical "existence" of the now "invisible" mass of material particles.

According to Euclidean geometry, as it was used by Sir Isaac Newton, this division of the original plank of wood can continue *indefinitely*, for the concept of infinity is fundamental to Euclidean geometry. Even with the most sophisticated scientific equipment, the empirical evidence for the ever-decreasing particle mass will eventually become "invisible" to detection. When material evidence becomes undetectable, an empirical skeptic like Hume can justifiably dismiss its existence. At this point, our intellectual capacity can continue the division through the abstract framework of mathematics. The rationalism of Descartes would dismiss the evidence of "extension" and its "modes,"* continuing the "division" indefinitely. Both the empirical realm of extension and the abstract reasoning of intellect are self-evident.

In 1918, the Nobel Prize was awarded to Max Planck (1858–1946) for his discovery of the smallest extension, the *Planck length* (1.616 x 10⁻³³ centimeters). Using today's technology, according to physicist Brian Greene, the Planck length is "some 17 orders of magnitude smaller than what we can currently access," and "we would need an accelerator the size of the galaxy" to see one.[1] Clearly, our acceptance of the Planck length cannot be verified by empirical evidence. Within a Euclidean world-view supported by abstract mathematics, there is no *reason* to accept a minimum length. The math can iterate infinitely. If our only modes of knowing were limited to either intellectual reflection or sensory perception of empirical evidence, neither would compel acceptance of the Planck length. So what is the third method of knowing?

The Realm of Mystery

Étienne Gilson credits William of Ockham (ca. 1288–1348) with distinguishing abstract knowledge from intuition. Using Ockham's logic, Gilson states, "intuition alone enables us to perceive the existence or non-existence of things."[2] This, however, sounds remarkably similar to Hebrews 11:1: "Faith is the substance of things hoped for, the

---

*Descartes stated: "I believe that body, figure, extension, motion, and place are merely fictions of the mind. What is there, then, that can be esteemed true? Perhaps this only, that there is absolutely nothing certain" ("Meditations II," in Roger Ariew and Eric Watkins, eds., *Modern Philosophy: An Anthology of Primary Sources* [Indianapolis, IN: Hackett Publishing, 1998], p. 30).

evidence of things not seen." Owen Barfield, empathizing with the "ago-nizing struggle" of Middle Age philosophers "to state the exact relation between spirit and matter," identifies words that reflect this struggle: "*essence, existence, intellect, intelligence, intention, intuition, motive, potential, transcend; abstract* and *concrete, matter* and *form, objective* and *subjective…, real* and *ideal, general, special* and *species, particu-lar, individual,* and *universal.*"[3]

The first instance of these words, according to Barfield, can be found in Latin translations of Greek terms, which led to his conclusion, mentioned earlier, that the internal and external meaning of words in Greek were separated in their Latin translations. For example, *intuition* in Latin (*intuitio*), as used by Plotinus, referred to contemplation as an act of thinking only, whereas in Greek the word connoted both thought and action (that is, both *theoria* and *praxis*). The difference can be seen in thinking about fire, as opposed to building a fire. The experience (*praxis*), as opposed to the concept (*theoria*), of intuition is understood by almost everyone in the twenty-first century. Have you ever *known* that someone was watching you without any evidence beyond intuition? If you are like most people, the obvious answer is yes. We recognize this mode of knowing, but it resists detection through empirical evidence and intellectual reflection. I call this the realm of mystery, in which I in-clude all experiences of intuition, divine revelation, faith, or simply that "gut feeling" that most of us are familiar with. In Chapter 6, the "data of Revelation" introduced by St. Bonaventure can best be understood through the experienced reality of mystery.

Acceptance of the realm of mystery leads to acceptance of unprovably mysterious conclusions. Accepting the Planck length as a minimum can only be "proved" through the realm of mystery. To both rationalists and empiricists, the realm of mystery is rejected out of hand, but quantum mechanics and non-Euclidean geometry can only be accepted through this realm of mystery. Science may prefer the term *probability*, but anything less than certainty belongs to the realm of mystery. The balance of this book will therefore refer to non-Euclidean geometry as "supra-Euclidean" to represent the fuller understanding of life that is experienced through all three realms of knowing.

Accepting the reality of the realm of mystery does not diminish the evidence of empiricism or the logic of rationalism. Legendary physicist Richard Feynman (1918–1988) demonstrated the precision of probability as follows:

> If you were to measure the distance from Los Angeles to New York to this accuracy, it would be exact to the thickness of a human hair. That's how delicately quantum electrodynamics has, in the past fifty years, been checked—both theoretically and experimentally.[4]

With such a demonstrable degree of accuracy, one could easily cross the line from the realm of mystery to the certainty of Euclid, but in so doing one would confuse or ignore the fundamental differences that distinguish perception from reality.

In the previous chapter, we followed reason's conquest of faith. But if reason is limited to intellectual reflection and sensory perception of empirical evidence, and if the realm of mystery is an essential part of temporal reality, there must be fundamental inaccuracies in Newton's physics. Newton's laws were on display for all to evaluate, and their ability to accurately predict movement that humanity naturally considers through Euclidean perception defined "classical physics" for two hundred years. But Newton's laws did not accurately predict *all* movement with certainty. Something was missing.

The Science of Mystery

In 1821, the discovery by Michael Faraday (1791–1867) of electrical and magnetic "force fields" was the first significant step beyond Newtonian physics. According to Albert Levi (1911–1988), a professor of philosophy at Washington University in St. Louis, "field theory provides the first assault upon a Newtonian doctrine of the independent existence of material particles."[5] Faraday's discovery was followed by the discovery of electromagnetic equations by James Clerk Maxwell (1831–1879). Albert Einstein (1879–1955), widely considered the greatest physicist of all time, credited Maxwell's equations with being the inspiration for his own theory of Special Relativity; Richard Feynman regarded Maxwell's equations as the most significant discovery of the nineteenth century; and Max Planck observed that Maxwell "achieved greatness unequalled."[6]

Maxwell can properly be credited with the second revolution in modern Western thought, as profound as the first revolution, inspired by Copernicus. Maxwell's electrodynamic theories proved that light was not Newtonian particles, but, in the words of Fritjof Capra, "a rapidly alternating electromagnetic field traveling through space in the form of waves."[7] Capra speculates that Maxwell "must have realized *intuitively*, even if he did not say so explicitly, that the fundamental entities in his theory were the fields and not the mechanical models."[8] I have added the italics to this statement to highlight Capra's implicit understanding of the realm of mystery.

The development of supra-Euclidean geometry by Russian mathematician Nikolai Lobachevsky (1792–1856) and others redefined scientific reality, providing the foundation for Einstein's famous theories of General and Special Relativity, which author and academic David Bodanis (1939–) summarizes as follows: "The speed of light becomes the fundamental speed limit in our universe: nothing can go faster."[9]

Bodanis uses a colorful illustration to demonstrate the implications of this:

> To catch up with a streak of light and see it standing still would be like saying, "I want to see the blurred arcs of a thrilling juggling act, but only if the balls are not moving." You can't do it. The only way you'll see a blur from the juggling balls is if they're moving fast. Einstein concluded that light can exist only when a light is actively moving forward.[10]

In today's "politically correct" world, respected scientists do not want to criticize classical physics. For example, Brian Greene writes:

> It would be naïve to say that Newton's theory was wrong.... Einstein invoked a whole new conceptual schema, one that radically altered our understanding of space and time. But the power of Newton's discovery within the domain he intended it for (planetary motion, commonplace terrestrial motion, and so on) is unassailable.[11]

In the chaotic environment of the 1960s, the fearless scientist Thomas Kuhn (1922–1996) wrote, "Einstein's theory can be accepted only with the recognition that Newton's was wrong."[12] Beyond political correctness and in pursuit of absolute truth, can Newton and Einstein coexist? The answer depends on which view constitutes reality.

Within Newtonian physics, absolute space and absolute time are completely separate and distinct. Brian Greene provides an example of the implications:

> If the sun were suddenly to explode, the earth—some 93 million miles away—would instantaneously suffer a departure from its usual elliptical orbit. Even though it would take light from the explosion eight minutes to travel from the sun to the earth, in Newton's theory knowledge that the sun had exploded would be instantaneously transmitted to the earth through the sudden change in the gravitational force governing its motion.[13]

But Einstein's theories determined that nothing moves faster than light. Proposing a new framework for considering space, time, and gravity, Einstein recognized that space can never be considered independently of time, and that time can never be considered independently of space. Thus, he proposed the concept of *space-time* and attributed movement to gravitational fields. Greene writes:

> Even though Newtonian physics seemed to capture mathematically much of what we experience physically, the reality it describes turns out not to be the reality of our world. Ours is a relativistic reality…. But utility and reality are very different standards. As we will see, features of space and time that for many of us are second nature have turned out to be figments of a false Newtonian perspective.[14]

This was not the first time that the cooperation between three concepts was challenged by the competition of separate and distinct concepts. Newtonian physics posited that space and time were separate and distinct: a duality. Einstein saw a cooperative relationship in space-time. Seventeen hundred years earlier, Arius of Alexandria (ca. 250–335 A.D.) challenged Athanasius of Alexandria (ca. 298–373 A.D.) at the First Ecumenical Council of Nicaea by rejecting the Trinitarian understanding of One as Three and Three as One, since he believed that the modes of Father and Son are as separate and distinct as Newton believed space and time to be. The conclusions of both Arius and Newton make rational sense, but ultimately their understanding of "separate and distinct" represents an inadequate understanding of cooperative supra-Euclidean reality.

Athanasius's views were accepted and adopted by the First Ecumenical Council, but Arius's were not. Einstein's theories are recognized as superior to Newton's. Just because people are inclined toward Arius's or Newton's incomplete views of reality does not mean that perception *is* reality. The science of quantum dynamics and the early Christian paradigm share a common understanding of absolute truth. Like the Trinity of Un-Begotten Father, Only-Begotten Son, and Proceeding Holy Spirit, space, time, and gravity are not additive, nor is one mode superior to the others.

In Chapter 4, we saw that the three modes of an electron (mass, charge, and spin) demonstrate the commonality between early Christian theology and quantum mechanics. Similarly, the three modes of the Trinity can seamlessly underlie the relationships of space, time, and gravity, as well as the alternating procession of electromagnetic impulses that we know as light. If there is such a thing as absolute truth, then scientific inquiry and at least one of the many religious alternatives should point in the same direction.

Another example of supra-Euclidean cooperation and the early Christian paradigm can be seen in the Heisenberg Uncertainty Principle. Greene explains the implications of the famous principle:

> Unlike the framework of Newton or even of Einstein, in which the motion of a particle is described by giving its location and its velocity, quantum mechanics shows that at a microscopic level *you cannot possibly know both of these features with total precision.*[15]

In other words, at the quantum level of reality, nothing is certain! If you know with certainty the location of a particle, it is impossible to know its velocity. If you know its velocity, it is impossible to know its location.

There is *no* amount of additional information that will remove the uncertainty identified by Werner Heisenberg (1901–1976). The boundary between the knowable and the unknowable can be accurately recognized by quantum mechanics. Only in the realm of mystery can the concept of knowledge beyond intellect be accepted. If one rejects the realm of mystery, Heisenberg and quantum reality become unprovable theories easily dismissed by rigid empiricists and rationalists.

Reality in Relativity

For those unfamiliar with quantum reality, the idea that what we perceive to be real is actually incomplete seems obviously false. Capra explains it this way:

> In everyday life, the impression that we can arrange the events around us in a unique time sequence is created

by the fact that the velocity of light—186,000 miles per second—is so high, compared to any other velocity we experience, that we can assume we are observing events at the instant they are occurring. This, however, is incorrect.[16]

Our relative perception of both space and time is unique. Everyone's perception of reality is relative!

When two automobiles crash, each driver presents his or her relative version of what happened. If there were two other observers of the accident kitty-corner from each other, the police would also document their relative perceptions of what happened. However, each of the four individuals would have a different understanding of the events, since each understanding would be relative to the person's place in space and speed in time. Thus, no observer can "objectively" summarize what actually happened. Greene explains:

> Identical wristwatches worn by two individuals in relative motion will tick at *different rates* and hence will not agree on the amount of time that elapses between chosen events. Special relativity demonstrates that this statement does not slander the accuracy of the wristwatches involved; rather, it is a true statement about time itself. Similarly, observers in relative motion carrying identical tape measures will not agree on the lengths of distances measured.[17]

The uncertainty principle represents a significant challenge to our Euclidean perception of evidence. But its implications are more significant than simply eliminating the concept of certainty from our understanding of absolute truth. Heisenberg recognized that the very act of *observing* events influences outcomes. The idea that one can objectively consider anything is false. Physicist John A. Wheeler (1911–2008) comments on this truth:

> Nothing is more important about the quantum principle than this, that it destroys the concept of the world as "sitting out there," with the observer safely separated from it by…a plate of glass. Even to observe so miniscule an object as an electron, he must shatter the glass. He must reach in…. To describe what has happened, one has to cross out that old word "observer" and put in its place the new word "participator." In some strange sense the universe is a participatory universe.[18]

So-called objectivity separates *theoria* from *praxis*, but in quantum reality they are one. In other words, quantum mechanics in effect recombines *theoria* and *praxis*!

Einstein spent the last thirty years of his life in search of the Unifying Theory that would unite the findings of General Relativity with those of Special Relativity. General Relativity explains cosmic motion in terms of space-time and gravitational fields that produce predictable results with apparent certainty. Special Relativity, at best, offers the probability of movement at the quantum level. But are these two theories really so far apart? At the quantum level, all variables have been controlled, and still the act of observing alters what is seen. At the cosmic level, it is not only impossible to account for all variables, but the act of observing continues to alter what is seen. Capra and Greene assert that we do not notice the uncertainty principle of the quantum level in our daily lives. Perhaps that explains why each of us *sees* reality in *relative* Euclidean terms. What we actually *see* are our own relative interpretations of the options embodied in Heisenberg's uncertainty principle!

Euclidean Competition Versus Supra-Euclidean Cooperation

Empirical evidence, intellectual reflection, and Heisenberg's principle of uncertainty demonstrate their respective limits when modern physicists discuss gravity, about which Richard Feynman observed:

> The theory of gravitation…was not understandable from the laws of motion, and even today it stands isolated from the other theories. Gravitation is, so far, not understandable in terms of other phenomena.[19]

Gravity is described as a "feeble force" by Brian Greene,[20] yet the modern scientific theory of the Big Bang depends on gravity exerting a repulsive force of such magnitude that it "explains" the initial moments of our universe and underlies the theory of "inflationary cosmology." We know that gravity exists, yet there is no tangible evidence of gravitons. We recognize gravity as a feeble force, yet inflationary cosmology theories require repulsive gravity to create the universe we know today. Clearly, our understanding of gravity is speculative at best.

Euclidean perception seeks a "graviton" particle to account for gravitational fields. Levi observed, "In the absence of gravitational forces, space-time may be considered as Euclidean."[21] In other words, examining space-time as if gravity did not exist yields precise Euclidean measurements. However, gravity *cannot* be separated out from space-time, and so those measurements are an illusion. On the other hand, supra-Euclidean cooperation between the three ways of knowing (intellectual reflection, sensory perception of empirical evidence, and intuition of the realm of mystery) accepts the mystery of gravity. If the realm of mystery is inaccessible by either empirical evidence or intellectual reflection, what is science to do? Brian Greene looks to Nobel Prize winner Niels Bohr (1885–1962) for comfort:

> [As] one of the central pioneers of quantum theory and one of its strongest proponents, [Bohr] once remarked that if you do not get dizzy sometimes when you think about quantum mechanics, then you have not really understood it.[22]

The inability to explain the inexplicable is not unique to modern physicists. Recall St. John Cassian's acceptance of cooperation between divine grace and free will that so frustrated Prosper of Aquitaine at the beginning of the fifth century A.D.. Interestingly, St. John Damascene (676–749 A.D.) offered a similar observation after attempting to explain the unity of the Trinity:

> We shall both of us be stricken with madness for prying into the mystery of God…. The Son is begotten, the Holy Spirit *proceeds* from the Father. This is sufficient to distinguish them.[23]

The implications of quantum mechanics are difficult for most people to appreciate. I suspect that even most physicists have not applied these implications to their daily lives. If reality is defined by Euclidean geometry, then what we *perceive* to be real *is* absolute reality. In that case, infinity exists; classical physics is perfect; all that can be known can be determined with certainty through either empirical evidence or intellectual reflection; and, with enough information, rigid determinism will ensure accurate predictions.

But if reality is defined by supra-Euclidean cooperation, then what we perceive to be real is actually incomplete and relative. In that case, infinity does *not* exist; the relative physics of quantum mechanics provides, at best, probabilities of outcomes; knowledge can be acquired through empirical evidence, intellectual reflection, *and* the realm of mystery; there is no temporal cosmic certainty; free will trumps all inferences of determinism; and no amount of information can remove uncertainty.

Human volition represents a particularly interesting contrast. We have shown that if the Euclidean world is ultimately real, then an implied determinism is also real. If so, free will is a false concept, and beliefs that describe predestination and fate represent absolute truth. Therefore, if one has enough information, one will see that events unfold in a determined way. The information can come through genetic investigation, environmental evolution, or some other product of empirical evidence and intellectual reflection. In this scenario, missing evidence that accurately predicts genetic and evolutionary conclusions with certainty will be found with enough scientific investigation.

On the other hand, if the supra-Euclidean world is ultimately real, then the best we can do to predict events is to measure probabilities. In that case, free will exists as an absolute truth in choosing between alternatives. Foreknowledge of decisions that a person will make can be viewed as probabilities that lack the rigid implications of determinism. More specifically, predictions made through genetic investigation and environmental evolution will be undermined by the influence of the realm of mystery. Furthermore, in this scenario, there is no tangible missing evidence to prove the veracity of genetic engineering and evolution.

Brian Greene summarizes the scientific dilemma this way:

> According to quantum mechanics, the universe evolves according to a rigorous and precise mathematical formalism, but this framework determines only the probability that any particular future will happen—not which future actually ensues.[24]

There is tremendous difficulty in seeing the world exclusively through either a Euclidean or supra-Euclidean lens. The Euclidean perspective sees the glass of water as either half empty *or* half full, and the certainty of either conclusion can be empirically determined. The supra-Euclidean view requires cooperation to see the glass as simultaneously half empty *and* half full. We want the certainty promised by the Euclidean lens, but life is fundamentally uncertain. Recall from Chapter 5 how Maximus the Confessor distinguished the heart-centered *nous* from intellection. Intellect can analyze and judge evidence, but the *nous* experiences being before intellection can analyze it. The heart experiences life; the head explains what is experienced. In the scientific world of cause and effect, the heart always precedes intellection! Competition or cooperation between the heart and the head represent very difficult choices.

An example will demonstrate the difficulties that arise when the heart and the head compete. Graduating seniors take standardized tests for university admissions. If average test scores go up four percent from one year to the next, everyone understands what this means. But if I tell you that I love you four percent more this year than I did last year, what have I really said? Do I *want* you four percent more? Am I willing to sacrifice for you four percent more? What is four percent of love and sacrifice? Words are inadequate in matters of the heart. Intellect's ability to precisely communicate ideas can intimidate the inexpressible *feelings* of the heart.

Heartfelt feelings are not simply primal or instinctual, as they are typically categorized by a Euclidean lens. Rather, they are the actual experience of being, from which intellect analyzes and judges. If the Euclidean lens represents the only scientific understanding of feelings, then the illusion of duality represented by a glass of water as half empty or half full represents the spectrum of alternatives, the modern version of the poles of Aristotle's Doctrine of the Mean. But if the supra-Euclidean lens puts the heartfelt experience of life *before* intellection, then intellection can rationalize and justify any inclination that the heart experiences. Paradigms frame the heart's experience of life. That is why concepts like "reason" and "freedom" mean different things to different people.

It is clear that intellect communicates ideas much more powerfully than the heart can. Euclidean clarity can employ the "objective" standard of "rational persons," since our perception of objectivity and logical determinism is innate. Our Euclidean perspective gives a decided edge to intellection. Cooperation between the heart and the head, represented by the Heisenberg uncertainty principle, also remains an intellectual concept. In the supra-Euclidean world, however, objectivity and determinism are rejected, and willful cooperation between the heart and the head avoids conflict. On the occasions when they *do* compete, however, the heart is ultimately in charge.

This point was dramatically represented in a radio interview between Terry Gross, host of National Public Radio's *Fresh Air*, and Elizabeth Weil, a guest who had written an article about abortion. When Ms. Gross asked the author about her personal struggle with this very emotional issue, Ms. Weil said that she had been over forty and pregnant with her second child when she was diagnosed with an infection that represented a significant threat to the fetus. Told that her baby would probably be born deaf, blind, and severely mentally retarded, she and her husband "dove into doing tons and tons of research…, assuming that if we researched enough, we would get to really firm ground with it. But we never did."[25] The point is that no amount of information was going to make this a simple decision. Ultimately, intellect can analyze evidence, but the heart makes the decisions. Asked by Ms. Gross if she had any ethical reservations about deciding to abort the pregnancy, Ms. Weil replied, "I had lots of fears of feeling endless sadness about the decision, but I didn't feel it was unethical."[26]

This example brings up a number of issues. The real implications of Heisenberg's uncertainty principle are far more significant than simply discussing the intellectually abstract boundary between the knowable and unknowable. Questions of feelings and ethical judgments require a paradigm to identify right conduct and appropriate enforcement mechanisms. Judging Ms. Weil's decision is completely dependent on which paradigm guides one's heart. Believers within each paradigm will not necessarily agree on a common judgment. This is particularly true in our modern paradigm of self, in which each person has a unique interpretation of reality. The point of the example is not to judge Ms. Weil, but rather to distinguish the heart's ultimate experience of life from the intellect's interpretation of the experience.

Accepting the Realm of Mystery

In this chapter, using scientific methods of inquiry, we have continued the pursuit of absolute truth that defined the ancient Greek and early Christian paradigms. Science is the only discipline recognized as authoritative by the paradigm of self. Science pursues absolute truth through empirical evidence and intellectual reflection. These dual approaches complement Euclidian perception and find comfort in the illusion of certainty. Applying Euclidian logic reveals a great deal about the dual reality of rationalism and empiricism, but is useless in accepting the realm of mystery. Perhaps the heart-centered *nous* has a place in our modern understanding of absolute truth!

The term *probability* accounts for uncertainty, but does not require acceptance of the realm of mystery. I believe, however, that accepting the realm of mystery is necessary for one to completely understand reality. Richard Feynman described the accuracy of prediction provided by the science of probability and the limits of knowledge identified by Heisenberg, but he did not necessarily accept the third realm of mystery.

A simple abstract mathematical problem will offer an example of the differences between perception and reality. In Euclidean geometry, two plus two always equals four. There is complete certainty in this additive formula. The great visionary Buckminster Fuller, however, spoke at length about synergy, the idea that a result can be greater than the sum of its parts. As evidence he cited the tensile strength of the chrome-nickel-steel alloy, which is lighter and stronger than any of its component parts. Synergy can only be considered within a supra-Euclidian reality, and when it occurs, two plus two exceeds four!

Accepting the realm of mystery does not require one to abandon intellectual reflection or empirical evidence. But these two realms are not obligated to accept the unprovable existence of a heart-centered *nous*. Once again, the choice of cooperation or competition defines reality. The decision to accept mystery seems to require a fundamental subordination of evidence and intellection, but such a conclusion is based on Euclidian competition.

To fully illustrate the Euclidian and supra-Euclidian understandings of reality, recall Werner Jaeger's summary of cosmic origins, discussed in Chapter 3:

> The Logos [of the Hebrews] is a substantialization of an intellectual property or power of God the creator, who is stationed *outside* the world and brings that world into existence by his own personal fiat. The Greek gods [described by Hesiod] are stationed *inside* the world; they are descended from Heaven and Earth, the two greatest and most exalted parts of the universe…. Thus they are already subject to what we shall call natural law.[27]

Jaeger is presenting us here with a false Euclidean choice between an external and an internal God. The supra-Euclidean understanding accepts a God who is both external *and* internal. Reality is either a separate and distinct Euclidian duality or a cooperative supra-Euclidian trinity. The scientific concept of *probability* becomes merely a secular placeholder for the realm of mystery.

Accepting the realm of mystery, the data of revelation, and the heart-centered *nous* as equal to evidence and intellection requires a supra-Euclidean commitment to cooperation. Those unwilling to cooperate are condemned to eternally argue about the evidence found in the glass of water.

❖ ❖ ❖

Chapter 9

Implications of the Modern Paradigm

The Illusion of Certainty Versus the Uncertainty of Relativity

Accepting the reality revealed by supra-Euclidian physics neces-sarily leads to uncomfortable conclusions. Empirical evidence and in-tellectual reflection can point to scientifically repeatable examples of cause and effect, but the realm of mystery offers no such comparable evidence. In fact, mystery is beyond evidence and inaccessible by rea-son. Certainly, inexplicable events happen, but it is far easier for science to ignore such phenomena as statistical anomalies than to accept them as evidence of mystery.

On the other hand, there is a multiplicity of faith-based explanations about the realm of mystery. So, who is right? In the United States, we are theoretically free to subscribe to any belief system we wish. Consis-tent with the victory of the Sophists, we can each pick and choose what we believe and adhere to our self-proclaimed beliefs as ardently or casu-ally as we wish. We truly are the measure of all things.

Like the citizens of the early Roman Empire, we sift through the competing claims of absolute truth with nothing more than our head and heart to guide us. The internal struggle between self-interest and self-sacrifice persists, but today we rely on our head to guide our heart. The modern paradigm of self shares the same faith in reason that guided the ancient Greek paradigm. It lacks, however, two fundamental principles that held the ancient Greek *polis* together: (1) there is no organic or transcendent sense of duty to others; and (2) supra-Euclidean physics cannot be proven by empiricism or rationalism. Simply distinguishing perception from reality, as we did in Chapter 8, does not oblige modern citizens to accept the uncertainty of relative reality. We prefer the illusion of certainty to the uncertainty of relativity.

Setting aside the quest for absolute truth of the ancient Greeks, the early Christians, and modern physicists, we can believe that all truth is culturally or even personally relative. It is fitting that the hottest word in 2005 and 2006 was *truthiness*.* Invented, copyrighted, and trademarked by faux reporter Stephen Colbert (1964–), "truthiness," in his words, "is what you want the facts to be, as opposed to what the facts are. What feels like the right answer as opposed to what reality will support."[1] If, in fact, the heart experiences life, and the intellect explains what is experienced, the idea of relative truth is consistent with our modern paradigm of self. Our intellect "rationally" investigates the evidence and supports its superiority over an irrationally inferior heart. Contradictory experience is ignored; mystery is dismissed; duty is personalized; and scientists discount the evidence and implications of supra-Euclidean reality as much as religionists disregard the theory of evolution.

The battle lines between faith and reason have grown rigid over the past thousand years, so that now there is little room for common ground and little interest in cooperation. The sociological necessity described by Werner Jaeger, which I applied in Chapter 6 to the Holy Roman Empire, continues to frame the debate between faith and reason.[2] Since the duty to cooperate is not intrinsic to the paradigm of self, why should we? An individual may believe in a divine duty to "love thy neighbor," but such a duty cannot be imposed on someone who believes it is foolish.

In the ancient Greek paradigm, the obligation of duty to the state cooperated with the personal motivations of *aidos* ("holy shame") and *areté* ("virtue") to moderate self-interested behavior. But even in that environment, allowance was made for the innate motive of

---

Truthiness was voted word of the year by Merriam-Webster in 2006 (see http://www. m-w.com/info/06words.htm) and in 2005 by the American Dialect Society (see http:// americandialect.org/Words_of_the_Year_2005.pdf).

self-preservation. As the ancient Greek paradigm waned, so did the influence of *aidos* and *areté*. But self-preservation, the ultimate defender of self-interest, never lost its authority.

Only the most ardent believers in the early Christian paradigm accepted the personal responsibility of unconditional love without regard for temporal self-preservation. Martyrdom was celebrated as the highest expression of the Divine Trinity through faith, reason, and humility. The organic unity of the ancient Greek paradigm and the transcendent unity of the early Christian paradigm have been lost in the modern paradigm of self, in which there is no generally accepted civic obligation to others and no innate self-imposed responsibility.

The Common Good After the Enlightenment

After the triumph of self-reliance as espoused by Emerson, his contemporary Auguste Comte (1798–1857) attempted to reestablish the importance of duty to others through his Positivistic Philosophy. In ways that remind us of the ancient Greek paradigm, he believed that all societies have an organic character and move through three stages of intellectual development: theological, metaphysical, and scientific. He further believed that this development must lead to altruism's triumph over egoism.[3] *Altruism*, a term popularized by Comte, implies an interest in the well-being of others that is self-initiated. Where humility historically served a divine purpose, the idea of altruism represented a feeble attempt by Comte to explain our social character. Self-interest is compelling; altruism is not.

Our modern paradigm frames both humility and altruism in a similar light. For example, Nancy E. Snow, a professor of philosophy at Marquette University, attempted to justify humility by modern standards when she wrote, "Central to the role of humility is the acknowledgement of error or personal deficiency and its negative impact on others."[4] Snow distinguishes narrow from existential humility. The former accepts personal deficiency but disregards its impact on others. The latter represents that personal sense of smallness "before the greatness of nature."[5] Both examples of humility are self-centered, and Dr. Snow's attempt to unify them relies on an appeal to the communal benefits of compassion and sympathy and the personal benefit in recognizing one's deficiencies. Unfortunately, there is no compelling reason to recognize personal deficiencies, and there is no obligation to others. While self-interest remains compelling, modern explanations of humility and altruism are deficient. By being self-centered, they lack any role for a transcendent divinity and, appropriately, would not be justifiable on the basis of Euclidean knowledge.

In 1943, psychologist Abraham Maslow (1908–1970) proposed his now famous hierarchy of needs, according to which, once basic needs were met, an individual would progress through Love, Esteem, and Self-actualization.[6] This formula, like those offered by Comte and Dr. Snow, lacks a compelling rationale, and there has been little scientific evidence to support the existence of any such hierarchy.[7]

The idea of divine motivation simply has no place in the modern paradigm of self. Although Maslow considered himself an atheist, he thought that transcendence represented a cooperative middle ground (my interpretation) between science and religion. Secular psychologists discredit vague ideas of transcendence as psychobabble that belongs to the domain of religious belief.[8] Theories of motivation that are based on biological instinct, evolution, and self-interest are more compatible with the modern paradigm of self. In fact, the field of modern psychology distinguishes two familiar disciplines: rationality and empiricism.[9] Over time, these splintered and moved from Ernst Cassirer's general to the particular, today including such disciplines as Functional

Psychology inspired by William James (1842–1910) and Depth Psychology introduced by Sigmund Freud (1856–1939).[10]

In the ancient Greek paradigm, the psyche (soul) shared a common essence with the divine and served as the bridge between the visible and invisible. In the early Christian paradigm, the soul was created simultaneously with the body. The eye of the soul, or *nous*, was only capable of seeing the divine energy if it experienced purification. With Freud, the psyche acquired a new trinity of ego, id, and superego that navigates our conscious and unconscious mental systems. In Freudian psychoanalysis, man is the measure of all things, and there is no requirement for a divine realm, a *nous*, or mystery. Of course, no one is obliged to accept Freud's structural theories.

The subordination of self-interest by the ancient Greek and the early Christian paradigms remains constant, whether viewed through a Euclidean or a supra-Euclidean lens. But in the paradigm of self, each of us defines reality, acceptable behavior, and which institutions and belief systems deserve our respect. In Western society, institutions that historically defined right conduct no longer influence individual behavior with the same authority as in earlier generations. Religious authority, respect for elders or traditions, and cultural understandings of marriage and child rearing have given way to our personal freedom to choose. Confusing "choice" with "freedom," modern individuals employ Euclidean distinctions to compare and contrast alternatives rather than to identify common ground that is compatible with supra-Euclidean cooperation.

The success of Euclidean influences on modern society is exemplified in our educational system, which emphasizes "critical thinking"—a concept defined by the Foundation for Critical Thinking as:

> that mode of thinking—about any subject, content, or
> problem—in which the thinker improves the quality

of his or her thinking by skillfully taking charge of the structures inherent in thinking and imposing intellectual standards upon them.[11]

The effort "is based on universal intellectual values that transcend subject matter division: clarity…, consistency…, sound evidence, good reasons, depth, breadth, and fairness."[12] Although it is a noble effort to identify areas of cooperation, critical thinking is ultimately limited by its reliance on intellect. It suffers from the same vague notion of transcendence that secular psychologists use to dismiss Maslow, for there is no compelling reason to improve one's thinking and no objective standard to measure that improvement.

This limitation becomes evident in the foundation's concluding summary:

> Critical thinking is, in short, self-directed, self-disciplined, self-monitored, and self-corrective thinking. It presupposes assent to rigorous standards of excellence…. It entails…a commitment to overcome our native egocentrism and sociocentrism.[13]

Self-interest remains native and compelling; "assent to rigorous standards of excellence" and "transcendence" does not.

One should not, however, view the above comments as an assault on intellect and reason. Rather, one must recognize that every modern philosopher who investigates the universal questions that ancient Greeks called wisdom is simply offering one version of truth. None of us is obligated to share any belief or conform to any standard of right conduct. More accurately, each of us defines what we believe. Have you ever heard faithful Roman Catholics distance themselves from particular dogmatic pronouncements of the Pope? Unless we accept a particular belief system unconditionally, we are all versions of "cafeteria Catholics," picking and choosing what we believe in. Like Emerson, we are gods, creators of the finite.

Modern Examples of Cooperation

Human beings apparently have an innate desire to cooperate, and there are clearly benefits to doing so. Unfortunately, our social character—that is, our desires for companionship, relationship, acceptance, and that "good feeling" we get when we do something nice for others—has no compelling intellectual rationalization. There is no compelling reason to endure self-sacrifice for the common good when there is no common standard. The supra-Euclidean reality that accepts the realm of mystery cannot force individuals to accept mystery.

Simply stated, reason does not know what it does not know. The Euclidean assumption that everything can be known with enough information cannot be reconciled with Heisenberg's uncertainty principle. We may intellectually repeat Heisenberg's principle, but it is far more difficult to wear it, instill it in our heart, and accept that there is knowledge beyond intellect and that we are solely responsible for our decisions. To better understand cooperation independently of modern science, but consistently with my understanding of paradigms and belief systems, let us consider the desire to cooperate and the benefits of cooperating at their most basic level: the religious hermit and the couple who seek harmony.

The religious hermit avoids society, exercising complete individual freedom to practice his (or her) beliefs. The hermit's internal struggle between self-interest and self-sacrifice is reconciled by the deferred reward of his guiding belief system. The hermit is free from external oppression and the judgments of others, free to endure the internal struggle. The consequence of this freedom, however, is the forfeiture of human companionship. The hermit strives for harmonious cooperation between self-will and the divine will through his commitment to the path of humility.

So long as the ruling elites leave the hermit alone, there will be no conflict between them. If, however, the ruling elites interfere with the hermit's isolation, he will not resist. There will, in fact, be no limit to his humble cooperation—even to the point of martyrdom.

As for the couple who choose to share a living space, in effect forming a miniature society, harmony between them will depend on their willingness to cooperate and endure sacrifice. Husbands and wives who share common understandings of ethics, morality, and conduct enjoy harmonious relationships. Sharing a common belief system defines their individual roles, the right conduct necessary to maintain a stable union. The strength of their marriage directly depends on their individual willingness to accept their role, their willingness to sacrifice personal freedom in return for the comfort and stability of a strong union.

If each member of this relationship is unconditionally committed to the well-being of the other, their union experiences a synergy that is unattainable by either one alone.* If I am selflessly committed to your well-being, and you are selflessly committed to mine, each of us experiences a degree of comfort and security that exceeds our individual capacities. There is no room for conflict when there is unconditional cooperation. This would be the purest form of a "win-win" strategy of cooperation.

The degree to which each member of the union considers his or her own needs first will directly challenge his or her commitment to

---

*In this example, we can assume that each member willingly subordinates self-interest without coercion and also enjoys a healthy level of self-esteem. Otherwise, it would not be possible for both members to be *unconditionally* committed to the well-being of the other.

unconditional cooperation. The less committed the two are to each other, the less secure their relationship is, and each one becomes more responsible for his or her own well-being. The spectrum from unconditional self*less*ness to unconditional self*ish*ness represents the alternatives that result from personal decisions to cooperate or compete. Unconditional cooperation and competition may seem like extreme alternatives, but they frame each individual's willingness to sacrifice self-interest for some understanding of a common good.

The stability of any society depends on the willingness of individuals to cooperate. The more that individuals accept a common understanding of ethics, morality, and conduct, the greater communal harmony there will be. While harmonious coexistence depends on personal willingness to endure sacrifice for the common good, the more emphasis there is on personal sacrifice and common good, the less emphasis there is on individualism.

In each of these two examples, the religious hermit and the devoted couple, there is a common goal of harmonious cooperation. The Euclidean inclination to emphasize differences willingly cooperates with the supra-Euclidean realm of mystery in the pursuit of harmony. There is no conflict between the various paradigms that interpret reality, because all of the participants willingly choose cooperation. As more people are introduced into the community, however, the opportunities to cooperate or compete become more complex.

Cooperation Requires Willing Sacrifice

We endure the sacrifices, the boundaries to self-interest, hoping to achieve an harmonious union. The religious hermit sacrifices all companionship, hoping to attain eternal salvation through the path of humility. The rest of us seek a balance between cooperation and competition in our relationships with others. We are free to impose our belief systems on our own behavior and navigate the internal struggle of self-interest and self-sacrifice. When we impose our beliefs on others, however, we violate their freedom to navigate their own belief systems. The problem is that, over time, the fabric of sacrifice that holds couples, families, tribes, and nations together ultimately wears thin.

Clearly, the more homogeneous a community is, the greater the likelihood of cooperation. But in the paradigm of self, each of us consciously or unconsciously relies on competing belief systems that seek to influence our heart. The ancient Greek and early Christian paradigms represent different understandings of duty that offer unifying relationships between individuals and communities. The paradigm of self, however, has no organic or transcendent character, no strategy for cooperation. The heart continues to experience being, but the head assumes it has the leadership role. Actually, the head only considers alternatives, but as in the example of Ms. Weil in Chapter 8, who chose to abort her seriously vulnerable fetus, the heart continues to call the shots.

In the paradigm of self, there is no organic understanding of common good, no common understanding of "American values," and no transcending concern for others. The question of duty remains unanswered, and each of us rationalizes whatever our hearts decide. The United States seeks to unite the many, as seen in its motto *E Pluribus Unum* ("Out of Many, One"). Our society is made up of people from all walks of life and all communities on Earth. Thus, there is no consensus about what constitutes duty. Some Americans satisfy their duty to a personally defined divine authority, others to the rule of law. I suspect that most do not spend a lot of time thinking about duty at all. If the only principle that unites Americans is our common interest in self-interest, there is precious little fabric left in our American quilt.*

---

*In a future work, I intend to explore American values through the lens of competition, cooperation, and paradigms.

A Clash of Paradigms

Self-interest continues to be compelling. For example, President Bush successfully manipulated fears of self-preservation in the aftermath of the 9/11 tragedy in order to justify invading Iraq. For a while, Americans were united against an enemy who "hates our way of life." But as the situation in Iraq became more complicated, the divisions within our own society began to manifest themselves, and our personal allegiances moved in competing directions. The perceived separation between religion and government has been clouded. Many Americans are Muslim, many are not religious at all, and many who are religious have varying personally defined standards for military engagement. "Enemies" are more complicated than simplistic slogans portray them.

So, what do cooperation and competition really mean? I heard a tragic example of the choice between cooperation and competition while listening to National Public Radio. The 1999 civil war in Yugoslavia sent Kosovar refugees into Albania, while back in the United States daily news reports tried to explain the reasons for the conflict to an American audience. As NPR's Melissa Block reported allegations of rape by Serbian soldiers and police, the clash of paradigms between our two societies was dramatically revealed. Interviewing the mother of an 18-year-old daughter who had been shot and killed by three Serbian soldiers, Block reported:

> Her mother refuses to believe that [her daughter] was raped. Neighbors say the soldiers tried to attack her, but she resisted. When the neighbors brought back her body, [she] was dressed and her mother says she had a peaceful smile on her face.… Her mother says when she saw [her] being led away, she was terrified her daughter would be raped.[14]

Through a translator, the mother explained, "It's better that she's dead than if they raped her and gave her back to me alive, because then I would wish to die, too." Block commented, "This is such a stunning declaration that I asked [her] again if she really means that she rather her daughter die than survive a rape. The mother says, 'Yes.'"[15]

Our nation was founded during the Enlightenment and inspired by it. We celebrate the individual and encourage self-reliance. The idea that a mother would actually want her daughter to die rather than survive a rape is so foreign to an American audience that it is no wonder Block was stunned. Limited by her own belief system, the reporter could not understand how a mother could feel relief at the loss of her daughter. The daughter's life, *any* individual's life, is the most basic component of our American belief system. To Americans, individual life should be cherished above all else, especially by a mother for her child.

Limited by her communal belief system, however, this mother would never value the life of her daughter above that of the family and community. The shame of the rape would dishonor the family and village. Self-sacrifice for the common good demanded that the individual subordinate her life for the well-being of the community. Assuming that the daughter accepted this belief system, she would herself have preferred death to rape. Notice here the powerful authority of the ancient Greek enforcement mechanisms: *aidos* and *areté*. Judging the mother's society as good or bad, right or wrong, will depend on which paradigm one uses to interpret the evidence. The reader can share the mother's or the reporter's belief system. The choice is as clear as the proverbial glass of water that is either half empty or half full: that is, one must decide whether to live as a rape victim or die for some understanding of common good.

Competition: The Euclidean Lens

In the ancient Greek paradigm, self-sacrifice for the common good was the communal standard. A daughter's willingness to die rather than be dishonored is no different from Socrates' willingness to die rather than leave Athens. In the early Christian paradigm, faith in divine mercy endures any degree of temporal suffering. In the modern paradigm of self, each of us judges right conduct, and that judgment can justify any belief system's determination of right and wrong. But cooperation resists judgment. The glass can be half empty *and* half full. It is not a question of who is right. If your intention is to cooperate, then right is irrelevant. In the clash of civilizations that confront leaders around the globe, it is much easier to mobilize a nation through an appeal to self-preservation than through a message of international cooperation.

With Euclidean certainty, self-preservation can become a belief system, and then "right conduct" can seek to eliminate threats to one's well-being. In fact, if one perceives a national or cultural or religious community as a threat, then one could regard genocide as right conduct! The enforcement mechanism of hope and fear described by Hume would ensure right conduct—that is, the fear that inspires genocide so long as the threat exists, and the hope of peace once the threat is eliminated. The duality of hope and fear represents the spectrum of enforcement alternatives through a Euclidean lens. Cooperation and coexistence are supra-Euclidean alternatives that are rejected outright by individuals who see the world through Euclidean certainty.

Other examples of self-interested belief systems that woo our heart include the economic motivations of capitalism and communism or the theological principles of coexistence and cooperation. Employing the clarity of the Euclidean lens, right conduct and enforcement mechanisms can be readily identified. Capitalism is defined as the personal accumulation of wealth, and in this context right conduct would be determined through a "cost-benefit" analysis. The enforcement mechanisms would be the hope of accumulating more wealth and the fear that others might benefit at your expense. In such a view of reality, right conduct would encourage prostitution and drug dealing. In fact, it would be immoral to sacrifice personal profit because of the weaknesses of others.

Communism promotes communal at the expense of individual well-being. In this context, right conduct is determined by some kind of communal hierarchy. All members of the society are expected to accept their duty to the state, which can enforce its judgments by any means necessary.

Lacking *areté*, *aidos*, and a personal commitment to unconditional love, capitalism and communism are both compatible with self-interest. Whether one works hard or hardly works remains a question of self-interest.

The Euclidean lens recognizes the struggle between capitalism and communism. For one perspective to win, the alternative must be defeated. There is no room for cooperation or compromise. From the perspective of the early Christian paradigm, however, both capitalism and communism will be undermined by extreme greed and self-interest. Neither economic system can ensure communal well-being as reliably as can the principle of loving one's enemy. This principle can only be considered from a supra-Euclidean perspective and will be swiftly dismissed by Euclidean clarity.

The theological principles of coexistence and cooperation are problematic when viewed from the perspective of the paradigm of self. Leaving behind the certainty of Euclidean perception, we must navigate the supra-Euclidean realm of mystery. The obvious problem is the absence of a common standard of behavior. There is no duty owed to any civil or religious authority. If man is the measure of all things, then individuals define their own acceptable standards of coexistence and cooperation.

Philosophers and poets may fill the void with rationales for morality and ethical behavior, but they lack any effective enforcement mechanisms.

Fanaticism

If individuals are accountable only to themselves, they can arbitrarily choose to make sacrifices only when it is convenient for them. Coexistence and cooperation imply some degree of personal sacrifice in the service of some personally defined sense of common good. The internal struggle to balance self-interest and self-sacrifice continues in our modern paradigm of self. While maintaining a healthy balance between self-interest and self-sacrifice might be called normal, what happens when there is no such internal struggle? Any principle, philosophy, or religion that is embraced with extreme and uncritical enthusiasm lacks the normal internal struggle between self-interest and self-sacrifice.

The problem with fanatics is the uncritical nature of their enthusiasm. Fanatics are "true" believers who ignore the evidence of reason. Empirical and rational proofs are irrelevant to them. In the realm of mystery, their extreme and uncritical ardor blinds them to reason's logic. Their belief system resolves the struggle between self-interest and common good. Fanatics see themselves as divine arbiters of the guiding principles that govern common good, and so they believe they exercise divine authority in the administration of justice. Fanatics can seamlessly cross the line from being martyrs (who make the ultimate self-sacrifice) to being murderers (the ultimate determiners of life itself). They can turn a belief system that clearly states "Thou shalt not kill" into a rationalization for mass murder.

Whether they are religious extremists or uncritical enthusiasts for unlimited individual freedom or unlimited self-interest, all fanatics believe that those who disagree with their interpretation of right conduct are simply wrong. Fanatics are unable to recognize inconsistencies in their own behavior. They are essentially unable to distinguish rationality from irrationality. These ideologues believe that they alone possess the supreme truth of their belief system. Individuals who live in extreme uncritical enthusiasm are beyond the influence of any reasoned argument.

The United States allows individuals to freely choose their belief systems. Our Constitution and rules of law offer no guidance in this area beyond the separation of church and state. Under the shield of individual freedom, however, fanatics reject any limits on their individual conduct. They dismiss national instability as a real threat or, more dangerously, regard it as an acceptable sacrifice. We recognize American fanatics like Timothy McVeigh (1968–2001), the convicted Oklahoma bomber, or Eric Rudolph (1966–), the convicted Atlanta Olympics bomber, as dangerous. We must similarly recognize uncritical enthusiasts for unlimited individualism as equally dangerous.

The behavior of Timothy McVeigh and Eric Rudolph makes sense only within the terms of their personal belief systems. Both claimed to be Christians, yet neither was part of a traditional Christian sect that defines "right conduct." They merged their self-styled belief systems and fanatical self-righteousness to become divine arbiters of justice, self-righteous murderers. To the general public, their actions are neither rational nor reasonable, since there is no rational explanation for their behavior outside of their self-styled belief systems.

Because our forefathers trusted individuals to willingly shoulder responsibility toward each other for the collective good, our Constitution and Bill of Rights provide no guidance on personal responsibility. Thus, our national psyche has evolved from a culturally relative sense of responsibility to scientific explanations of life. Lost in this evolution is an explanation of purpose. What is the meaning of life? Why do we exist? Our forefathers sidestepped these questions and declared secular inalienable rights of life, liberty, and the pursuit of happiness with no enforceable underlying belief system beyond culturally relative communal standards.

A survey conducted in 2001 by the City University of New York calculated that 29.4 million people in this country identified themselves as having no religion at all—a number that had more than doubled from the 14.3 million who had so identified themselves in 1990.[16] Noting the religious pluralism of the United States, American Atheist, Inc., cautioned those who insist that the United States is a Christian nation:

> The ranks of those who reject religious doctrines and
> movements is thriving in the United States…. This is a
> diverse and politically independent group…. Larger than
> many denominations, and for the most part un-organized,
> it is a potential sleeping giant waiting to flex its political
> and cultural influence.[17]

The increasing political and cultural influence of modern-day atheists, like that of the ancient Sophists before them, has already undermined traditional religious institutions that promote standards of right conduct for the common good. As these traditional institutions have lost influence, spirituality has begun to replace religion. As Robert Fuller, Professor of Religious Studies at Bradley University, has noted:

> *Spiritual* gradually came to be associated with the pri-
> vate realm of thought and personal experience, while
> the word *religious* came to be connected with the public
> realm of membership in religious institutions.[18]

These definitions of *spiritual* and *religious* correspond directly with the paradigm of self and the breakdown of traditional forms of social order. As with Timothy McVeigh and Eric Rudolph, the problem with self-styled belief systems is their serious lack of accountability. Traditional religious institutions clearly articulate standards of right conduct and consequences for wrong conduct. Self-styled belief systems are beyond the influence of any external institutional standard of conduct. Fanatics, who bow to no one, balance self-interest and self-sacrifice with an arbitrary self-righteousness that is dangerous to the rest of us.

Modern Arbiters of Justice

How do we maintain "American values" in a way that allows a nation of individuals to agree on a belief system that unites our society? Within secular America, the highest authority is the rule of law as interpreted by the judicial branch of government. Among our citizenry, there is broad-based acceptance of the rule of law as supreme. When revolutionary forces sought to overthrow the rule of law, our nation endured a civil war. Over our 200-year history, revolutionary fervor has been pacified (through force when necessary) to submit to the highest authority in the land, the rule of law. Louis Menand (1952–), author of *The Metaphysical Club*, asks, "How do we trust the claim that a particular state of affairs is legitimate?" Or, to paraphrase him, how do we trust that the authority of the rule of law is legitimate? Menand's answer is both brilliant and insightful:

> The solution has been to shift the totem of legitimacy
> from premises to procedures. We know an outcome
> is right, not because it was derived from immutable

principles, but because it was reached by following the correct procedures.... If the legal process was adhered to, the outcome is just. Justice does not preexist the case at hand; justice is whatever result just procedures have led to.[19]

The rule of law is the final arbiter of right conduct, and we collectively respect the authority with which judgment is passed. We trust the process to arbitrate justly. Whether or not O. J. Simpson committed murder or George W. Bush lost the presidential election in 2000, the rule of law deemed both of them victorious.

The reliance of the rule of law on the premise that just process results in just outcomes highlights a conflict between the spirit and the letter of the law. Honesty may be a precept that Americans share, but there is no legal requirement in this country to be honest. For example, there is no law against telling a lie, except when that lie is perjury. And perjury can occur only under a specific set of conditions—namely, "the willful utterance of a false statement under oath before a competent tribunal, upon a point material to a legal inquiry."[20] Perjury is therefore an example of a secular principle with a clear standard of right conduct (it is unlawful to lie under oath) and a reliable enforcement mechanism (a perjurer is subject to prosecution and imprisonment by a court of law). All this is accomplished by creating a clear context within which the principle can be enforced. We cannot go into a man's house and arrest him for lying to his wife. But if he lies in court, he can be prosecuted.

The rule of law enshrined in the U.S. Constitution has outlined a secular process that navigates conflicting personal belief systems, as is demonstrated by the fact that our Constitution has been embraced and respected by citizens of different faiths, including atheists and agnostics. The rule of law wisely remains secular through its separation of religious and civil authority. It does not presume to determine if Jesus is the Son of God, whether God created the world in six days, or how many angels can dance on the head of a pin.

Our Constitution provides the secular philosophy that defines our societal guiding principles, our moral obligations to each other. The separation of church and state, our multi-religious culture, and especially the inherently irrational character of the realm of mystery preclude our establishing consensus principles of right conduct based on religious unity. If we wait for religion to unite our nation, we will not survive. Historically, American secular politics has been less dangerously divisive and less subject to fanaticism than politics in other parts of the globe. As with the ancient Greeks, however, our dual allegiances to the divine and to the state are not in harmony. Where religion and politics intersect, the Constitution and our acceptance of the legal process rest on shaky common ground, as in the debate over abortion today.

The inalienable right to life is proclaimed in our Declaration of Independence. Without the rudder of a consensus secular belief system, we face nearly insurmountable problems identifying and accepting common ground. One need simply start with the "inalienable right to life" to recognize the difficulty in using any particular standard of right conduct that most Americans would accept. The Supreme Court has attempted to balance individual rights and culturally relative communal standards through *Roe v. Wade*, but it is safe to say there is no consensus on the issue of abortion.

The American electorate is passionately divided over the constitutional meaning of the inalienable right to life. From the status of a fetus to capital punishment, adversaries use arguments to support or dismiss heart-centered positions without ever questioning the "logical" inconsistencies along the way. Both sides claim moral superiority to rally their troops throughout the political battles. Both sides employ logic and reason to justify their competing belief systems.

Expecting any society to agree on the meaning of our right to life with scientific clarity is an impossible objective without a common faith-based frame of reference. Our right to life may be "inalienable," but it is not self-evident and cannot be relied on to build a national consensus. Living one's personal belief system is consistent with supra-Euclidean cooperation. Imposing one's belief system on others is consistent with Euclidean competition.

Our society relies on courts to resolve major conflicts between parties, but from moment to moment we all make our own decisions and decide what is right conduct. Each of us follows multiple belief systems. For example, an individual can simultaneously be a Christian, a capitalist, and a self-preservationist. When these various belief systems conflict, the individual has to arbitrate among them to decide which one will prevail. However, ten minutes later, the same individual, confronted with a similar issue, may decide it differently. Ultimately, which belief system is most deeply instilled in one's heart will guide one's decisions. Religious hermits consciously choose their austere lifestyle to discipline their minds so that their principal belief system will prevail most of the time. This requires cooperation between reason, faith, and humility to work toward this common goal.

The religious hermit only has to arbitrate between his or her own internal competing belief systems. When a second person is added, as in a couple, the arbitration of right conduct becomes more complex. As more parties are added to the community, the arbitration becomes even more complex. Different belief systems have empowered different kinds of arbiters to resolve these complexities. That is precisely the moral challenge of the ancient Greeks and Romans, as we have seen in previous chapters. Religious systems have empowered clergy. Legal systems have empowered judges. Mental health systems have empowered therapists.

Throughout history, the wisest or fastest or strongest or oldest have all been called on to arbitrate conflicts. The stronger one's faith is in a particular belief system, the more readily will one accept the judgments of the arbiters of that faith. In a perfect relationship between believers and arbiters, judgments will always be consistent and just, and societies will live happily ever after.

Problems arise when arbiters are inconsistent, unjust, or above the laws they arbitrate. Arbitrary judgments break down trust. As the glue of trust breaks down, coercion and intimidation must be used to enforce obedience. This move from willing sacrifice for the common good toward coerced sacrifice demonstrates the transition from a positive to a negative enforcement mechanism, from hope to fear.

When the arbiters of justice violate their own rules of right conduct, accepting mystery becomes highly confusing to believers' reason and logic, for they can clearly see the inconsistencies in such behavior. Faith, however, does not provide any means of challenging the authority of the defining belief system. Faith demands submission, acceptance, conformity, and humility. Individual believers therefore only have two choices: submit to the authorities or leave the faith. The fear of the unknown that is inherent in the decision to leave can be terrifying. As the saying goes, "The devil you know is better than the devil you don't know."

Consider the case of a woman in an abusive relationship. Clearly, the abuse is inconsistent with American ideals of individual freedom. No one would rationally choose to remain in such a relationship, yet many women do. If a woman submits to a belief system whereby the man defines right conduct, she has limited herself to two alternatives: remain with him and endure the abuse, or leave him and face the world alone. Anyone who has worked with women in such relationships knows how real the fear of the unknown is.

Each of us is guided consciously or unconsciously by heart-centered belief systems that define right conduct for us. Our gnomic will evaluates the evidence, arbitrates self-interest and self-sacrifice, and accepts the enforcement mechanism of hope or fear that ensures compliance. Our relationship with others is guided by some personalized version of paradigms and belief systems.

There are many examples of communal arbiters of justice who are universally recognized as deranged, but the elements of belief systems are nevertheless apparent. One need only think of Jim Jones (1931–1978) and the terrible Jonestown tragedy in Guyana on November 18, 1978. Like all self-appointed arbiters of justice, Jones claimed to be a true interpreter of his own divine authority. The members of his cult had the free will to accept or reject his claimed authority. Those who accepted his authority submitted completely to it. Jones was the sole determiner of right conduct and exercised his own version of *aidos* and *areté*. Individual submission was so complete that hundreds of people committed suicide at his command.

Given the potential for abuse, why do rational people accept an arbiter's belief system? Despite the evidence that human beings are both rational and irrational, we have an innate need for each other that cannot be easily resisted. Genetics, instinct, and evolution provide a rationale that is consistent with both the ancient Greek paradigm and the modern paradigm of self. Creation in the image and likeness of the Triune God provides the rationale for the early Christian paradigm. Through whatever paradigm one interprets reality, the fact is that each of us seeks communion with others. Even religious hermits struggle to redirect this basic human tendency away from other humans and toward their Creator.

Inevitable Loneliness

Recall that reason eventually conquered faith and gave birth to our modern paradigm of self. The move from organic communal obligation through transcendent responsibility to our modern duty to self will eventually undermine our willingness to endure self-sacrifice for the common good. In the brutal reality presented by the Kosovar daughter's "choice," it is easy to recognize that, one day, her society will choose self-preservation over self-sacrifice.

Our national rhetoric about "human rights" appeals directly to self-interest around the world, transcending couples, families, tribes, and nations. As the message of self-interest spreads, the authority of the various arbiters of justice, including clergy, elders, and judges, declines. Communal customs and traditions, all of which impose an expectation of duty through *areté* and *aidos*, also lose influence. We reject obligations and responsibilities, choosing instead our own aimless agendas. We drift through time, avoiding sacrifice and asserting rights. The remaining void leaves our innate need for community unsatisfied.

The evidence is overwhelming that our modern paradigm leads to loneliness. The Census Bureau's 2007 edition of *The Statistical Abstract of the United States* provides 999 pages of evidence that documents how alienated Americans are from each other. For example, we spend more time today engaged with electronics than with other people.[21] Reacting to the *Statistical Abstract*, Gerald Celente, founder of the Trends Research Institute, lamented, "We're trying to make technology replace what we've lost humanly. We're getting more and more isolated and less and less human."[22] In line with this trend, a recent study has found that today's college students are more self-centered than their predecessors. "Current technology fuels the increase in narcissism," said Professor Jean Twenge of San Diego State University, the study's lead author. "By its very name, MySpace encourages attention-seeking."[23] No generation in history has had more material wealth and been more alone.

❖ ❖ ❖

Chapter 10

Final Thoughts on Cooperation

Losing God in the Twentieth Century

We have covered a lot of territory in our exploration of paradigms, and the last chapter may have left the reader with serious questions about an uncertain future. There are many facts we interpret as evidence to support heart-centered belief systems. We seem to collectively accept the physics of quantum mechanics even if few of us understand it. The appeal of Euclidean certainty provides a perception of stability and security that offers comfort. The supra-Euclidean acceptance of mystery and relativity holds us all accountable to navigate an uncertain existence without a safety net.

The modern paradigm continues to assimilate scientific discoveries. In the past one hundred years, humanity has had much to absorb and reconcile. The implications of quantum mechanics, our reliance on reason, and the lack of consensus regarding personal duty have combined to support personal versions of reality. In this chapter, we will sift through the evidence, identify areas of compatibility and conflict between the paradigms, and offer some final thoughts.

By the middle of the twentieth century, the atomic bomb had killed hundreds of thousands of people, and humanity's inhumanity was embodied in the atrocities committed by Adolf Hitler. Nazi Germany represented an evil that the world could recognize as such. But the events of World War II did not occur in a vacuum, were not black and white, good and bad, separate and distinct. There was a great deal of gray within the spectrum. The universal condemnation of Hitler could unite the world, while allowing individuals to sidestep questions about personal responsibility by ignoring any consideration of an internal struggle between the heart and the head. People were not obligated to question their own deficiencies and personal struggles, for Hitler set the standard of inhumanity so low that the rest of us could feel good about our own relative standards of morality and ethics.

In summarizing modern philosophy, Professor Albert Levi identified supporters of the ancient Greek paradigm and the modern paradigm:

> All cyclic theories, whether Vico's doctrine of *ricorsi* (recurrences), Nietzsche's theory of *die ewige Wiederkunft* (the eternal recurrence), or Pareto's theory of the upward and downward paths of the ruling elites, are Greek in inspiration. All directional theories, whether those of Marx, Comte, or Hegel, are the consequence of a secularization of theological principles.[1]

Note the absence here of the early Christian paradigm. Levi accurately summarized the "secularization of theological principles." In Chapter 7, we identified how reason conquered faith, and we concluded that every attempt to "explain" reality thereafter was the personal interpretation of each author. Another book will have to describe the historical events of the past two hundred years and the personal contributions of Charles Darwin, William James, Sigmund Freud, and many others in light of the paradigms described in this book. Levi's summary is valuable in providing an historical snapshot of mid-twentieth-century philosophical thought. In comparing Oswald Spengler's (1880–1936) *The Decline of the West*[2] with Arnold Toynbee's (1889–1975) *A Study of History*,[3] Levi summarizes Spengler's philosophy of history as "a denial of absolute values...[and] a pervasive historical skepticism."* According to Levi, Toynbee looked for cooperation between nature and nurture. "It is clear," Toynbee wrote, "that if the geneses of civilizations are not the result of biological factors or of geographical environment acting separately, they must be the result of some kind of interactions between them..., not an entity but a relation."[4] For Toynbee, the study of history was "a vision...of God revealing Himself in action to souls that were sincerely seeking Him."[5]

Adhering to the modern paradigm, Levi did not find Toynbee persuasive:

> He does not take the Augustinian path of a strict separation between the City of God and the earthly city, but tries naively to establish a correspondence between the "Law of God" and the "laws of Nature."[6]

Levi's observation seems to channel the logic of fifth-century Prosper of Aquitaine's defense of Augustine against St. John Cassian, which we discussed above in Chapter 4. In the final analysis, Levi found *The Decline of the West* and *A Study of History* very similar:

> Between the Stoic endurance [of Spengler] and the lesson of early Christian humility [of Toynbee] there is really not much to choose; no more perhaps than we find between Toynbee's gloomy radiance and Spengler's radiant gloom.[7]

---

*Albert Levi, *Philosophy and the Modern World* (Bloomington, IN: Indiana University Press, 1959), p. 131. The "decline in absolute values" is an acknowledgment of the relative values in our modern paradigm, and of the higher standard that absolute values enjoyed in prior paradigms.

Yet, Levi considered Spengler and Toynbee the "two greatest contemporary philosophers of history."[8]

Levi did not live to consider the historical work of Jared Diamond (1937–).[9] It is interesting to note the different level of interest in Toynbee and Spengler forty years after Levi wrote about them. In *Guns, Germs and Steel*, Diamond refers to Toynbee only at the end of his book, in his suggestions for further readings, and he does not mention Spengler at all. Both Levi and Diamond find Toynbee's theology unconvincing, but more revealing is Diamond's nominal inclusion of religion in history.

Diamond identifies "kleptocrats" as governing elites who maintain their superior position in society by manipulating public support for their privileges. To secure their position in centralized societies, they construct an institutional ideology or religion, which has three tangible results for them and their societies. First, it justifies the transfer of wealth to them. Second, it provides common ground for unrelated individuals to "live together without killing each other—by providing them with a bond not based on kinship."[10] Third, "it gives people a motive, other than genetic self-interest, for sacrificing their lives on behalf of others."[11] Diamond's kleptocrats are reminiscent of the Sophists' argument that religion is only a clever invention of the politicians.

Diamond is an historian who is fully immersed in a secular version of the modern paradigm. History, for him, is a series of coincidences, an evolution of tribalism. Self-interested kleptocracy, evolutionary survival of the fittest, and genetic self-interest provide little evidence of an innate struggle between self-interest and self-sacrifice. Toynbee accepted a transcendent Creator, and in his day was highly regarded. By the twenty-first century, there would be no room in academia for religious psychobabble.

Every belief system that relies on faith alone seems to be either dismissed or relegated to mythology by modern philosophers and scientists. One prominent Doctor of Cultural Anthropology who addressed religion head-on was Ernest Becker (1924–1974), who, in his Pulitzer Prize–winning book *The Denial of Death*, proposed a fundamental truth about modern society—namely, that man's refusal to acknowledge his own mortality is a necessary "vital lie."[12] "We don't want to admit," Becker wrote, "that we are fundamentally dishonest about reality, that we do not really control our own lives."[13] This statement precisely summarizes the appeal of Euclidean perception.

Instead of accepting our mortality, Becker argues, humanity busies itself with seemingly "important" tasks, such as relationships, careers, and financial investments, in an effort to ignore the terrifying reality of death.[14] To Becker, the vital lie is a neurotic defense that transfers the importance of our activities into a life-enhancing illusion.[15] Becker makes a compelling argument for religion as the best vital lie because it "solves the problem of death."[16] Mindful of his academic peers, Becker assures them of his allegiance to the modern paradigm:

> Let me hasten to assure the reader that I am not developing an apologia for traditional religion but only describing the impoverishment of the modern neurotic and some of the reasons for it.[17]

Mental illness, Becker argues, results from individuals' inability to maintain the vital lie:

> Once you accept the truly desperate situation that man is in, you come to see not only that neurosis is normal, but that even psychotic failure represents only a little additional push in the routine stumbling along life's way.[18]

Becker summarizes the dilemma confronting psychotherapy by quoting Otto Rank (1884–1939), the Austrian psychologist who was originally one of Sigmund Freud's closest disciples, but eventually became one of his sharpest critics. The question, said Rank, is not whether a patient can be cured, but whether a patient *should* be cured![19] Rank was not specifically addressing the vital lie here, but he may as well have been.

Interestingly, Becker identifies a three-step process whereby psychology itself can become a belief system:

> One of them is to be a creative genius as a psychologist and to use psychology as the immortality vehicle for oneself—as Freud and subsequent psychoanalysts have done. Another is to use the language and concepts of psychotherapy in much of one's waking life, so that it becomes a live belief system. We see this often, as ex-patients analyze their motives in all situations when they feel anxious…. The third and final way is…to take psychology and deepen it with religious and metaphysical associations so that it becomes actually a religious belief system with some breadth and depth.[20]

Ultimately, however, Becker believes that there cannot be a truthful union between psychology and religion because scientific skepticism cannot honestly be married to mystical belief.

Nevertheless, I cannot help respecting the courage and honesty of Becker's effort to create such a union, as is evident in the following passage from the end of his book:

> In the mysterious way in which life is given to us in evolution on this planet, it pushes in the direction of its own

expansion. We don't understand it simply because we don't know the purpose of creation. We only feel life straining in ourselves and see it thrashing others about as they devour each other. There is a driving force behind a mystery that we cannot understand, and it includes more than reason alone. The urge to cosmic heroism, then, is sacred and mysterious and not to be neatly ordered and rationalized by science and secularism.... The most that any one of us can seem to do is to fashion something— an object or ourselves—and drop it into the confusion, make an offering of it, so to speak, to the life force.[21]

Fifty years ago, Levi identified Toynbee as one of the greatest contemporary philosophers of history, despite Toynbee's religious beliefs. Twenty-five years later, Becker referred to religion as a vital lie, yet could not dismiss the mysteries that lie beyond science and secularism. After another quarter of a century, Diamond regards institutional religion as a vehicle to transfer wealth to "kleptocrats." Diamond's version of history is much more compatible with Hesiod's than with the *ex nihilo* creation of early Christianity.

Ex Nihilo *and* Eternal?

Another example of our modern paradigm's deference to Hesiod can be seen in the debate about nature versus nurture. Both genetic predisposition and environmental conditions contribute to a person's "success" in life and are compatible with Hesiod. There is, however, another factor that is independent from either of those options: choice. For example, the exercise of free will explains how one child can thrive when his or her siblings, reared in a foster-care environment, do not. Clearly, nature and nurture both contribute to who we are. Children born with an inherited drug addiction and raised in foster care have two strikes against them. But some succeed. If one argues the false duality of nature and nurture, that will not provide any insight into the supra-Euclidean acceptance of free will and choice. Attributing drive and determination solely to genetic predisposition would be the scientific version of un-verifiable psychobabble.

Every day, new theories are presented to explain everything. Clearly, there have been tremendous advances in medicine, and science continues to identify cause-and-effect relationships. We have come a long way from preparing for death after hearing a diagnosis of cancer. The belief in science gives us hope that cures to any malady are imminent. Science can predict one's risk for a particular cancer to be one in a thousand. But there are two problems with this information. First, if you're the *one*, you find little comfort in the good luck of the other 999. Probability is not certainty; life and death are. Second, knowledge of how our bodies work does not assure a healthy outcome. The abyss between how our bodies work and why life is so unpredictable represents a tangible demonstration of the gap between the illusion of Euclidean certainty and the acceptance of supra-Euclidean reality. Theory and practice in the ancient Greek tradition of *theoria* and *praxis* required a union between contemplation and action. Knowing how the body works does not substitute for exercise. Knowing how to make a fire will not keep you warm. Finally, there is no amount of medical knowledge that will overcome the certainty of death. Becker's vital lie represents a visceral truth that attempts to bridge perception and reality.

Becker describes the inherent despair of our modern paradigm when he offers his utopian fantasy:

If I wanted to give in weakly to the most utopian fantasy I know, it would be one that pictures a world-scientific body composed of leading minds in all fields, working under an agreed general theory of human unhappiness. They would reveal to mankind the reasons of human un-happiness.... Then men might struggle, even in anguish, to come to terms with themselves and their world.[22]

This depressing utopian vision is all that is left for the modern paradigm of self. The ancient Greek and the early Christian paradigms made life meaningful through stories of transcendent mystery. For Becker, that was not an option.

Modern-day individuals seek meaning in life through personalized stories that are based on either *ex nihilo* creation or eternal cosmology. Since the modern paradigm of self lacks a transcending standard, either creation story will find its share of supporters. The legions of conflicting voices that both claim and deny divine truth undermine efforts to unite societies. Undeterred, academics and scientists continue to hypothesize, analyze, and judge.

Intellectual judgment is a truly powerful ability. However, discernment and discrimination, the characteristics of intellect, too easily degenerate into condemnation and arrogance. Hubris inflates one's self-importance, undermining the social value inherent in humility. Intellectual hubris leads well-meaning believers in the divine on a quest to prove God's existence. Yet, each attempt fails to achieve intellectual harmony. In fact, we saw in Chapter 7 how competing rationales for the divine undermined all efforts at proof. Empiricist David Hume was right when he said that there is not enough evidence in the world to allow us to infer the existence of an infinitely good, wise, powerful, and perfect God. Of course, Hume's suggestion to burn metaphysical beliefs supported by the supra-Euclidean realm of mystery demonstrates the hubris of his intellect!

We may intellectually accept Heisenberg's uncertainty principle, yet insist that everything can be known with enough information. We may appreciate the ultimate authority of our heart-centered belief system as exemplified by Ms. Weil, who chose to abort her possibly impaired fetus, yet insist on intellectually analyzing alternatives. We may exhibit certain impulsive behaviors without understanding the relationship between belief systems, right conduct, and enforcement mechanisms. We may value the perceived objectivity of empiricism and rationalism, but be reluctant to accept objectivity itself as an illusion. We may speak of "theory and practice" or "perception and reality" without the visceral consciousness of life experienced through our heart-centered *nous*. We may acknowledge the choice between cooperation and competition, but insist on a middle strategy that successfully balances self-interest and common good.

High-Entropy As the Natural State of Being

This book has traced the human exploration of wisdom over the past three thousand years. The movement from organic unity, through transcendent responsibility, to personal belief systems can be understood as a progression from communal unity to the celebration of individuality. Cassirer has accurately described this as movement from the general to the particular. Interestingly, this corresponds to another scientific principle known as the Second Law of Thermodynamics, or entropy, whose essential features Brian Greene describes as follows:

> First, entropy is a measure of the amount of disorder in
> a physical system.... Second, in physical systems with

many constituents…, there is a natural evolution toward greater disorder, since disorder can be achieved in so many more ways than order. In the language of entropy, this is the statement that physical systems tend to evolve toward states of higher entropy.[23]

The organic unity found in ancient Greek society can be described as highly ordered, having low entropy. The relationship between the individual and the community was generally recognized and accepted by everyone. As a result, *areté* ("virtue") and *aidos* ("holy shame") were sufficient to enforce cooperation.

Greene finds entropy intriguing because it implies an arrow of time that "points to increasing entropy."[24] There is no need to explain the move from highly ordered systems to highly disordered systems because "high-entropy is the natural state of being."[25] We may believe that there is a middle strategy that balances self-interest and the common good, but if high-entropy is the natural state of being, then movement toward a highly disordered reality is inevitable. Greene affirms this when he writes:

> The future is indeed the direction of increasing entropy. The arrow of time—the fact that things start like this and end like that but never start like that and end like this— began its flight in the highly ordered, low-entropy state of the universe at its inception.[26]

Of course, this brings us back to the familiar question of creation. The early Christian paradigm's acceptance of creation *ex nihilo* might be compatible with the scientific evidence of a "big bang" inception of the universe, but is absolutely incompatible with the ancient Greek paradigm's eternal cosmology of Hesiod.

In different ways, our modern paradigm of self finds compatibility with each of the previous paradigms. In Chapter 8, we identified an understanding of phenomena shared by both the early Christian paradigm and quantum mechanics. The faith-based acceptance of Heisenberg, the orthodox understanding of Trinity (which accepts three as one, but never two), and the shared inability to explain phenomena such as gravity and the divine Persons through intellect or evidence are all areas of compatibility.

In Chapter 9, we acknowledged a common faith in reason shared by our modern paradigm and the ancient Greek paradigm. The early Christian paradigm of *ex nihilo* creation represents a clear conflict with the ancient Greek paradigm. Modern secularists, despite the accumulating scientific theories that point to an initial moment, must dismiss the *ex nihilo* implications of the "big bang" theory. Theories of evolution are broad enough to "explain" biological, genetic, and environmental changes over time. Evolution of an eternal universe is far more compatible with the ancient Greek cosmology of Hesiod.

Parallel with faith in reason's compulsive need to explain everything is the expanding embrace of spiritualism. The breakdown of organized religion has not only led to skepticism but also to an increasing acceptance of some personally defined "spiritual" realm. Eastern beliefs such as Buddhism, Hinduism, Taoism, and Confucianism, and the increasing interest in yoga and meditation, are filling the spiritual void. Indigenous belief systems that venerate Mother Earth elevate the importance of Nature. All of these examples are compatible with Hesiod.

The growing spiritualism also blends a number of beliefs concerning life after death. We have seen how, in ancient Greek mythology, the soul is reunited after death with the transcendent divine. Modern seekers of spiritual truth may accept a role for a heart-centered *nous* that is compatible with personal interpretations of Buddhism and other Eastern or indigenous philosophies. Such seekers may also reinterpret aspects of Christianity and adapt them to their spiritual beliefs. For example, they may split off the "proceeding Holy Spirit" from the Christian Trinity and identify it with their vague understanding of eternal Oneness. The cosmology of Hesiod is highly compatible with the realm of mystery and our modern paradigm of self. In fact, all vague notions of cosmic oneness, fate, and destiny can co-exist comfortably under the umbrella of the ancient Greek paradigm.

What Is Truth?

In this book, I have intentionally not traced the evolution of Christianity as a unique belief system after the creation of the Holy Roman Empire. In fact, I have identified many competing understandings under the umbrella of the Roman Catholic Church, and these differences were only compounded after the Protestant Reformation and the Enlightenment. What distinguished the early Christian paradigm was its unity. The lack of unity after the Great Schism of 1054 created an environment that eventually ushered in our modern paradigm of self. Now each of us has some degree of familiarity with some aspect of Christianity. Modern Christians who ponder wisdom regard various aspects of Christian mystery and dogma with varying degrees of reverence.

What I find particularly interesting is how each paradigm interprets the experience of life. The idea of divine providence provides a rationale for life's twists and turns only so long as people accept the existence of a divine authority. The guardianship of the Creator for the created is clearly consistent with the early Christian paradigm, which seeks human cooperation with the operation of divine grace. There is, however, no requirement for a Triune Creator to accept the idea of a divine plan.

The idea of a divine plan is totally compatible with the Euclidean implications of fate and predestination.

The famous Swiss psychotherapist Carl Jung (1875–1961) wrote about experiences of meaningful coincidence as examples of what he called "synchronicity."[27] Clearly, meaningful coincidence does not require a Creator as much as a belief in some vague universal oneness or in some unifying idea such as the ancient Greek paradigm. Thinking about someone as you drive home, only to find a message from that person on your answering machine when you arrive, can be interpreted as an example of divine providence, synchronicity, or merely random chance, depending on which paradigm you use to interpret the experience.

Another, more dramatic example of how competing belief systems can offer alternative interpretations of evidence is to be found in the Christian belief in Armageddon as opposed to environmentalists' belief in what they call the Sixth Extinction. The latter refers to the rapid extinction of plants and animals anticipated within the next one hundred years.[28] Geologists have determined that mass extinctions due to natural disasters have occurred five times since the emergence of complex life on Earth. The upcoming extinction, however, is man-made, for the planet simply cannot sustain the level of consumption that humanity seems to require.

Most people who are concerned about the environment fear the prospect of an ecological disaster that will alter or end life on Earth as we know it. Efforts to remove our dependence on oil and to reduce our consumption of other natural resources all share an underlying motivation to avoid the anticipated extinction. But those who interpret the end of life as Armageddon find hope in the second coming of Christ. Professing personally defined Christian-sounding sentiments, they look forward to the predicted disaster because they expect it to end with their own salvation.

The evidence for Armageddon and the Sixth Extinction is the same. Whether one is hopeful or fearful depends on which paradigm one uses. In this example, however, the choices represent blended alternatives within our modern paradigm. One's personalized Christianity and environmental commitment determine the ardor of one's hope or fear. Early Christian writings described the end of time as if it were imminent. The early Christian paradigm, however, did not emphasize *when* this would happen so much as *how* prepared one should be for it. Modern academics and philosophers will point to the fact that after two thousand years the end hasn't happened yet, so the early Christian belief in the second coming must therefore be false. Those who subscribe to the early Christian paradigm, however, observe that everyone who has died in the past two thousand years has in fact run out of time, and the eternity of all individuals will be judged on how they lived the time they had. When that final judgment will come, however, is known only to our Creator.

This book will have succeeded to the degree that the reader considers the role of paradigms in interpreting history, evidence, and reality itself. According to the modern paradigm, each of us can justify whatever we believe. Whether we then choose to cooperate or compete is a matter of personal choice. Understanding the roots of personally defined belief systems that guide our hearts becomes the real challenge to "know thyself."

Final Thoughts

Where do we go from here? Recall in Chapter 2 that ancient Greece employed three paths to knowledge of divine perfection. Material evidence (*pistis*) was the least respected and considered mere opinion. Mathematical thought (*dianoia*) could provide abstract understanding and was therefore considered superior to material evidence. These two ways of knowing have an underlying faith in reason and continue to frame the modern paradigm's interpretation of reality. But the ancient Greeks believed that the highest path to knowledge of divine perfection (or revelation) was the heart-centered *nous*.

We have seen how our modern paradigm has "freed" itself from any transcendent acceptance of divinity. One's belief in the *nous* is personal and relative at best. The ancient Greeks elevated justice as the tangible standard of noble *areté*. In fact, voluntary subordination to the higher communal good was the necessary prerequisite for justice. No comparably compelling commitment to justice permeates our modern paradigm.

The decision to cooperate or compete has been traced in this book throughout the past three thousand years. In the personal struggles created by the ancient Greek and early Christian paradigms, cooperation was an internal struggle between self-interest and self-sacrifice, between our head and our heart. Compared to competition, cooperation has always been the more difficult road. The decision to cooperate rejoins the ancient Greek relationship between *theoria* and *praxis*, for more than simply contemplating positive thoughts, one makes a commitment to action. Simply imagining a better reality is not enough. Improving reality is a conscious commitment to positive *praxis*, an affirmative action.

But the harder road of cooperation lacks a compelling motive. The appeal of self-interest and the Euclidean illusion of certainty and objectivity overwhelmingly encourages competition. For example, competition between men and women and the economic glass ceiling are real obstacles when Euclidean perception defines relationships. Dualities require one to compete and "do what it takes to win." Negative campaigning successfully influences political contests by advertising the perceived deficiencies of an opposing candidate. There is no obligation to broadcast the truth or educate the electorate. Political candidates and consultants who will do anything to win will not hesitate to engage in negative campaigning, because it works.

The stability of supra-Euclidean acceptance relies on the trinity of intellectual reflection, empirical evidence, and the realm of mystery. Believing that the realm of mystery is co-equal stabilizes this trinity. Plato framed freedom as a choice between our higher sense of duty and our lower inclinations. But in our modern paradigm there are three "authorities" that vie for our duty: the state, the divine, and the self. Self-righteous, self-centered individuals will look to the state, the divine, and other people to satisfy their need for companionship, but without any willingness to make sacrifices for others. Therefore, loneliness is unavoidable for them. Over time, since high entropy is the natural condition, more and more people will become self-righteous and self-centered—unless, that is, they make a conscious decision to cooperate. Conscious cooperation is the only way to overcome the natural state of being.

Freedom does not pose a choice between two false dualities, but underlies the personal willingness to accept some noble purpose in life. Individuals who are committed to humility will never be first, for they will always be willing to sacrifice self-interest for some understanding of the common good. On the other hand, self-proclaimed Christians who indiscriminately consume natural resources in the belief that they are somehow facilitating Armageddon have blended self-interest and self-righteousness. No amount of evidence or rationalization will persuade them to see and admit their arrogance. Of course, life has a way of humbling the self-righteous. The early Christian paradigm would interpret such humbling life experiences as opportunities to reconsider one's beliefs.

Most arrogant of all are the intellectuals, who are so full of self-righteous hubris as they discern the deficiencies of others. Blinded by Euclidean certainty, they are unable to accept wisdom that is beyond the reach of reason and evidence. As with the self-proclaimed Christians above, in the absence of a humbling life experience, no amount of evidence or rationalization will persuade them to see and admit their arrogance. The truth of supra-Euclidean reality can only be accepted through conscious cooperation between mystery, reason, and evidence.

If the three paradigms described in this book adequately summarize the plethora of belief systems that govern behavior, are there any lessons to be learned from this? I believe that an historical pattern of humility demonstrates the essential fabric of strong communities. Two thousand years ago, ancient Greece, although militarily weak, conquered the emerging Roman Empire with culture and philosophy. Five hundred years later, only the weak Pope of Rome supported Maximus the Confessor in challenging the authority of the Emperor in Constantinople. The Eastern Orthodox Church survives to this day only through its temporal weakness. In the long run, humility has kept communities strong and stable.

The life of Maximus the Confessor provides a particularly revealing example of humility. His steadfast support of divine truth had absolutely no self-serving motive. He did not suffer from low self-esteem, nor was his uncompromising adherence to Christian dogma an act of self-promotion. Accepting the political compromise of the Emperor with regard to the two wills of Christ would have been the painlessly easy way out. Maximus, however, was a monk committed to subordinating his will to cooperation with divine grace. Ascetic monks like Maximus accomplish this through prayer and fasting. Fasting humbles the body and disciplines the mind, which prayer directs toward the Triune God. Maximus's ultimate triumph of humility came when the Sixth Ecumenical Council, without a mention of his name, accepted his cosmology regarding the issue of the two wills of Christ.

One force that *seems* to be strong and stable but actually dissolves communities is nationalism. For example, Isocrates' appeal to Greek nationalism undermined the Athenian city-state and advanced the conquest of Macedonian King Phillip II and his son Alexander the Great. Charlemagne's nationalization of the Holy Roman Empire under a Latin umbrella fragmented Western Europe over the next thousand years and established the Enlightenment victory of our modern paradigm. Today, nationalism continues to emphasize differences at the expense of cooperation.

Essentially, life is a series of choices between cooperation and competition. We remember appeals to love when we consider cooperation. But the word *love* is hollow without the praxis of humility, which is the essence of love. Those who decide to cooperate should do so with no expectation of acknowledgment, accepting humility as a virtue. The biblical commandment is not to help others so that they will like you, but to help others even if they are your enemies. There are many reasons, conscious and unconscious, to compete, but the decision to cooperate can only be conscious. St. Paul recalls the Lord's words in 2 Corinthians 12:9: "My strength is made perfect in weakness." Ultimately, the choice between cooperation and competition is an internal struggle within one's heart-centered *nous*. According to the modern paradigm of self, there are as many realities as there are people, for reality is only an interpretation of experience filtered through each individual's blend of belief systems. Unless, of course, there really *is* an absolute truth transcending the cosmos.

❖ ❖ ❖

Epilogue

Three Paradigms of Reality represents a summary of the belief paradigms that I have experienced over the past fifty years. I discovered these points of view along the path of my own spiritual journey. Both nature and nurture contributed greatly to my religious growth until I accepted the truth of Orthodox Christian cooperation. This epilogue traces my journey.

My mother's parents emigrated from Palestine to the United States in the 1930s and settled on the East Coast, where my Mom was born. At the age of 18, in 1947, my Dad emigrated from Palestine to the United States and settled in San Francisco. My parents met and married in Detroit and drove to San Francisco for their honeymoon. I was born nine months later in San Francisco. Blessed with natural beauty, ethnic diversity, eccentric charm, and high ideals of personal freedom and social justice, San Francisco has few places in the world to match it. I was raised in the Eastern Orthodox Christian faith of my parents. But San Francisco, the epicenter of the turbulent 1960s, was the place that defined me as an American youth.

I grew up a few miles from the Haight-Ashbury, almost across the street from Golden Gate Park. In my virtual backyard, the Jefferson Airplane and the Grateful Dead performed free concerts for thousands of hippies. Allen Ginsberg, Timothy Leary, and other cultural icons hosted the culminating event that celebrated the high idealism of that era: the legendary San Francisco Be-In.

The Six Day War imposed a national and cultural identity on me that I would learn to wear, however uncomfortably at first. People held me accountable for events beyond my control or judged me according to standards I knew nothing about. It took me another decade before I could accept my ancestry with confidence.

Meanwhile, in 1968, when I was in seventh grade, future U.S. Senator from California Sam Hayakawa sent the National Guard onto the campus of San Francisco State University against student antiwar demonstrators. Vietnam was a divisive, gaping wound in the American psyche. Martin Luther King, Jr., and Robert Kennedy were assassinated in that year. Two years later, four students were shot and killed by National Guard units at Kent State University while they were protesting Nixon's bombing of Cambodia.

My junior and senior high school years encompassed an array of conflicting messages: "Make love, not war," "Overthrow the establishment," and "Question authority" were a few of the popular, if contradictory, slogans of the era. There were communes, "mind-expanding" drugs, racial discrimination, radical student movements, antiwar protests, riot police, National Guardsmen, homegrown political terrorists, Peace Corps members, and a very nervous population at large. In my school, long hair, tie-dye shirts, bell-bottom pants, and peace symbols were the fashion, drugs were easily bought on campus, and racial fights were a regular occurrence. Dealing drugs was a career option among my classmates.

At the same time, there was a passionate idealism that shone clearly through the chaos, reflecting our nation's highest principles, which inspired me and my generation. I cherished the ideal of a society that recognizes and protects individual freedoms. Watching our government punish individuals who exercised their protected freedoms was appalling, but it allowed me to discover that real heroes demonstrate their courage and integrity by enduring the consequences of their principled decisions.

The best American example of this heroism at the time, I thought, was Muhammad Ali, who relinquished his heavyweight boxing title at the height of his career and was ready to face a prison sentence rather than betray his principles. His willing sacrifice of short-term glory and his courage to endure the consequences of his principles were a standard of integrity that few people sought then or seek now. Muhammad Ali set the standards I adopted for myself. I expected others, especially people "in charge," to seek these same principles of conscience, honor, integrity, and courage. However, I was continually disappointed by the nation's political leadership.

One by one, my generation witnessed its highest ideals being betrayed by those in power for a variety of supposedly noble objectives—whether to "stop the spread of communism" or "safeguard America's interests abroad." The consequences were often something quite different. Thus, cynicism became a popular defense mechanism for constant disappointment.

By 1978, the reality of my nation routinely violating its most cherished ideals in order to achieve short-term benefits had become too confusing for me to deal with and too painful to accept. For six months, I backpacked around the country, exploring 32 states and 64 cities. While on the road, I began to explore religion as a solution for the world's ills. Modern society had demonstrably sacrificed its noblest ideals to the principle of expedience, that popular euphemism for self-interest. I wanted to go to the source of those ideals and see what was true when you stripped them down to their core. At bottom, I wanted to discover if God were real or not. Surely, one of the many religions claiming divine truth would lead me to that perfect blend of reason and faith in which values are consistently professed and practiced.

In my spiritual search, I studied Christianity, Buddhism, Judaism, and Islam, read the Bhagavad-Gita and the Way of Lao Tzu, and even looked at Transactional Analysis for answers. My search finally brought me back to Eastern Orthodox Christianity, the faith of my youth, which I continue to embrace with the fervor of a convert. The wisdom of that decision has only increased with the passage of time. Accepting humility as a virtue completed my understanding of my identity as an Orthodox Christian American citizen of Arab ancestry.

The formative life-events recounted above have all led, in one way or another, to the writing of this book. As a child of my time and tradition, I have both great respect for reason and a living faith in the Triune God. These two fundamental precepts, reason and faith, are not irreconcilable, and we do not have to choose between them, as fundamentalists in both the reason and the faith camps often claim. I have come to appreciate that the competition between reason and faith is actually a human struggle between the head and the heart. The early Christian paradigm navigates this Euclidian duality and finds cooperation through a commitment to humility—the Trinitarian strategy for eternal salvation.

While humility may be a virtue, it is not an American value. But without humility, champions of reason or faith battle endlessly, while the rest of us wrestle with unanswered questions. After writing this book, I read two others that are representative of the combatants: Karen Armstrong's *A History of God* and Richard Dawkins' *The God Delusion*. Those two books and mine cover the same territory and reference many of the same scientific examples and historical events. But what a difference there is among them!

Armstrong employs an air of objectivity and a faith in reason that threads various beliefs about God into a cosmic quilt, but ultimately ends with the observation that since "human beings cannot endure emptiness and desolation, they will fill the vacuum by creating a new focus of meaning."[1] Armstrong is similar to Ralph Waldo Emerson in her attempts to reconcile reason and faith in the modern paradigm. Her explanation of faith is grounded in the Biblical Abraham's trust in God. Faith is not found in a particular creed, but in a "leap in the dark toward a reality that had to be taken on trust."[2]

Dawkins would hardly find this argument compelling. To the contrary, he seethes with disdain for anyone who harbors a belief in the divine. Dawkins repeatedly identifies atheists as intellectually superior and trusts only the evidence of evolution as the foundation for his reliance on reason. In fact, he would reject having *faith* in reason, because faith, he writes, "is an evil precisely because it requires no justification and brooks no argument."[3] Nevertheless, his trust in reason can only be described as a form of faith.

Armstrong identifies herself as a "freelance monotheist…, draw[ing] sustenance from all three of the faiths of Abraham."[4] She is a contemporary example of the ancient Greek paradigm's acceptance of a transcendent law and of faith in reason. Dawkins' intellectual hubris is consistent with that of Laplace and Hume. The *faith* of both Dawkins and Armstrong provides reason a purpose that justifies both the ancient Greek paradigm, on the one hand, and the modern paradigm of self, on the other. Reasoned attempts to convince our head, our intellectual capacity, of the respective wisdom in these competing versions of reality will ultimately fail, as this book has demonstrated.

Faith springs from the realm of mystery beyond Euclidean certainty. Faith is not an intellectual concept, but an innate characteristic of our heart-centered *nous*. Like typical philosophers, Armstrong and Dawkins speculate about faith but never experience *theoria*—participation with the divine. Faith comes from the experience of being and living. *Three Paradigms of Reality* provides a window into the hope of faith. Accepting faith, embracing humility, and employing reason will not win arguments, but this trinity provides a steadfast foundation for cooperation.

My religious ardor is not fanatically blind to empirical evidence or reasoned logic. But my life experience convinces me that there is something greater. The 2,000-year-old Orthodox Christian narrative, perfected by Maximus's cosmology, represents the perfect collaboration of reason, faith, and humility. For me, the scientific concepts of entropy, quanta, and gravity are not only compatible with Maximus's cosmology but evidence of its truth. My faith threatens no one because I strive not to judge others, nor do I impose my beliefs on others. Reason and faith cooperate through humility. As Maximus wrote, reason does not bend to self-determination, nor is reason at variance with naturally free will, but willingly submits to humility as the only reliable path to salvation.

My struggle is to emulate the unconditional love of my Creator, without judgment, knowing that I fail miserably every day and hoping that my feeble efforts earn His perfect mercy. The hope of eternal well-being, despite my constant failings, has kept me grounded throughout the turbulence of the past fifty years.

❖ ❖ ❖

Acknowledgments

When I began this project, I never intended to write a book. The process, however, helped me to make sense of my life's contradictory experiences, which are identified in the Epilogue. This final product is the culmination of fifteen years and three drafts of arduous effort. Along the way, I received advice and assistance from Ruth, Doug, Byron, Robert, Sean, and Rick, although they are probably unaware of their contributions.

Thank you to all the people I met throughout my involvement in politics. Thanks to those who supported me every step of the way, including the 10,000+ voters, 500+ contributors, and hundreds of volunteers, family members, friends, and well–wishers. In particular, I'd like to thank those who opposed me with an irrational fervor, whose depths I have never known. You have unintentionally contributed to my well–being, and I am truly appreciative. The City of San Francisco remains a place of high thought and idealism, despite the sometimes stifling political correctness of its plantation politics.

The literary quality of this final effort relied on the art and precision of my editor, Paul Weisser, Ph.D.

My final acknowledgment goes to Metropolitan Nikitas of the Patriarch Athenagoras Orthodox Institute at the Graduate Theological Union in Berkeley, California, for his generous support of my effort to serve our faith.

To you, the reader, I hope the described paradigms help you to embrace the virtue of humility: the highest purpose of our rational capacity.

❖ ❖ ❖

Historical Glossary

Avicebron (1020–1070 A.D.): Jewish philosopher interested in Aristotle.

Alexander the Great (356–323 B.C.): Son of Macedonian King Phillip II and tutored by Aristotle.

Al-Kindi (ca. 813–873 A.D.): The first Arab philosopher to explore Aristotle's metaphysics within his Islamic beliefs.

Allen, Reginald (1931–2007): Professor of Classics and Philosophy, Emeritus, at Northwestern University.

Ammonius Saccas (ca. 175–242 A.D.): Philosopher; credited with founding the Neo-Platonic school in Alexandria that taught Plotinus and Origen.

Anaximander of Miletus (ca. 610–546 B.C.): Student of Thales; believed in opposites balanced by time.

Anaximenes of Miletus (585–525 B.C.): Student of Anaximander; believed that a thick mist, Aer, was the source of everything.

Aquinas, Thomas (1225–1274 A.D.): Philosopher and theologian; united reason and faith in his *Summa Theologica*.

Aristotle (384–322 B.C.): Student of Plato; tutor of Alexander the Great; inspired cosmology in his treatise *On the Heavens*.

Arius of Alexandria (ca. 250–335 A.D.): Theologian; challenged the dogma of the First Ecumenical Council regarding the relationship between the Un-Begotten Father and the Only-Begotten Son.

Armstrong, Karen (1944–): Former Roman Catholic nun and current "freelance monotheist."

Athanasius of Alexandria (ca. 298–373 A.D.): The most dominant theologian at the First Ecumenical Council of Nicaea, in 325 A.D.

Averroes (Ibn Rushd) (1126–1198 A.D.): Arab philosopher and author of Commentaries that became the template for Aquinas's *Summa Theologica*.

Avicenna (Ibn Sina) (980–1037 A.D.): Arab philosopher translated into Latin; initiated the revival of interest in Aristotle.

Bacon, Francis (1561–1626 A.D.): English statesman, essayist, and philosopher; distinguished God's works from natural works.

Barfield, Owen (1898–1997): British philosopher, author, poet, and critic.

Becker, Ernest (1924–1974): Author and professor of Cultural Anthropology.

Bodanis, David (1939–): Best-selling author and academic.

Bohr, Niels Henrik David (1885–1962): Renowned physicist who won the Nobel Prize for Physics in 1922.

Campenhausen, Hans von (1903–1989): Early church historian at the University of Heidelberg.

Capra, Fritjof (1939–): Physicist who considers himself both a Buddhist and a Catholic.

Cassirer, Ernst (1884–1978): French philosopher unique in his equal consideration of both mathematics and natural sciences, on the one hand, and the humanistic discipline of aesthetics, on the other.

Chadwick, Henry (1920–2008): Distinguished historian and former Dean of Christ Church, University of Oxford.

Charlemagne (742–824 A.D.): Emperor; the primary figure behind the declaration of the Holy Roman Empire in 800 A.D., which ultimately led to the Great Schism of 1054 A.D.

Clement of Alexandria (ca. 150–215 A.D.): An early Christian philosopher and theologian who was comfortable with the ambiguity that existed before philosophy and theology were separated.

Colbert, Stephen (1964–): Comedian and faux reporter.

Combéfis, François (1605–1679): A Dominican patristic scholar.

Comte, Auguste (1798–1857): Philosopher; attempted to reestablish the importance of duty to others through his Positivistic Philosophy.

Constantine the Great (ca. 274–337 A.D.): First Christian emperor of the Roman Empire; defeated Licinius, the eastern Roman Emperor, and reunited the ancient Roman Empire throughout the Mediterranean.

Copernicus, Nicolas (1473–1543 A.D.): Astronomer; challenged the "science" of Aristotle and Claudius Ptolemy, which recognized the Earth as the center of the universe. In so doing, Copernicus also challenged the authority of the Roman Catholic Church, which had accepted Ptolemy's cosmic relationships.

Darwin, Charles (1809–1882): Naturalist; proposed the evolution of man, which did not require a divine creator.

Dawkins, Richard (1941–): Outspoken atheist, evolutionary biologist, and popular author.

Descartes, René (1596–1650): Philosopher and mathematician; defined the modern understanding of Cartesian rationalism, which challenged the relationship between philosophy and theology.

Diamond, Jared (1937–): Evolutionary biologist and author.

Dobbs, E. R. (1893–1973). Irish classical scholar.

Donatus Magnus (ca. 311–ca. 355 A.D.): Christian heretic; supported an unyielding standard of perfection for the clergy, which was opposed by St. Augustine and condemned as heresy.

Einstein, Albert (1879–1955): Nobel Prize–winning physicist; author of relativity theory; widely considered the greatest physicist of all time.

Emerson, Ralph Waldo (1803–1882): Essayist, poet, and leader of the Transcendentalist movement.

Empedocles (490–430 B.C.): Philosopher and statesman; believed that reason and material evidence are "real."

Epicurus (341–270 B.C.): Philosopher; founded Epicureanism, which promoted material happiness and hedonism.

Euclid of Alexandria (ca. 325–265 B.C.): Mathematician; founded Euclidean geometry, which defined "reality" for two thousand years.

Eutyches (ca. 380–ca. 346 A.D.): A priest in Constantinople who did not agree with the dogma of equal divine and human wills for Jesus, for which he was excommunicated by Flavian, Patriarch of Constantinople.

Faraday, Michael (1791–1867): Chemist and physicist; discovered electric and magnetic "force fields," which began the move away from Newton's Euclidean reality toward Einstein's relativistic reality.

Feynman, Richard (1918–1988): Nobel Prize–winning physicist; known for particle theory and quantum electrodynamics.

Flavian (d. 449 A.D.): Patriarch of Constantinople; excommunicated Eutyches.

Flavius Claudius Constantinus (316–340 A.D.): Oldest son of Constantine the Great; known as Constantine II; ruled Britannia, Gaul, and Hispania.

Flavius Julius Constans (ca. 320–350–A.D.): Youngest son of Constantine the Great; known as Constans I; ruled Italia, Africa, and Illyricum.

Flavius Julius Constantius (317–361 A.D.): Middle son of Constantine the Great; known as Constantius II; ruled the East.

Fourth Council of Lateran (1215 A.D.): Formalized a legal formula for pardons and indulgences for the Roman Catholic Church.

Freud, Sigmund (1856–1939): Neurologist; father of psychoanalysis.

Fuller, Robert (n.d.): Professor of Religious Studies at Bradley University, in Peoria, Illinois.

Gilson, Étienne (1884–1978): Philosopher and historian.

Gnosticism: A religious sect that attempted to find middle ground between Christianity and Neo-Platonism, but was rejected by both. Mani was the most prominent Gnostic.

Goudsmit, Samuel Abraham (1902–1978): Dutch physicist who, with George Uhlenbeck, recognized three modes intrinsic to our understanding of electrons: mass, electric charge, and spin.

Greene, Brian (1963–): Physicist and author.

Hegel, Georg Wilhelm Friedrich (1770–1831): A post-Kantian idealist philosopher, who published many writings from a "logical" perspective. He inspired Karl Marx, who manipulated Hegel's ideas into communism.

Heisenberg, Werner (1901–1976): Nobel Prize–winning physicist; one of the founders of quantum mechanics; author of the uncertainty principle.

Heraclitus (ca. 535–475 B.C.): Philosopher; believed divine logos united the cosmos.

Hesiod (ca. 800 B.C.): Greek poet and historian, second only to Homer.

Homer (9th–8th? cent. B.C.): Most celebrated pre-Socratic poet and historian.

Hume, David (1711–1776): Philosopher and historian; defined the modern understanding of empiricism.

Isocrates (436–338 B.C.): Athenian orator; promoted Greek nationalism as an alternative to Plato's philosopher king.

Jaeger, Werner (1888–1961): Professor of classics; author of *Paidea: The Ideals of Greek Culture*.

James, William (1842–1910): Psychologist and philosopher; father of functional psychology.

Jones, Jim (1931–1978): Cult leader; created Jonestown tragedy in Guyana.

Jung, Carl G. (1875–1961): Famous Swiss psychotherapist.

Kant, Immanuel (1724–1804): The "last" philosopher; merged science and philosophy.

Kireyevsky, Ivan (1806–1856): Nineteenth-century Russian philosopher.

Kuhn, Thomas (1922–1996): Professor of philosophy and history; author of *The Structure of Scientific Revolutions.*

Laplace, Pierre Simon (1749–1827): Mathematician; rejected the idea of a divine creator.

Leibniz, Gottfried Wilhelm (1646–1716): Philosopher, mathematician, and logician; believed in, and attempted to prove, the existence of a transcendent God.

Levi, Albert (1911–1988): Professor of philosophy at Washington University, in St. Louis.

Lobachevsky, Nikolai (1792–1856): Mathematician; contributed to the refinement of supra-Euclidean geometry.

Locke, John (1632–1704): Philosopher; challenged the authority of all institutions, religious and civil.

Lossky, Vladimir (1903–1958): Professor of dogmatic theology.

Louth, Andrew (1944–): Professor of theology and religion at Durham University, England.

Luther, Martin (1483–1546 A.D.): German Reformation leader.

Maimonides (1135–1204 A.D.): Jewish philosopher interested in Aristotle.

Mani (ca. 215–ca. 274 A.D.): The most influential Gnostic; proclaimed himself the latest incarnation of God's messengers; executed by Zoroastrian priests.

Maslow, Abraham (1908–1970): Humanistic psychologist; best known for his actualization theories and his proposal of a hierarchy of human needs.

Maximus the Confessor (580–662 A.D.): Christian monk, theologian, and scholar; supported the position that Jesus had both a human and a divine will.

Maxwell, James Clerk (1831–1879): Scottish physicist; built on Faraday's theories and discovered electromagnetic equations that became the foundation of Einstein's theory of Special Relativity.

McVeigh, Timothy (1968–2001): The convicted Oklahoma bomber.

Menand, Louis (1952–): Author of *The Metaphysical Club.*

Monothelitism: The heresy that one divine will guides the two natures of Jesus.

Newton, Isaac (1642–1727): English physicist; identified laws of motion that explained the mechanics of the cosmos.

Nietzsche, Friedrich (1844–1900): German philosopher who challenged traditional morality and Christianity.

Origen (ca. 185–232 A.D.): An early Christian philosopher who sought to clarify the ambiguity between philosophy and theology, only to be discredited by both communities.

Parmenides (b. ca. 515 B.C.): Greek philosopher; found reality only through abstract reason.

Pelagius (ca. 354–ca. 420 A.D.): British monk and theologian; believed that Original Sin did not taint human nature and that Jesus set a good example in contrast to the bad example set by Adam. The heresy of Pelagianism was condemned at several local synods and opposed by St. Augustine.

Petrarch, Francesco (1304–1374 A.D.): Italian poet; reacquainted Western Europe with Classical Greek and Latin culture; regarded as an early representative of Renaissance humanism.

Phillip II (382–336 B.C.): Macedonian king who conquered ancient Greece; father of Alexander the Great.

Philo (ca. 13 B.C.–ca. 50 A.D.): Jewish philosopher in Alexandria; merged Judaism and Platonic theology.

Planck, Max (1858–1946): Nobel Prize–winning physicist who discovered the smallest extension, the *Planck length* (1.616×10^{-33}).

Plato (ca. 428–ca. 348 B.C.): Celebrated author, philosopher, and student of Socrates.

Plotinus (ca. 205–270 A.D.): Roman philosopher; fine-tuned Plato's theology into the religion of Neo-Platonism.

Plutarch (ca. 46–ca. 119 A.D.): Greek biographer and moralist.

Pope Leo the Great (d. 461 A.D.): Roman Catholic pope; wrote the *Tome of Leo,* which was adopted at the Fourth Ecumenical Council of Chalcedon in 451 A.D.

Popkin, Richard (1923–2005): Philosopher and historian.

Prosper of Aquitaine (390–465 A.D.): A Latin layman who rejected co-operation between divine grace and free will, believing he was supporting St. Augustine against St. John Cassian.

Protagoras (ca. 485–410 B.C.): Greek philosopher whose belief that man is the measure of all things became the guiding principle of the Sophists.

Ptolemy, Claudius (ca. 90–ca. 168 A.D.): Alexandrian astronomer; perfected Aristotle's cosmic system and popularized the relationships of the universe with the Earth as the center.

Rank, Otto (1884–1939): Austrian psychologist; originally one of Sigmund Freud's closest disciples, but eventually one of his sharpest critics.

Richard II (1367–1400 A.D.): King of England; during his reign, differences between civil and religious authority became sharper.

Romanides, John (1927–2001): Orthodox priest, scholar, and professor of dogmatic theology at the University of Thessaloniki, Greece.

Rousseau, Jean-Jacques (1712–1778): **P**reeminent Romantic philosopher; influenced the French Revolution and inspired such diverse thinkers as Hegel, Emerson, and Freud.

Rudolph, Eric (1966–): The convicted Atlanta Olympics bomber.

Saccas, Ammonius (ca. 175–242 A.D.): A Neo-Platonic philosopher; the teacher of both Plotinus and Origen.

Scotus, Duns (aka John Duns Scotus, 1270–1308): Ninth-century philosopher.

Seneca, Lucius Annaeus (ca. 4 B.C.–65 A.D.): Roman statesman, dramatist, and philosopher; believed in Stoicism constrained by the boundaries of natural law.

Sherrard, Philip (1922–1995): Poet, translator, literary scholar, theologian, and interpreter of the Orthodox tradition.

Skeptics: Ancient Greek philosophers who rejected final judgment about every belief system.

Snow, Nancy E. (n.d.): Professor of philosophy at Marquette University.

Socrates (470–399 B.C.): Greek philosopher; example of moral discipline that inspired Plato.

Solon (638–558 B.C.): Plato's ancestor and legendary example of *areté* (virtue).

Sophists: Ancient Greek philosophers who challenged the authority of the divine and undermined the concept of *areté*.

Sophocles (ca. 496–406 B.C.): Renowned Greek poet and playwright.

Spengler, Oswald (1880–1936): Historian and author of *The Decline of the West.*

Spinoza, Baruch (1632–1677): Jewish philosopher who believed in and attempted to prove the existence of a transcendent God.

St. Ambrose (ca. 340–397 A.D.): An early Latin theologian, who was fluent in Greek.

St. Augustine (354–430 A.D.): An early Latin theologian, who had no knowledge of Greek.

St. Basil the Great (329–379 A.D.): A Greek-speaking theologian in the Roman Empire.

St. Benedict of Nursia (ca. 480–543 A.D.): A Latin theologian who was significantly influenced by St. John Cassian; developed the Rule as a legislative code of conduct; founded the Benedictine Order.

St. Bernard of Clairvaux (1090–1153 A.D.): Founder of the Cistercian movement.

St. Dominic (1170–1221 A.D.): Founder of the Dominican Order.

St. Francis of Assisi (1182–1226 A.D.): Founder of the Franciscan Order.

St. Gregory of Nazianzus (ca. 325–389 A.D.): A Greek-speaking theologian in the Roman Empire.

St. Gregory of Nyssa (d. ca. 386 A.D.): A Greek-speaking theologian in the Roman Empire.

St. Helena (ca. 248–ca. 329 A.D.): The mother of Emperor Constantine the Great; traditionally credited with finding the relics of the True Cross.

St. Jerome (ca. 340–420 A.D.): An early Latin theologian, who was fluent in Greek.

St. John Cassian (ca. 360–435 A.D.): An early Latin theologian, who was fluent in Greek.

St. John Climacus (ca. 525–606 A.D.): Abbot of St. Catherine's Monastery on Mount Sinai and author of *The Ladder of Divine Ascent*.

St. John Damascene (676–749 A.D.): Christian theologian.

St. Thomas Aquinas (see Aquinas, Thomas).

Tarnas, Richard (1950–): Professor of philosophy and psychology at the California Institute of Integral Studies (San Francisco).

Thales of Miletus (624–547 B.C.): Greek philosopher who believed that water was the source of everything.

Thucydides (ca. 460–ca. 400 B.C.): Greek historian of the Peloponnesian War (431–404 B.C.) fought between Athens and Sparta and their allies.

Toynbee, Arnold J. (1889–1975): British historian.

Transcendentalist Movement: A movement in philosophy and literature that flourished in America, especially New England, during the early to middle years of the nineteenth century. It stressed the existence of an indwelling God and the significance of intuitive thought.

Uhlenbeck, George Eugene (1900–1988): Dutch physicist who, with Samuel Goudsmit, recognized three modes intrinsic to our understanding of electrons: mass, electric charge, and spin.

Vlachos, Hierotheos (1945–): Theologian, professor, and Orthodox priest who has published over sixty books in Greek.

Wheeler, John A. (1911–2008): Recognized as one of the finest American physicists.

Whitehead, Alfred North (1861–1947): British mathematician and philosopher; collaborated with Bertrand Russell on the writing of the three-volume *Principia Mathematica* (1910, 1912, 1913).

Wilken, Robert Louis (1936–): Professor of early Christian history at the University of Virginia.

William of Ockham (ca. 1288–1348): English philosopher; speculated about the differences between abstract knowledge and intuition.

Wyclif, John (1324–1384 A.D.): English religious reformer and theologian; challenged the accumulation of wealth and authority by the Archbishop of Canterbury.

Xenophanes of Colophon (ca. 560–ca. 478 B.C.): Pre-Socratic Greek philosopher who believed that one god controlled the universe through thought.

❖ ❖ ❖

Bibliography

Allen, Reginald, ed. *Greek Philosophy: Thales to Aristotle*, 3rd ed. New York: Free Press, 1991.

Ariew, Roger, and Watkins, Eric, eds. *Modern Philosophy: An Anthology of Primary Sources*. Indianapolis, IN: Hackett Publishing, 1998.

Aristotle. *Metaphysics*, ed. J. A. Smith and W. D. Ross. Cambridge: Harvard University Press, 1935.

Aristotle. *The Nicomachean Ethics of Aristotle*, trans. David Ross. Oxford, England: Oxford University Press, 1959.

Aristotle. *On the Heavens*, trans. W. K. C. Guthrie. Cambridge: Harvard University Press, 1970.

Aristotle. *Physics*, ed. J. A. Smith and W. D. Ross. Cambridge: Harvard University Press, 1934.

Armstrong, Karen. *A History of God: The 4,000-Year Quest of Judaism, Christianity and Islam.* New York: Ballantine Books, 1993.

Barfield, Owen. *History in English Words.* Barrington, MA: Lindisfarne Books, 1967.

Barfield, Owen. *Saving the Appearances: A Study in Idolatry*, 2nd ed. Middletown, CT: Wesleyan University Press, 1988.

Becker, Ernest. *The Denial of Death* New York: Free Press, 1973.

Becker, Ernest. *Escape from Evil.* New York: Free Press, 1975.

Bible, The. New King James Version. Nashville, TN: Thomas Nelson, 1997.

Bodanis, David. *E=mc2: A Biography of the World's Most Famous Equation*, 3rd ed. London: Pan Books, 2001.

Bowersock, G. W. *Hellenism in Late Antiquity.* Ann Arbor, MI: University of Michigan Press, 1996.

Campenhausen, Hans von. *The Fathers of the Greek Church*. New York: Pantheon, 1955.

Capra, Fritjof. *The Tao of Physics*. Boston: Shambhala, 1991.

Cassirer, Ernst. *The Philosophy of the Enlightenment*, trans. Fritz Koelln and James P. Pettegrove. Princeton: Princeton University Press, 1951.

Ceram, C. W. *Gods, Graves, and Scholars: The Story of Archaeology*, trans. E. G. Garside. New York: Knopf, 1951.

Chadwick, Henry. "Philosophical Tradition and the Self." In *Interpreting Late Antiquity: Essays on the Postclassical World*, ed. G. W. Bowersock, Peter Brown, and Oleg Grabar. Cambridge: Harvard University Press, 2001.

Climacus, St. John. *The Ladder of Divine Ascent*. Brookline, MA: Holy Transfiguration Monastery, 1991.

Crary, David. "Self-esteem Has Run Rampant, Study Says." *San Francisco Chronicle*, February 27, 2007, p. A2.

Dawkins, Richard. *The God Delusion.* New York: Houghton Mifflin, 2006.

Descartes, René. "Meditation Two: Concerning the Nature of the Human Mind: That It Is Better Known than the Body." In Roger Ariew and Eric Watkins, eds., *Modern Philosophy: An Anthology of Primary Sources* (pp. 30–34). Indianapolis, IN: Hackett Publishing, 1998.

Diamond, Jared. *Guns, Germs, and Steel: The Fates of Human Societies.* New York: W. W. Norton, 1999.

Dodds, E. R. "Tradition and Personal Achievement in the Philosophy of Plotinus." *Journal of Roman Studies,* 50, nos. 1 and 2 (1960), 1–7.

Feynman, Richard P. *QED: The Strange Theory of Light and Matter.* Princeton: Princeton University Press, 1988.

Gibbons, Edward. *The Decline and Fall of the Roman Empire.* New York: Modern Library, 1987.

Gilson, Étienne. *The Unity of Philosophical Experience.* San Francisco: Ignatius Press, 1964.

Greene, Brian. *The Elegant Universe.* New York: W. W. Norton, 1999.

Greene, Brian. *Fabric of the Cosmos: Space, Time, and the Texture of Reality.* New York: Knopf, 2004.

Gross, Terry. "Wrongful Birth and Early Testing." *Fresh Air* transcript, March 16, 2006. National Public Radio. Available at http://www. npr. org/templates/story/story.php?storyId=5283840/

Heylighen, Francis. "A Cognitive Systematic Reconstruction of Maslow's Theory of Self-Actualization." *Behavioral Science,* 37 (1992), 39–58.

Hume, David. "An Inquiry Concerning Human Understanding." In Roger Ariew and Eric Watkins, eds., *Modern Philosophy: An Anthology of Primary Sources* (pp. 491–557). Indianapolis, IN: Hackett Publishing, 1998.

Jaeger, Werner. *Early Christianity and Greek Paideia*. Cambridge: Harvard University Press, 1961.

Jaeger, Werner. *Paideia: The Ideals of Greek Culture*, 2nd. ed., 3 vols., trans. Gilbert Highet. New York: Oxford University Press, 1945.

Jaeger, Werner. *The Theology of the Early Greek Philosophers*. New York: Oxford University Press, 1967.

Jung, C. G. *Synchronicity: An Acausal Connecting Principle*, trans. R. F. C. Hull. Princeton: Princeton University Press, 1952.

Kant, Immanuel. *Critique of Pure Reason*, trans. Norman Kemp Smith. London: Palgrave Macmillan, 1985.

Kuhn, Thomas. *The Structure of Scientific Revolutions*, 3rd ed. Chicago: University of Chicago Press, 1996.

Lamb, Brian. "*Islam: A Short History* by Karen Armstrong." *Booknotes* transcript, September 22, 2000. Available at http://www.booknotes.org/Transcript/?ProgramID=1636, 7.

Levi, Albert. *Philosophy and the Modern World*. Bloomington, IN: Indiana University Press, 1959.

Locke, John. "An Essay Concerning Human Understanding." In Roger Ariew and Eric Watkins, eds., *Modern Philosophy: An Anthology of Primary Sources* (pp. 270–373). Indianapolis, IN: Hackett Publishing, 1998.

Lossky, Vladimir. *In the Image and Likeness of God*. New York: SVS Press, 1974.

Lossky, Vladimir. *The Mystical Theology of the Eastern Church*. New York: SVS Press, 2002.

Louth, Andrew. *The Origins of the Christian Mystical Tradition: From Plato to Denys*. New York: Clarendon, 1981.

Louth, Andrew, ed. and trans. *Maximus the Confessor*. New York: Routledge, 1996.

Maximus. *Maximus Confessor: Selected Writings*, trans. George C. Berthold. New York: Paulist Press, 1985.

Menand, Louis. *The Metaphysical Club: A Story of Ideas in America*. New York: Farrar, Straus and Giroux, 2001.

Mittelman, W. "Maslow's Study of Self-Actualization: A Reinterpretation." *Journal of Humanistic Psychology*, 31, no. 1 (1991), 114–135.

Philo. *The Works of Philo*, trans. C. D. Yonge. Peabody, MA: Hendrickson, 1993.

Plato. *Cratylus*. In *The Collected Dialogues of Plato*, trans. Benjamin Jowett, ed. Edith Hamilton and Huntington Cairns. Princeton, NJ: Princeton University Press, 1969.

Plato. *Laws*. In *Plato, The Collected Works*, trans. A. E. Taylor, ed. Edith Hamilton. Princeton, NJ: Princeton University Press, 1969.

Plato. *Lesser Hippias*, trans. Benjamin Jowett. Princeton, NJ: Princeton University Press, 1969.

Plato. *Letters*, trans. L. A. Post. Princeton, NJ: Princeton University Press, 1969.

Plato. *Meno*, trans. K. C. Guthrie. Princeton, NJ: Princeton University Press, 1969.

Plato. *Phaedo*, trans. Hugh Tredennick. Princeton, NJ: Princeton University Press, 1969.

Plato. *Phaedrus*, trans. R. Hackforth. Princeton, NJ: Princeton University Press, 1969.

Plato. *Protagoras*, trans. K. C. Guthrie. Princeton, NJ: Princeton University Press, 1969.

Plato. *Republic*, trans. Paul Shorey. Princeton, NJ: Princeton University Press, 1969.

Plato. *Symposium*, trans. Michael Joyce. Princeton, NJ: Princeton University Press, 1969.

Popkin, Richard. *The History of Skepticism from Erasmus to Descartes*. New York: Humanities Press, 1964.

Pseudo-Dionysius. *Divine Names*, trans. N. Janowitz. Chicago: University of Chicago Press, 1991.

Reese, William, ed. *Dictionary of Philosophy and Religion*. Atlantic Highlands, NJ: Humanities Press, 1996.

Schilpp, Paul Arthur, ed. *Albert Einstein: Philosopher-Scientist*, 3rd ed. La Salle, IL: Open Court, 1970.

Sherrard, Philip. *From Theology to Philosophy in the Latin West: From the Greek East and the Latin West—A Study in the Christian Tradition*. New York: Oxford University Press, 1959.

Snow, Nancy E. "Humility." *Journal of Value Inquiry*, 29 (1995), 203–216.

Spengler, Oswald. *The Decline of the West*, trans. C. F. Atkinson. New York: Knopf, 1939.

St. Augustine. *On Trinity*, trans. Thomas Merton. New York: Random House, 2000.

St. Nikodimos of the Holy Mountain and St. Makarios of Corinth, comps. *The Philokalia*, 5 vols., trans. G. E. H. Palmer, Philip Sherrard, and Kallistos Ware. London: Faber and Faber, 1983.

Tarnas, Richard. *The Passion of the Western Mind.* New York: Ballantine, 1991.

Toynbee, Arnold J. *A Study of History*, 12 vols. New York: Oxford University Press, 1934–1954.

Vlachos, Hierotheos. *Orthodox Psychotherapy*, trans. Esther Williams. Levadia, Greece: Birth of the Theotokos Monastery, 1994.

Vlachos, Hierotheos. *The Person in the Orthodox Tradition*, trans. Esther Williams. Levadia, Greece: Birth of the Theotokos Monastery, 1998.

Wheeler, John A. "From Relativity to Mutability." In *The Physicist's Conception of Nature*, ed. Jagdish Mehra. New York: Springer, 1973.

Wilken, Robert Louis. *The Spirit of Early Christian Thought: Seeking the Face of God*. New Haven, CT: Yale University Press, 2003.

Yollin, Patricia. "The Way We Live: Census Bureau Says Americans Love Electronics and Prefer the Internet to People." *San Francisco Chronicle*, December 15, 2006, p. 12. Available at http://www.sfgate.com/cgi-bin/article.cgi?f=/c/a/2006/12/15/MNGSBN09321.DTL&hw=The+Way+We+Live&sn=001&sc=1000/

❖ ❖ ❖

Notes

Chapter 1: The Ancient Greek Paradigm

[1]Werner Jaeger, *Paideia: The Ideals of Greek Culture*, 2nd. ed., trans. Gilbert Highet, vol. 1 (New York: Oxford University Press, 1945), p. xiv.

[2]Jaeger, *Paideia*, vol. 1, p. xxi.

[3]Jaeger, *Paideia*, vol. 1, p. xvii.

[4]Jaeger, *Paideia*, vol. 1, p. xx.

[5]Jaeger, *Paideia*, vol. 1, p. 9.

[6]Jaeger, *Paideia*, vol. 1, p. 88.

[7]Jaeger, *Paideia*, vol. 1, p. 83.

[8]Plutarch, *Lycurgus* 25, quoted here from Jaeger, *Paideia*, vol. 1, p. 83.

[9]Jaeger, *Paideia*, vol. 1, p. 83.

[10]Jaeger, *Paideia*, vol. 1, p. 418, note 10.

[11]Jaeger, *Paideia*, vol. 1, p. 8.

[12]Jaeger, *Paideia*, vol. 1, p. 7.

[13]Jaeger, *Paideia*, vol. 1, p. 59.

[14]Jaeger, *Paideia*, vol. 1, pp. 59–61.

[15]Jaeger, *Paideia*, vol. 1, p. 69.

[16]Jaeger, *Paideia*, vol. 1, p. 75.

[17]Jaeger, *Paideia*, vol. 1, p. 99.

[18]Jaeger, *Paideia*, vol. 1, p. 100.

[19]Jaeger, *Paideia*, vol. 1, p. 150.

[20]Quoted here from Plato, *Cratylus* 386a, in *The Collected Dialogues of Plato*, edited by Edith Hamilton and Huntington Cairns (Princeton, NJ: Princeton University Press, 1969).

[21]Jaeger, *Paideia*, vol. 1, p. 291.

[22]Jaeger, *Paideia*, vol. 1, p. 128.

[23]Jaeger, *Paideia*, vol. 1, p. 92.

[24]Jaeger, *Paideia*, vol. 1, p. 279.

[25]Jaeger, *Paideia*, vol. 2, p. 366.

[26]Jaeger, *Paideia*, vol. 1, p. 55.

[27]Jaeger, *Paideia*, vol. 2, p. 157.

[28]Jaeger, *Paideia*, vol. 1, p. 106.

[29]Jaeger, *Paideia*, vol. 2, p. 54.

[30]Plato, *Laws* 10.904c, in *The Collected Dialogues of Plato*, edited by Edith Hamilton and Huntington Cairns (Princeton, NJ: Princeton University Press, 1969).

[31]Jaeger, *Paideia*, vol. 1, p. 326.

[32]Jaeger, *Paideia*, vol. 1, p. 344.

[33]Jaeger, *Paideia*, vol. 3, p. 122.

[34]Jaeger, *Paideia*, vol. 1, p. 328.

[35]Jaeger, *Paideia*, vol. 1, p. 330.
[36]Jaeger, *Paideia*, vol. 2, p. 173.

Chapter 2: From Hesiod to Aristotle

[1]Werner Jaeger, *Paideia: The Ideals of Greek Culture*, trans. Gilbert Highet, vol. 1 (New York: Oxford University Press, 1945), p. 453, note 2.
[2]Jaeger, *Paideia*, vol. 1, p. 65.
[3]Jaeger, *Paideia*, vol. 1, p. 68.
[4]Jaeger, *Paideia*, vol. 1, p. 453, note 2.
[5]Reginald Allen, ed., *Greek Philosophy: Thales to Aristotle*, 3rd ed. (New York: The Free Press, 1991), p. 2.
[6]Allen, *Greek Philosophy*, p. 4.
[7]Allen, *Greek Philosophy*, p. 6.
[8]Allen, *Greek Philosophy*, p. 3.
[9]Aristotle, *Physics* 204b 24.
[10]Allen, *Greek Philosophy*, p. 4.
[11]Jaeger, *Paideia*, vol. 1, p. 65.
[12]Jaeger, *Paideia*, vol. 1, p. 152.
[13]Allen, *Greek Philosophy*, p. 17.
[14]Jaeger, *Paideia*, vol. 1, p. 255.
[15]Plato, *The Laws* 9:875.a, in *Plato, The Collected Works*, edited by Edith Hamilton (Princeton, NJ: Princeton University Press, 1969), Bollingen Series LXXI, p. 1434.
[16]Jaeger, *Paideia*, vol. 2, p. 206.
[17]Plato, *The Laws* 9.875.b.
[18]Plato, *Protagoras* 358.c.
[19]Plato, *Protagoras* 345d; *Lesser Hippias* 373c, 375a–b.
[20]Jaeger, *Paideia*, vol. 2, p. 69.
[21]Plato, *The Republic* 8.549.b.
[22]Jaeger, *Paideia*, vol. 2, p. 242.
[23]Plato, *Letters* 7:341e.
[24]Jaeger, *Paideia*, vol. 2, p. 230.
[25]Plato, *Phaedrus* 246a. Cf. 247d.
[26]Plato, *Phaedrus* 246b.
[27]Jaeger, *Paideia*, vol. 2, p. 367.
[28]Plato, *Meno* 81b, 85e; *Phaedo* 85e, 87, 92, 105; *Phaedrus* 245c; *Republic* 10:608c.
[29]Plato, *Phaedo* 81; *Phaedrus* 250c.
[30]Plato, *The Laws* 10.892a–896c, 12.959a; *Phaedrus* 248–250a; *Symposium* 212a.
[31]Plato, *Phaedo* 85d; see Jaeger, *Paideia*, vol. 2, p. 340, note 81.
[32]Jaeger, *Paideia*, vol. 2, p. 165.

[33]Plato, *Letters* 7:341c–d.

[34]Plato, *Republic* 511c.

[35]Jaeger, *Paideia*, vol. 2, p. 290.

[36]Richard Tarnas, *The Passion of the Western Mind* (New York: Ballantine Books, 1991), p. 55.

[37]Plato, *Republic* 6.509b.

[38]Jaeger, *Paideia*, vol. 2, p. 293. See Plato, *The Republic* 7.514 sq., 532b–7.539e.

[39]Jaeger, *Paideia*, vol. 2, p. 169.

[40]Tarnas, *Passion*, p. 60.

[41]Owen Barfield, *History in English Words* (Barrington, MA: Lindisfarne Books, 1967), p. 107.

[42]New King James Version (Nashville, TN: Thomas Nelson, 1997), p. 218.

[43]Barfield, *History*, p. 117.

[44]Barfield, *History*, p. 108.

[45]Jaeger, *Paideia*, vol. 3, p. 262.

[46]Aristotle, *Nicomachean Ethics* Book I, Chapter IV, 1095b. See Allen, *Greek Philosophy*, p. 387.

[47]Jaeger, *Paideia*, vol. 1, p. 293.

[48]Aristotle, *Metaphysics* Book II. See Allen, *Greek Philosophy*, pp. 320–323.

[49]Albert Levi: *Philosophy and the Modern World* (Bloomington, IN: Indiana University Press, 1959), p. 527.

[50]Aristotle, *Nicomachean Ethics* Book I, Chapter IV. See Allen, *Greek Philosophy*, p. 387.

[51]Jaeger, *Paideia*, vol. 3, p. 104.

[52]Allen, *Greek Philosophy*, p. 3.

[53]Aristotle, *Nicomachean Ethics* Book II.

[54]Jaeger, *Paideia*, vol. 2, p. 120.

[55]Plato, *The Republic* 433b.

[56]Jaeger, *Paideia*, vol. 2, p. 240.

[57]Jaeger, *Paideia*, vol. 2, p. 242.

[58]Jaeger, *Paideia*, vol. 1, p. 9.

[59]Aristotle, *Nicomachean Ethics* Book V.

[60]Owen Barfield, *Saving the Appearances*, 2nd ed. (Middletown, CT: Wesleyan University Press, 1988), p. 49.

[61]Levi, *Philosophy*, p. 86.

[62]Jaeger, *Paideia*, vol. 3, p. 51.

[63]Jaeger, *Paideia*, vol. 3, p. 215.

[64]Jaeger, *Paideia*, vol. 3, pp. 252–253.

Chapter 3: From Middle Platonism to Neo-Platonism

[1]Werner Jaeger, *Paideia: The Ideals of Greek Culture*, trans. Gilbert Highet, vol. 1 (New York: Oxford University Press, 1945), p. 149.

[2]Jaeger, *Paideia*, vol. 1, p. 147.

[3]Plato, *The Republic* 5:460c.

[4]Jaeger, *Paideia*, vol. 2, p. 250.

[5]Jaeger, *Paideia*, vol. 2, p. 250.

[6]Quoted here from Jaeger, *Paideia*, vol. 2, p. 200.

[7]Plato, *The Laws* 10:907d–909d.

[8]Jaeger, *Paideia*, vol. 2, p. 390, note 53.

[9]Jaeger, *Paideia*, vol. 2, p. 339.

[10]Jaeger, *Paideia*, vol. 3, p. 119.

[11]Jaeger, *Paideia*, vol. 2, p. 264.

[12]Jaeger, *Paideia*, vol. 3, p. 240.

[13]Jaeger, *Paideia*, vol. 1, p. 227.

[14]Jaeger, *Paideia*, vol. 3, p. 46.

[15]Jaeger, *Paideia*, vol. 3, p. 93.

[16]Jaeger, *Paideia*, vol. 3, p. 52.

[17]Jaeger, *Paideia*, vol. 3, p. 80.

[18]Jaeger, *Paideia*, vol. 3, p. 93.

[19]Jaeger, *Paideia*, vol. 3, p. 82.

[20]Jaeger, *Paideia*, vol. 1, p. xvii.

[21]Edward Gibbons, *The Decline and Fall of the Roman Empire and Other Selections* (New York, Washington Square Press, 1963) p. 55.

[22]Jaeger, *Paideia*, vol. 1, p. 149.

[23]Jaeger, *Paideia*, vol. 2, p. 122.

[24]William Reese, ed., *Dictionary of Philosophy and Religion* (Atlantic Highlands, NJ: Humanities Press, 1996), p. 202.

[25]Reese, *Dictionary*, p. 734.

[26]Reese, *Dictionary*, p. 707.

[27]Werner Jaeger, *Early Christianity and Greek Paideia* (Cambridge: Harvard University Press, 1961) p. 41–42.

[28]Andrew Louth, *The Origins of the Christian Mystical Tradition: From Plato to Denys* (New York: Clarendon, 1981).

[29]Owen Barfield, *History in English Words* (Barrington, MA: Lindisfarne Books, 1967), p. 118.

[30]Numbers 12:3; Isaiah 57:15; Psalms 9:12, 10:12, 25:9, 147:6, et al.

[31]Louth, *Origins*, p. 25.

[32]Henry Chadwick, "Philosophical Tradition and the Self," in *Interpreting Late Antiquity: Essays on the Postclassical World*, ed. G. W. Bowersock, Peter Brown, and Oleg Grabar (Cambridge: Harvard University Press, 2001), available at http://www.myriobiblos.gr/texts/english/chadwick_tradition.html/

[33]Reese, *Dictionary*, Cit. Gnosticism, p. 260.

[34]E. R. Dodds, Tradition and Personal Achievement in the Philosophy of Plotinus', *The Ancient Concept of Progress*, Oxford, 1973), 126. Quoted in Louth *Origins*, p. 36.

[35]Louth, *Origins*, p. 51.

[36]Louth, *Origins*, p. 51.

[37]Louth, *Origins*, p. 38.

[38]Barfield, *History*, p. 58.

[39]Barfield, *History*, pp. 92–93.

[40]Reese, *Dictionary*, pp. 203–204.

[41]Reese, *Dictionary*, pp. 734–735.

[42]Reese, *Dictionary*, p. 260.

[43]Werner Jaeger, *The Theology of the Early Greek Philosophers: The Gifford Lectures, 1936* (New York: Oxford University Press, 1967), p. 16.

[44]Richard Popkin, *The History of Skepticism from Erasmus to Descartes* (New York: Humanities Press, Inc. , 1964).

[45]Chadwick, "Philosophical Tradition," Accessible through http://www.myriobiblos.gr/texts/english/chadwick_traditions.html/

Chapter 4: The Christian/Neo-Platonist Era

[1]Philo, *Spec. Leg.* i, 43ff. translated by C. D. Yonge, *The Works of Philo* (Oxford: Hendrikson, 1993), p. 538.

[2]Hans von Campenhausen, *The Fathers of the Greek Church* (New York: Pantheon Books, 1955), p. 29.

[3]Vladimir Lossky, *In the Image and Likeness of God* (New York: SVS Press, 1974), p. 19.

[4]Von Campenhausen, *Fathers*, p. 33.

[5]Plato, *Timaeus* 28c.

[6]Plato, *Phaedrus* 251a.

[7]Galatians 1:11–24.

[8]Louth, *Origins*, p. 193.

[9]Plato, *Meno* 81b, 85e; *Phaedo* 85e, 87, 92, 105; *Phaedrus* 245c; *Republic* 10:608c.

[10]Plato, *Phaedo* 81; *Phaedrus* 250c.

[11]Plato, *Laws* 10.892a–896c, 12.959a; *Phaedrus* 248–250a; *Symposium* 212a.

[12]Plato, *Meno* 81b; *Phaedo* 70c, 81; *Phaedrus* 248c; *Republic* 10:617d.

[13]Henry Chadwick, "Philosophical Tradition and the Self," in *Interpreting Late Antiquity: Essays on the Postclassical World*, ed. G. W. Bowersock, Peter Brown, and Oleg Grabar (Cambridge: Harvard University Press), available at http://www.myriobiblos.gr/texts/english/chadwick_tradition.html/

[14]Louth, *Origins*, p. 53.

[15]Louth, *Origins*, p. 53.

[16]Vladimir Lossky, *The Mystical Theology of the Eastern Church* (New York: SVS Press, 2002), p. 32.

[17]Louth, *Origins*, p. 61.

[18]Origen, quoted here from Lossky, *Mystical Theology*, p. 32.

[19]Werner Jaeger, *Early Christianity and Greek Paideia* (Cambridge: Harvard University Press, 1961), p. 65.

[20]Von Campenhausen, *Fathers*, p. 43.

[21]Von Campenhausen, *Fathers*, p. 56.

[22]Von Campenhausen, *Fathers*, p. 47.

[23]Von Campenhausen, *Fathers*, p. 47.

[24]Von Campenhausen, *Fathers*, pp. 50–51.

[25]Plotinus's biographer Porphyry, quoted in Von Campenhausen, *Fathers*, p. 43.

[26]Brian Greene, *The Elegant Universe* (New York: Norton, 1999), p. 171.

[27]Greene, *Elegant Universe*, p. 171.

[28]Von Campenhausen. *Fathers*, pp. 67 and 70.

[29]Von Campenhausen. *Fathers*, p. 68.

[30]Von Campenhausen. *Fathers*, p. 74.

[31]Von Campenhausen. *Fathers*, p. 77.

[32]Von Campenhausen. *Fathers*, p. 72.

[33]Von Campenhausen. *Fathers*, p. 74.

[34]Louth, *Origins*, p. 78.

[35]Werner Jaeger, *Paideia: The Ideals of Greek Culture*, trans. Gilbert Highet, vol. 3 (New York: Oxford University Press, 1945), p. 262.

[36]Lossky, *Mystical Theology*, p. 82

[37]St. John Climacus, *The Ladder of Divine Ascent* (Brookline, MA: Holy Transfiguration Monastery, 1991), Step 8:27, p. 85.

[38]George Berthold, ed., *Maximus the Confessor* (New York: Paulist Press, 1985) p. 106 (Commentary on the Our Father, #4).

[39]William Reese, ed., *Dictionary of Philosophy and Religion* (Atlantic Highlands, NJ: Humanities Press, 1996), p. 260.

[40]www.newadvent.organization.

[41]Louth, *Origins*, p. 133.

[42]Berthold, *Maximus the Confessor*, p. 11.

[43]Ivan V. Kireyevsky, "On the Character of European Civilization," in *Complete Works of I. V. Kireyevsky*, vol. 1 (Moscow: Progress Publishers, 1911), quoted here from Rose, *Blessed Augustine*, p. 33.

[44]Rose, *Blessed Augustine*, p. 34.

[45]Quoted here from Rose, *Blessed Augustine*, p. 40.

[46]Cassian, Conferences, XIII, 11. Quoted here from Rose, *Blessed Augustine*, p. 41.

[47]Augustine, Letter 214. Quoted here from Rose, *Blessed Augustine*, p. 41.

[48]Philip Sherrard, *From Theology to Philosophy in the Latin West: From The Greek East and the Latin West—A Study in the Christian Tradition* (New York: Oxford University Press, 1959). Available at http://www.myriobiblos.gr/texts/english/sherrard_philosophy.html#38_bottom.

[49]Owen Barfield, *History in English Words* (Barrington, MA: Lindisfarne Books, 1967), p. 98.

[50]Étienne Gilson, *The Unity of Philosophical Experience* (San Francisco: Ignatius Press, 1964), p. 220.

[51]Augustine, *Confessions*, Book II.

Chapter 5: The Early Christian Paradigm

[1]Hans von Campenhausen, *The Fathers of the Greek Church* (New York: Pantheon Books, 1955), p. 159.

[2]Werner Jaeger, *The Theology of the Early Greek Philosophers: The Gifford Lectures 1936* (Oxford, England: Clarendon Press, 1947), p. 175.

[3]St. Leo the Great, *Tome of Leo*, quoted here from www.ewtn.com/faith/Teachings/incac1.htm/

[4]Andrew Louth, ed. and trans., *Maximus the Confessor* (New York: Routledge, 1996), p. 3.

[5]Louth, "Introduction," *Maximus the Confessor*, p. 17.

[6]Louth, "Introduction," *Maximus the Confessor*, p. 17.

[7]Louth, "Introduction," *Maximus the Confessor*, p. 18.

[8]Hierotheos Vlachos, *Orthodox Psychotherapy*, trans. Esther Williams (Levadia, Greece: Birth of the Theotokos Monastery, 1994), p. 209.

[9]Vlachos, *Orthodox Psychotherapy*, p. 209.

[10]Vlachos, *Orthodox Psychotherapy*, p. 211.

[11]Louth, "Introduction," *Maximus the Confessor*, p. 21.

[12]Louth, "Introduction," *Maximus the Confessor*, p. 60.

[13]Maximus, in St. Nikodimos of the Holy Mountain and St. Makarios of Corinth, comps., *The Philokalia*, trans. G. E. H. Palmer, Philip Sherrard, and Kallistos Ware (London: Faber and Faber, 1983), vol. 2, p. 82.

[14]Maximus, *Maximus Confessor: Selected Writings*, trans. George C. Berthold (New York: Paulist Press, 1985), p. 65.

[15]Louth, "Introduction," *Maximus the Confessor*, p. 52.

[16]Pseudo-Dionysius, *Divine Names*, trans. N. Janowitz (Chicago, University of Chicago Press, 1991).

[17]Maximus, "Letter to John the Cubicularius," in Louth, ed., *Maximus the Confessor*, p. 86.

[18]Maximus, "Letter to John the Cubicularius," in Louth, ed., *Maximus the Confessor*, pp. 86–87.

[19]Maximus, *Opscula* 26:277C, in Louth, ed., *Maximus the Confessor*, p. 60.

[20]Louth, "Introduction," *Maximus the Confessor*, p. 60.

[21]Maximus, "Letter to John the Cubicularius," in Louth, *Maximus the Confessor*, p. 87.

[22]Maximus, "Third Century on Love," in *Maximus Confessor*, p. 62.

[23]Maximus, "Third Century on Love," in *Maximus Confessor*, pp. 62 and 69.

[24]Hierotheos Vlachos, *The Person in the Orthodox Tradition*, trans. Esther Williams (Levadia, Greece: Birth of the Theotokos Monastery, 1998), p. 152.

[25]Maximus, "First Century on Love," in *Maximus Confessor*, p. 38.

[26]Maximus, "First Century on Love," in *Maximus Confessor*, p. 38.

[27]Louth, "Introduction," *Maximus the Confessor*, p. 42.

[28]Robert Wilken, *The Spirit of Early Christian Thought* (New Haven: Yale University Press, 2003), p. 295.

[29]Maximus, "First Century on Love," in *Maximus Confessor*, p. 44.

[30]Maximus, "Second Century on Love," in *Maximus Confessor*, p. 51.

[31]Vlachos, *Orthodox Psychotherapy*, p. 87.

[32]Louth, "Introduction," *Maximus the Confessor*, p. 25.

[33]Maximus, *Difficulty 10*, in Louth, ed., *Maximus the Confessor*, p. 126.

[34]Maximus, *Opuscule 7*, in Louth, ed., *Maximus the Confessor*, p. 185.

[35]Maximus, *Opuscule 7*, in Louth, ed., *Maximus the Confessor*, p. 183.

[36]Louth, "Introduction," *Maximus the Confessor*, p. 67.

[37]Louth, "Introduction," *Maximus the Confessor*, p. 61.

[38]Louth, "Introduction," *Maximus the Confessor*, p. 61.

[39]Werner Jaeger, *Paideia: The Ideals of Greek Culture*, trans. Gilbert Highet, vol. 1 (New York: Oxford University Press, 1945), p. 149.

[40]Maximus, *Opuscule 3*, in Louth, ed., *Maximus the Confessor*, p. 197.

[41]Maximus, *Opuscule 7*, in Louth, ed., *Maximus the Confessor*, p. 186.

[42]Maximus, *Opuscule 7*, in Louth, ed., *Maximus the Confessor*, p. 187.

[43]Maximus, *Opuscule 3*, in Louth, ed., *Maximus the Confessor*, p. 197.

[44]Maximus, "First Century on Knowledge," in *Maximus Confessor*, p. 138.

[45]Maximus, "Fourth Century on Love," in *Maximus Confessor*, p. 81.

[46]Maximus, "Commentary on the Our Father," in *Maximus Confessor*, p. 113.

[47]Maximus, "Commentary on the Our Father," in *Maximus Confessor*, p. 115.

[48]Maximus, "First Century on Love," in *Maximus Confessor*, p. 44.

[49]Maximus, "Second Century on Love," in *Maximus Confessor*, p. 50.

[50]St. John Climacus, *Ladder of Divine Ascent* (Brookline, MA: Holy Transfiguration Monastery, 1991), p. 259, Step 26.

Chapter 6: The Holy Roman Empire

[1]St. Augustine, *City of God*, trans. by Thomas Merton (New York: Random House, 2000), p. 141.

[2]On this, see Fr. Seraphim Rose, *The Place of Blessed Augustine in the Orthodox Church* (Platina, CA: Saint Herman of Alaska Brotherhood, 1996), p. 22.

[3]Will Durant, *The Age of Faith* (New York: Simon & Schuster, 1950), p. 123.

[4]Maximus, *Maximus Confessor: Selected Writings*, trans. George C. Berthold (New York: Paulist Press, 1985), p. 26.

[5]For a concise summary of conflicting belief systems, see G. W. Bowersock, *Hellenism in Late Antiquity* (Ann Arbor, MI: University of Michigan Press, 1996).

[6]*New Advent Catholic Encyclopedia*, available at http://www.newadvent.org, cit. St. Benedict/

[7]Encyclical on Faith and Reason, available at http://www.vatican.va/holy_father/john_paul_ii/ encyclicals/documents/hf_jp-ii_enc_15101998_fides-et-ratio_en.html/

[8]*New Advent Catholic Encyclopedia*, available at http://www.newadvent.org, cit. St. Bonaventure.

[9]Encyclical on Faith and Reason.

[10]Fr. John Romanides, *Franks, Romans, Feudalism, and Doctrine*, Part 1, available at http://www.romanity.org/htm/rom.03.en.franks_romans_feudalism_and_doctrine.01.htm/

[11]Romanides, *Franks, Romans, Feudalism, and Doctrine*, Part 1.

[12]Bishop Kallistos Ware, *The Orthodox Church* (Middlesex, England: Penguin Books, 1963), p. 54.

[13]Ware, *The Orthodox Church*, p. 54.

[14]Will Durant, *The Age of Faith* (New York: Simon & Schuster, 1950), p. 427.

[15]*Cambridge Medieval History*, vol. 2 (London: University Printing House, 1967).

[16]Étienne Gilson, *l'Étude de Saint Augustin* [The Work of St. Augustine] (Ann Arbor: University of Michigan Press, 2006), pp. 56 and 67.

[17]Philip Sherrard, *From Theology to Philosophy in the Latin West: From The Greek East and the Latin West—A Study in the Christian Tradition* (New York: Oxford University Press, 1959), p. 141, available at http://www.myriobiblos.gr/texts/english/sherrard_philosophy.html/

[18]St. Augustine, *On Trinity*, trans. Thomas Merton (New York: Random House, 2000), Book 15, chap. 25.

[19]For an extensive consideration of Essence and Energy in Augustinian thought, see Sherrard, *Latin West*, p. 129.

[20]Robert Louis Wilken, *The Spirit of Early Christian Thought* (New Haven: Yale University Press, 2003) p. 105.

[21]Werner Jaeger, *Early Christianity and Greek Paideia* (Cambridge: Harvard University Press, 1961), pp. 127–128.

[22]Aristotle, *On the Heavens*, trans. W. K. C. Gunthrie (Cambridge: Harvard University Press, 1970).

[23]Claudius Ptolemy: http://www-history.mcs.st-andrews.ac.uk/Mathematicians/Ptolemy.html/

[24]William Reese, *Dictionary of Philosophy and Religion: Eastern and Western Thought* (Atlantic Highlands, NJ: Humanities Press, 1996), p. 29.

[25]Reese, *Dictionary of Philosophy and Religion,* p. 29 (on Aquinas's Aristotelian interests) and p. 51 (on Augustine's Neo-Platonic tendencies).

[26]Terry Jones, *Who Murdered Chaucer? A Medieval Mystery* (New York: Thomas Dunne Books, 2004).

[27]Jones, *Who Murdered Chaucer?* p. 24.

[28]Jones, *Who Murdered Chaucer?* p. 35.

[29]Jones, *Who Murdered Chaucer?* p. 35.

[30]Will Durant, *Age of Faith*, pp. 762–765.

[31]Jones, *Who Murdered Chaucer?* p. 62.

[32]Jones, *Who Murdered Chaucer?* p. 71.

[33]Jones, *Who Murdered Chaucer?* p. 81.

[34]Jones, *Who Murdered Chaucer?* p. 89.

[35]Hans von Campenhausen, *The Fathers of the Greek Church* (New York: Pantheon Books, 1955), p. 129.

Chapter 7: The Enlightened Self

[1]See http://en.wikipedia.org/wiki/Renaissance/

[2]See http://en.wikipedia.org/wiki/Renaissance/

[3]Owen Barfield, *Saving the Appearances: A Study in Idolatry*, 2nd ed. (Middletown, CT: Wesleyan University Press, 1988), p. 50.

[4]Owen Barfield, *History in English Words* (Barrington, MA: Lindisfarne Books, 1967), p. 170.

[5]Étienne Gilson, *The Unity of Philosophical Experience* (San Francisco: Ignatius Press, 1964), p. 124.

[6]Gilson, *Unity*, p. 109.

[7]Ernst Cassirer, *The Philosophy of the Enlightenment* (Princeton, NJ: Princeton University Press, 1968), p. 29.

[8]Joel Myerson, ed., *A Historical Guide to Ralph Waldo Emerson* (New York: Oxford University Press, 2000), p. 25.

[9]John Locke, "An Essay Concerning Human Understanding," in Roger Ariew and Eric Watkins, eds., *Modern Philosophy: An Anthology of Primary Sources* (Indianapolis: Hackett Publishing, 1998), p. 271.

[10]David Hume, "An Inquiry Concerning Human Understanding," in Roger Ariew and Eric Watkins, eds., *Modern Philosophy: An Anthology of Primary Sources* (Indianapolis: Hackett Publishing, 1998), p. 557.

[11]Cassirer, *Philosophy*, p. 179.

[12]Gilson, *Unity*, p. 74.

[13]Gilson, *Unity*, p. 159.

[14]Gilson, *Unity*, p. 165.

[15]William Reese, ed., *Dictionary of Philosophy and Religion* (Atlantic Highlands, NJ: Humanities Press, 1996), p. 519.

[16]Paul Arthur Schilpp, ed., *Albert Einstein: Philosopher-Scientist*, 3rd ed. (La Salle, IL: Open Court, 1970), p. 595.

[17]Cassirer, *Philosophy*, p. 7.

[18]Cassirer, *Philosophy*, p. 22.

[19]Cassirer, *Philosophy*, p. 62.

[20]Brian Greene, *The Fabric of the Cosmos* (New York: Knopf, 2004), p. 79.

[21]Fritjof Capra, *The Tao of Physics: An Exploration of the Parallels Between Modern Physics and Eastern Mysticism* (Boston: Shambhala, 1991), p. 57.

[22]Capra, *Tao of Physics*, p. 58.

[23]Quoted here from Joel Myerson, ed., *A History of Ralph Waldo Emerson* (Cambridge: Harvard University Press, 1999), p. 13.

[24]Myerson, *History*, p. 23.

[25]Ralph Waldo Emerson, "Nature," in *Emerson: Essays and Lectures* (New York: Library of America, 1983), p. 7.

[26]Emerson, "Nature," p. 21.

[27]Emerson, "Nature," p. 41.

[28]Emerson, "The American Scholar," in *Emerson: Essays and Lectures* (New York: Library of America, 1983), p. 67.

[29]Emerson, "Divinity School Address," in *Emerson: Essays and Lectures* (New York: Library of America, 1983), pp. 77–78.

[30]Plato, *Republic* 526e.

[31]Cassirer, *Philosophy*, p. 181.

[32]Werner Jaeger, *Paideia: The Ideals of Greek Culture*, trans. Gilbert Highet, (New York: Oxford University Press, 1945), p. 262.

[33]Robert Hartman, trans., *Hegel: Reason in History* (Upper Saddle River, NJ: Prentice-Hall, 1997), p. xviii.

Chapter 8: Quantum Mechanics and Absolute Truth

[1]Brian Greene, *The Elegant Universe: Superstrings, Hidden Dimensions, and the Quest for the Ultimate Theory* (New York: Norton, 1999), p. 215.

[2]Étienne Gilson, *The Unity of Philosophical Experience* (San Francisco: Ignatius Press, 1964), p. 56.

[3]Owen Barfield, *History in English Words* (Barrington, MA: Lindisfarne Books, 1967), p. 139.

[4]Richard P. Feynman, *QED: The Strange Theory of Light and Matter* (Princeton: Princeton University Press, 1988), p. 7.

[5]Albert Levi, *Philosophy and the Modern World* (Bloomington: Indiana University Press, 1959), p. 488.

[6]For Einstein, Feynman, and Planck on Maxwell, see http://www.sco.wikipedia.org/wiki/James_Clerk_Maxwell/

[7]Fritjof Capra, *The Tao of Physics: An Exploration of the Parallels Between Modern Physics and Eastern Mysticism* (Boston: Shambhala, 1991), p. 61.

[8]Capra, *Tao of Physics*, p. 61.

[9]David Bodanis, *E=MC2: A Biography of the World's Most Famous Equation* (London: Macmillan, 2000), p. 49.

[10]Bodanis, *E=MC2,* p. 49.

[11]Brian Greene, *The Fabric of the Cosmos* (New York: Knopf, 2004), p. 328.

[12]Thomas Kuhn, *The Structure of Scientific Revolutions* (Chicago: University of Chicago Press, 1996), p. 98.

[13]Greene, *Elegant Universe*, p. 56.

[14]Greene, *Fabric of the Cosmos*, p. 10.

[15]Greene, *Elegant Universe*, p. 114, italics in the original.

[16]Capra, *Tao of Physics*, p. 165.

[17]Greene, *Elegant Universe*, p. 25.

[18]John A. Wheeler, "From Relativity to Mutability," in *The Physicist's Conception of Nature*, ed. Jagdish Mehra (New York: Springer, 1973), p. 244.

[19]Feynman, *QED*, p. 4.

[20]Greene, *Elegant Universe*, p. 12.

[21]Levi, *Philosophy*, p. 254.

[22]Greene, *Elegant Universe*, p. 88.

[23]Oration XXXI (Theologica V), 8', P.G., XXXVI, 141 B.

[24]Greene, *Elegant Universe*, p. 107.

[25]Terry Gross, "Wrongful Birth and Early Testing," *Fresh Air* transcript, March 16, 2006, National Public Radio. Available at http://www.npr.org/templates/ story/story.php?storyId=5283840/

[26]Terry Gross, "Wrongful Birth and Early Testing."

[27]Werner Jaeger, *The Theology of the Early Greek Philosophers: The Gifford Lectures, 1936* (New York: Oxford University Press, 1967), p. 16.

Chapter 9: Implications of the Modern Paradigm

[1]Stephen Colbert, *The Colbert Report*, October 17, 2005. Quoted here from http://www. wikiality.com/Truthiness/

[2]Werner Jaeger, *Paideia: The Ideals of Greek Culture*, 2nd. ed., trans. Gilbert Highet (New York: Oxford University Press, 1945).

[3]William Reese, *Dictionary of Philosophy and Religion* (Atlantic Highlands, NJ: Humanities Press, 1996) p. 131.

[4]Nancy E. Snow, "Humility," *Journal of Value Inquiry*, 29 (1995), 205.

[5]Snow, "Humility," p. 208.

[6]Abraham Maslow, "A Theory of Human Motivation," *Psychological Review*, 50, no. 4 (1943), 370–396.

[7]Francis Heylighen, "A Cognitive Systematic Reconstruction of Maslow's Theory of Self-Actualization." *Behavioral Science*, 37 (1992), 39–58.; W. Mittelman, "Maslow's Study of Self-Actualization: A Reinterpretation." *Journal of Humanistic Psychology*, 31, no. 1 (1991), 114–135; M. A. Wahba and L. G. Bridwell, "Maslow Reconsidered: A Review of Research on the Need Hierarchy Theory," *Organizational Behavior and Human Performance*, 15 (1976), 212–240;

[8]For example, see *Maslow's Hierarchy of Needs*, available at http://en.wikipedia. org/wiki/Maslow's_hierarchy_of_needs/

[9]Reese, *Dictionary of Philosophy and Religion*, pp. 617–618.

[10]Reese, *Dictionary of Philosophy and Religion*, pp. 617–618.

[11]The Foundation for Critical Thinking, *Defining Critical Thinking*, available at http://www.criticalthinking.org/aboutCT/definingCT.shtml/

[12]The Foundation for Critical Thinking, *Defining Critical Thinking*, available at http://www.criticalthinking.org/aboutCT/definingCT.shtml/

[13]The Foundation for Critical Thinking, *Defining Critical Thinking*, available at http://www.criticalthinking.org/aboutCT/definingCT.shtml/

[14]National Public Radio, *All Things Considered*, July 2, 1999.

[15]National Public Radio, *All Things Considered*, July 2, 1999.

[16]City University of New York, *American Religious Identification Survey*. Available at http://www.gc.cuny.edu/faculty/research_briefs/aris/key_findings. htm/

[17]American Atheists, *Flashline*. Available at http://www.atheist.org/flash.line/ atheist4.htm/

[18]Robert C. Fuller, *Spiritual, But Not Religious: Understanding Unchurched America* (New York: Oxford University Press, 2002).

[19]Louis Menand, *The Metaphysical Club: A Story of Ideas in America* (New York: Farrar, Straus and Giroux: 2001), p. 432.

[20]Quoted here from *The Random House Collegiate Dictionary*, revised edition (New York: Random House, 1980), p. 988.

[21]Patricia Yollin, "The Way We Live: Census Bureau says Americans Love Electronics and Prefer the Internet to People," *San Francisco Chronicle*, December 15, 2006, p. 12. Available at http://www.sfgate.com/cgi-bin/article. cgi?f=/c/a/2006/12/15/MNGSBN09321.DTL&hw=The+Way+We+Live&sn=0 01&sc=1000/

[22]Quoted here from Yollin, "The Way We Live," p. 12.

[23]Quoted here from David Crary, "Self-esteem Has Run Rampant, Study Says," *San Francisco Chronicle*, February 27, 2007, p. A2.

Chapter 10: Final Thoughts on Cooperation

[1]Albert Levi, *Philosophy and the Modern World* (Bloomington, IN: Indiana University Press, 1959), p. 108.

[2]Oswald Spengler, *The Decline of the West*, trans. C. F. Atkinson (New York: Knopf, 1939).

[3]Arnold J. Toynbee, *A Study of History*, 12 vols. (New York: Oxford University Press, 1934–1954).

[4]Toynbee, *Study of History*, vol. 1, p. 60

[5]Toynbee, *Study of History*, vol. 10, p. 1.

[6]Levi, *Philosophy*, p. 143.

[7]Levi, *Philosophy*, p. 145.

[8]Levi, *Philosophy*, p. 149.

[9]Jared Diamond, *Guns, Germs and Steel: The Fates of Human Societies* (New York: Norton, 1999).

[10]Diamond, *Guns, Germs and Steel*, p. 278.

[11]Diamond, *Guns, Germs and Steel*, p. 278.

[12]Ernest Becker, *The Denial of Death* (New York: Free Press, 1973).

[13]Becker, *Denial of Death*, p. 55.

[14]Becker, *Denial of Death*, p. 56.

[15]Becker, *Denial of Death*, pp. 57 and 158.

[16]Becker, *Denial of Death*, p. 203.

[17]Becker, *Denial of Death*, p. 201.

[18]Becker, *Denial of Death*, p. 269.

[19]Becker, *Denial of Death*, p. 270, citing Jesse Taft, *Otto Rank: A Biographical Study Based on Notebooks, Letters, Collected Writings, Therapeutic Achievements, and Personal Associations* (New York: Julian Press, 1958), p. 139.

[20]Becker, *Denial of Death*, pp. 272–273.

[21]Becker, *Denial of Death*, pp. 284–285.

[22]Ernest Becker, *Escape from Evil* (New York: Free Press, 1975), p. 168.

[23]Brian Greene, *The Fabric of the Cosmos* (New York: Knopf, 2004), p. 154.

[24]Greene, *Fabric of the Cosmos*, p. 158.

[25]Greene, *Fabric of the Cosmos*, p. 164.

[26]Greene, *Fabric of the Cosmos*, p. 175.

[27]C. G. Jung, *Synchronicity, An Acausal Connecting Principle*, trans. R. F. C. Hull (Princeton: Princeton University Press, 1952).

[28]Virginia Morell, "The Sixth Extinction," *National Geographic*, February 1999, available at http://www.nationalgeographic.com/ngm/9902/fngm/index.html/

Epilogue

[1]Karen Armstrong, *A History of God: The 4,000-Year Quest of Judaism, Christianity and Islam* (New York: Ballantine Books, 1993), p. 399.

[2]Armstrong, *History*, p. 278.

[3]Richard Dawkins, *The God Delusion* (Boston: Houghton Mifflin, 2006), p. 308.

[4]Brian Lamb, "*Islam: A Short History* by Karen Armstrong," *Booknotes* transcript, September 22, 2000, available at http://www. booknotes.org/ Transcript/?ProgramID=1636, 7.

❖ ❖ ❖

Index

❖ ❖ ❖